WHEN FOOTBALLERS
WERE SKINT

A JOURNEY IN SEARCH OF
THE SOUL OF FOOTBALL

WHEN FOOTBALLERS WERE SKINT

JON HENDERSON

Biteback Publishing

First published in Great Britain in 2018 by
Biteback Publishing Ltd
Westminster Tower
3 Albert Embankment
London SE1 7SP
Copyright © Jon Henderson 2018

Jon Henderson has asserted his right under the Copyright, Designs and Patents Act 1988 to be
identified as the author of this work.

ISBN 978-1-78590-384-7

10 9 8 7 6 5 4 3 2 1

A CIP catalogue record for this book is available from the British Library.

Set in Adobe Caslon Pro

Printed and bound in Great Britain by
CPI Group (UK) Ltd, Croydon CR0 4YY

MIX
Paper from
responsible sources
FSC® C020471

CONTENTS

A DEDICATION

This book is dedicated to Jimmy Hill.

As chairman of the Professional Footballers' Association (PFA), Hill, a Londoner born in 1928, did more than any other player to bring an end to the maximum wage in January 1961, by which stage it was £20 a week.

I knew him reasonably well in his later years, having a number of conversations with him when I was a sports journalist. I interviewed him for a profile in *The Observer* at a time when he was the country's most recognisable pundit on the game.

Also, I asked him one day if he might give away the awards after a fundraising event for a medical charity. 'Maybe you'd say a few words,' I said. He came, he charmed, he spoke movingly, alluding briefly to his own mid-life medical problems that he had overcome. He waved aside the charity's offer to pay for a taxi. But he did accept my offer to drop him off at Victoria Station.

I have a last image of him cheerily stepping out of the car into a windswept night. He had given freely of his services and turned what might have been a mundane evening into something a little special.

His views as a television pundit are what most people remember him for, overshadowing his relatively modest career as a player and his far greater legacy of having football's grossly unfair wage cap abolished.

As an innovative manager of Coventry City, and then as a media figure, he continued to have a considerable influence on the game's development.

I would have liked to have interviewed him for this book in his capacity as a key figure in its narrative, to whom today's multimillion-aire players owe so much and, I suspect, know very little of. Sadly, his failing health meant I was unable to do so.

Jimmy Hill died aged eighty-seven a week before Christmas in 2015.

INTERVIEWEES WHO MADE THIS BOOK POSSIBLE

They played all or some of their Football League careers in the era up to 1961 when wages were capped, never rising higher than £20 a week.

Colin Collindridge (b. 15 November 1920) Sheffield United 1938–50, Nottingham Forest 1950–54, Coventry City 1954–56

Johnny Paton (b. 2 April 1923, d. 2 October 2015) Celtic 1942–49, Chelsea 1946–47, Brentford 1949–52, Watford 1952–55

Jackie Sewell (b. 24 January 1927, d. 26 September 2016) Notts County 1946–51, Sheffield Wednesday 1951–55, Aston Villa 1955–59, Hull City 1959–61

Bill Slater (b. 29 April 1927) Blackpool 1944–51, Brentford 1951–52 & 1963–64, Wolverhampton Wanderers 1952–63

Frank O'Farrell (b. 9 October 1927) West Ham United 1948–56, Preston North End 1956–61, Manchester United (manager) 1971–72

Rex Adams (b. 13 February 1928, d. 14 January 2014) Blackpool 1948–51, Oldham Athletic 1953–54

Tony McNamara (b. 3 October 1929, d. 30 May 2015) Everton 1947–57, Liverpool 1957–58, Crewe Alexandra 1958, Bury 1958–59

Tommy Banks (b. 10 November 1929) Bolton Wanderers 1947–61

Roy Wood (b. 16 October 1930) New Brighton 1951, Leeds United 1952–60

Bill Leivers (b. 29 January 1932) Chesterfield 1948–53, Manchester City 1953–64, Doncaster Rovers 1964–66

Stan Anderson (b. 27 February 1933) Sunderland 1952–63, Newcastle United 1963–65, Middlesbrough 1965–66

Peter McParland (b. 25 April 1934) Aston Villa 1952–62, Wolverhampton Wanderers 1962–63, Plymouth Argyle 1963–64

Don Ratcliffe (13 November 1934, d. 19 October 2014) Stoke City 1954–63, Middlesbrough 1963–66, Darlington 1966–67, Crewe Alexandra 1967–69

Cliff Jones (b. 7 February 1935) Swansea Town 1952–58, Tottenham Hotspur 1958–68, Fulham 1968–70

Terry Allcock (b. 10 December 1935) Bolton Wanderers 1953–58, Norwich City 1958–69

George Eastham (b. 23 September 1936) Newcastle United 1956–60, Arsenal 1960–66, Stoke City 1966–73

Dave Whelan (b. 24 November 1936) Blackburn Rovers 1956–60, Crewe Alexandra 1962–66

Gordon Milne (b. 29 March 1937) Preston North End 1956–60, Liverpool 1960–67, Blackpool 1967–70

Alec Jackson (b. 29 May 1937) West Bromwich Albion 1954–64, Birmingham City 1964–67, Walsall 1967–68

Howard Riley (b. 18 August 1938) Leicester City 1955–65, Walsall 1965–66, Atlanta Chiefs 1967, Barrow 1968–69

Alex Dawson (b. 21 February 1940) Manchester United 1957–61, Preston North End 1961–67, Bury 1967–68, Brighton & Hove Albion 1968–71

Warwick Rimmer (b. 1 March 1941) Bolton Wanderers 1960–74, Crewe Alexandra 1974–79

Terry Neill (b. 8 May 1942) Arsenal 1959–70, Hull City 1970–73

'I need to understand the past. It illuminates the present.'

– GLEN COOK

'SIX POUNDS A WEEK! YOU CAN'T ASK FOR THAT!'

'Here, I want a word with you.'

The youth, his face freshened by a raw easterly wind, answered his trainer's call.

Stan Anderson understood that when Tommy Urwin barked a command after practice, you did as you were told.

Urwin was, though, for all his bluffness, a kindly man. His charitable nature reposed in the gentle upward curves of his mouth whenever he smiled, which was frequently. He was in his mid-fifties, having been born at the end of the nineteenth century, and came from the historic mining village of Haswell in Durham where people looked out for each other.

He had played as a forward for the north-east's three great clubs – starting off with Middlesbrough and Newcastle before making his debut for Sunderland at the age of nearly forty – and gained four caps for England in the 1920s. Now he trained the Sunderland B team and wanted the best for his callow charges.

His abrupt summons to Anderson, the most promising of the club's young recruits, who was coming up to seventeen, was at once commanding and avuncular.

'I know you and your father are going up to see George Crow about turning professional,' Urwin said. 'I'm telling you, ask for the biggest money you can get.'

Crow, a long-time servant of Sunderland AFC, was the club secretary but had also held other posts. Twelve years ago, in 1939, despite having no background in football, he had stood in as manager for three weeks after John Cochrane resigned. He would do so again in 1964 when Alan Brown quit the club.

'How much is that, Tom?' Anderson asked.

'He'll probably offer you three quid a week, maybe four. Ask for seven.'

Anderson also came from a mining community, Horden, not far from Sunderland, where his father, Jim, worked underground until the chest problems that were the coal miners' lot caught up with him.

When his health failed, Jim Anderson was found a job working above ground on what they called the Horden Aerial Flight. This was a ropeway suspended between pylons that carried coal waste to be dumped out in the North Sea. Not far enough out, though, to prevent the local beaches from wearing a heavy coat of black coal dust. For a full week's work, Anderson Sr received no more than £8.

'Are you sure, Tom?'

Anderson, a shy lad, did not relish the prospect of having to negotiate with Crow. Nobody did. Crow was small and grey-haired, with a face distinguished only by its pallor. If he had a lighter side, he regarded it as a vice to be exercised in private.

'Yeah, you'll get it,' Urwin assured him.

'OK, Tom.'

'But don't tell anyone I told you.'

Full of trepidation, despite having his father beside him, Stan Anderson knocked on the door of George Crow's office.

Crow greeted them with as much warmth as he could muster. 'We're going to sign you on as a full-time pro, Stanley,' he said.

'Thank you very much.'

'We're prepared to offer you four pounds a week.'

Anderson, who had shared Urwin's advice with the family, watched now as his father cleared his throat and prepared to speak. Anderson Sr was only marginally more worldly than his son, who held his breath waiting for the reply.

'Oh no, Mr Crow,' he said, but still could not quite find the courage to ask for the full, outrageous amount Urwin had suggested, 'I think Stan is worth six pounds a week.' Young Anderson looked on as George Crow froze, his face suddenly a rictus of incredulity. The usually phlegmatic secretary was struggling to keep his composure. For a moment Anderson thought Crow was going to faint.

'Six pounds a week! You can't ask for that!'

'Well, why not?' Jim Anderson asked with not a huge amount of conviction.

'Six pounds a week! Just a minute.'

At this point Crow hurriedly left the room.

He was gone for ten minutes.

'You've given me such a shock,' he said on his return. 'I can't possibly give you six pounds, but I'll tell you what I'll do: I'll give you five plus a ten-pound signing-on fee.'

Anderson looked at his father, willing him to say yes. He would have been perfectly happy to settle for the three or four pounds that Tommy Urwin said Crow would offer.

As his father hesitated, Stan thought: 'I'm working on a building site at the moment and getting one pound eight bloody shillings for a five-day week and here's a fella offering me five pounds plus a tenner for signing on to play football for a great club like Sunderland.'

Fortunately for young Stan, his father, who had never seen a £5 note in his life, was having roughly the same thoughts. It was all he could do not to reach out too quickly to shake on the deal. George Crow, meanwhile, fretted over whether he had set a precedent that would ruin the club despite resources that meant it was known as the Bank of England.

At the signing-on that followed, Crow handed over the two £5 notes that were Anderson's reward for committing himself to Sunderland. Anderson took them and handed them to his father: 'Here you are, Dad. You have them.'

'Are you sure?' his father asked.

The same two fivers stayed in Anderson Sr's pockets for the next ten years. He took them out only when he went to the Buffalo working men's club, the Buff, in Horden.

'Look at these,' he'd say to his mates.

No one else had a fiver around Horden in those days.

This story, told to me by Stan Anderson, was one of hundreds I heard as I travelled the country talking to the last generation of professional footballers who played in the era when their wages were capped. It was a story of a time when the men who played for the great football clubs of Britain shared a bond of borderline penury with the fans they entertained.

It was almost routine for players to travel to matches on the same public transport as the fans and after the game to return to homes that were as modest and basically equipped as those in which supporters lived. Quite possibly, player and fan were next-door neighbours in a street of working families' terraced houses.

Anderson signed for Sunderland in 1950, sixty-five years after a feebly enforced attempt to ban the payment of footballers for playing the game had come to an end. The Football Association announced after a special meeting on 20 July 1885 that it was 'in the interests of Association Football, to legalise the employment of professional foot-ball players, but only under certain restrictions'.

But not everyone benefited. To start with, players qualified for pay-ment only if they had been born within six miles of the ground – or had lived within the area for two years. More lasting restrictions were soon added, among them a maximum wage.

The fight for what might be termed pure, unbridled professionalism, as we now know it, was not won for nearly another eighty years. As Stan Anderson's story testifies, even as late as the 1950s it was simply not possible to make more than a very ordinary living from playing football.

The unbridling that eventually took place may no longer be to every-body's taste. But today the players' struggle to end the maximum wage seems as worthy as any of the centuries-old skirmishes undertaken by working people against mean-spirited employers.

At first, only the boards of some of the smaller teams, alarmed by the gulf between what they could pay their players and the wages of the bigger clubs, supported the maximum wage. In 1901, this con-cern led to the Football League delivering a hefty hit to the wage packets of many leading players when they upheld a request by Stoke City to cap earnings. The figure agreed was £4 a week.

For the next sixty years salaries mostly moved upwards – occasion-ally downwards – but never at a great pace.

Players agitating for more money would cite the huge crowds that paid to watch them – close to 150,000 for Scotland v. England in 1937 and 84,569 for an FA Cup tie between Manchester City and Stoke in 1934 – in pressing their case.

Even when the FA did raise the fee for international appearances after the Second World War, players still felt they were being exploited. England regular Tom Finney, not one of life's natural rabble-rousers, reflected caustically on the allocation of the £50,000-plus gate money the FA received from Wembley international matches.

'The eleven England players would share £550,' Finney said, 'and the rest, all £49,450, went somewhere else.'

As the war years receded, the Professional Footballers' Association, organised by the Association's secretary, Cliff Lloyd, and led by the Fulham forward Jimmy Hill, who mixed charm with iron resolve, stepped up their case for abolishing the maximum wage. By 1958 it had reached £20, a figure that survived until January 1961, when the PFA's threat of a players' strike effectively forced first the Football League and then the clubs to give way.

This landmark capitulation did not lead immediately to a massive surge in players' earnings; this came towards the end of the century, although some settlements did cause a brief outbreak of nervousness in club boardrooms across the country. The one most frequently cited is the deal agreed between Fulham and Johnny Haynes.

The story that has been passed down is that the chairman of Fulham, the comedian Tommy Trinder, was so confident that the maximum wage was a permanent fixture he boasted his star player was worth £100 a week. Haynes, a streetwise Londoner, kept the press cuttings and, straight after the PFA's victory, Trinder had to pay up.

When Trinder granted Haynes his substantial pay rise, officials of other clubs were outraged. Major H. Wilson Keys, West Bromwich Albion's chairman, was not alone when he harrumphed that Haynes's wage was 'dangerous and unsettling' and speculated that Fulham might have 'to starve other players' to finance it.

However, it was the advent of serious television money forty years later that eventually fuelled the supersonic inflation in wages – and turned the argument that players earned too little on its head.

For years the authorities had trembled at the idea of live football on TV, fearing it would mean no one showed up to stand on the terraces or sit in the stands. Alan Hardaker, the ultra-conservative Football League secretary who opposed English clubs entering European competitions because, in his privately expressed view, there were 'too many wogs and dagos', was adamant that 'regular live football [on TV] would undermine the game's health'.

But even adamant stances tend to crumble when Mammon really goes to work, which was what happened with the convergence of two significant arrivals: the Premier League and satellite television.

What looked to many like a reckless gamble by Rupert Murdoch's arriviste TV station, Sky, turned out to be the work of a savvy business brain. In 1992, Murdoch agreed to pay the newly formed league the thick end of £304 million, a stratospheric figure at the time, to secure live coverage of sixty matches a season over five years. The 2016–19 deal struck by Sky and BT Sports was worth £5.1 billion.

Sky has raked in massive winnings from its 1992 investment – and not just for themselves. The age of the multimillionaire footballer was ushered in.

In the hype and hysteria that came to surround the plutocrats who kick a ball around today, the Stan Andersons have been largely forgotten despite the fact they provided supporters with at least as compelling a diversion from everyday life as the modern game.

This book takes the first-hand accounts of a disappearing generation, before their stories are lost for ever, to tell what football was like when even the star players could earn not much more than the national average wage, lived next door to the fans and travelled with them to matches.

Some of their stories are scarcely believable. All of us who call ourselves football fans owe this book's multifarious cast our thanks for giving the national game such a rich and deeply human heritage.

CHAPTER ONE

TRAVELLERS' TALES

*In which Alec Jackson misjudges the size of a British Railways coffee cup –
Johnny Paton Sr refuses to batter down a front door with an axe – a night
at the Bolshoi Ballet opens the eyes of the Tottenham team – Terry Allcock
makes a hair-raising journey with a circus act in the driving seat.*

A film director charged with telling the story of football could do much worse than create a road movie. Travel has been at the heart of the game since the very beginning, a key element in precipitating its spread.

The palaces on wheels that convey the 21st-century footballer around the country lack the *Carry On* potential of the 1950s, when players and fans travelled in a ramshackle vehicle hired from the local coach company. The modern monsters that announce the opposition's arrival as they nose through the crowds suggest a rather sinister kind of movie, with its occupants lurking behind tinted windows. They exude the same sort of menace as prison vans taking criminals to court.

The old-style coach came with its obligatory operative, the driver with the massive gut straining his braces to snapping point. Likely as not, he had a fag pinched between his lips as, for mile on end, he intuitively directed his vehicle from behind a thick veil of smoke. In the passenger seats the finely honed athletes smoked just as devotedly while, almost without exception, they whetted their competitive juices by playing cards.

Plenty of comedians have picked up on the humorous possibilities of football teams and their followers on the move. Billy Connolly told the one about the drunken man, wrapped in a Celtic scarf, lying face down on the pavement, who was rescued by the supporters' bus as it travelled back to Scotland from an away fixture in England. On the outskirts of Glasgow the man mumbled his address, but when the bus got there no one was in. A neighbour, woken by the knocking, stuck his head out of an upstairs window: 'You'll nae find anyone there. They're in England on honeymoon.'

But, of course, it is the players themselves who are the main contributors to the great canon of football's road-trip stories. Tales involving journeys became a familiar motif of the reminiscences that fill this book.

In its earliest days, football was indebted to the railways for kindling mass interest in the game by providing fast, affordable travel. Acknowledging this, many clubs positioned themselves close to train stations. Manchester United, for example, moved to Old Trafford in 1909 to be near the rail network while most London clubs made sure they were adjacent to a railway or Underground station.

In recognition of the part the passenger train played in football's development in the early years, I chose, whenever possible, to use our unfairly defamed railway system to gather the material for this book.

In 1875, a young Glaswegian rode this system on a historic journey. Fergie Suter was bound for England where he would gain notoriety as the player credited with being football's first professional. On a late December morning he crossed the border to catch his first glimpse of England through the trailing smoke of a steam locomotive that was battling to reach a speed of more than forty miles an hour.

For over twenty years now it had been possible to go directly by train from Glasgow to London, a 400-mile journey that on a day with the weather set fair could be completed in a punchy twelve and a half hours.

In many instances I travelled down the same lines and gazed out at the same pastel landscapes as, decades earlier, the veteran footballers I was going to see had done on their way to matches. They were young men then, the heirs of Suter, full of hope and wonder. They were the stars of Saturday afternoons and yet their everyday lives were no different from those of the ordinary working men who idolised them.

The financial rewards for becoming a footballer would have been only marginally higher than driving the train on which the players travelled. For the Irishman Frank O'Farrell, being an engine driver was the aspiration that first consumed him.

During his boyhood in Cork in the 1930s, O'Farrell dreamed of being 'King of the Cab', just like his father. But after working his way up from engine cleaner to fireman shovelling coal into the firebox – just a footplate away from becoming a driver – he answered the call of his second great love. He signed as a professional footballer for one of England's great clubs, West Ham United, before some years later joining another, Preston North End. He played also for the Republic of Ireland and his posts as a manager included a stint at Old Trafford.

Still, though, what brings a look of trance-like rapture to O'Farrell's face, as he sits contentedly in his Torquay home, is not the memory of a sweetly struck goal. It is when he softly whispers the words 'steam engine'.

For many of the young men whose careers started either side of the Second World War, their first railway journeys as professional footballers were also the first time they had left the localities in which they grew up. The sense of departure must have been as keen as that of an astronaut being fired into space.

Such a man is Alec Jackson. Had he not become a professional footballer, Jackson might never have travelled by train for more than a few miles from his home in Tipton in the West Midlands, where he was born in 1937.

Jackson still lives in Tipton. The taxi ride from the station to his home in Hamilton Road is just long enough to conduct a brief analysis of the state of Sri Lankan cricket with the driver, a native of that beautiful island, before he drops me in front of Jackson's house. Even an imaginative estate agent would probably go no further than to describe the property as modest and compact.

Jackson's wife, June, greets me and shows me through to the front room where her husband, in an armchair drawn close to a full-on electric fire, is watching the Australian Open tennis. His legs are not quite what they were, he says, straightening up gingerly. But, he adds, he still manages to do an hour or so each day in the allotment that he has worked for nearly forty years. Beans are his speciality.

Jackson's father was a factory worker and 'my mum was just a mum'. Jackson himself was educated in Tipton and worked in the town as a machinist for the engineering firm W. G. Allen. His earliest football memory was kicking a tin can about because 'we couldn't afford a ball'.

He tells how he was discovered playing for the St John's Church team at Princes End in Tipton. 'I never got any proper coaching when I was young,' he says. 'After we'd seen how the top players did it, we'd go down the fields and we'd have a go at it.'

He says he did go to train briefly at Walsall when that club showed an interest in him. Apart from this, the furthest he had ever been until West Bromwich Albion spotted him was Great Bridge, a village just down the road but still within Tipton.

Once signed as a professional as a seventeen-year-old in September 1954, Jackson's progress to speeding past some of the Football League's best full-backs was rapid. Two months later he boarded a train to London to make his First Division debut for Albion against Charlton Athletic. 'I couldn't believe what was happening to me,' he says. 'It was unreal, putting me out of contact with the life I'd been used to. A new world hit me.'

He says that at times he found it hard to cope with being so suddenly thrust into the spotlight of professional football. 'But my football got me out of trouble.'

The journey to London for the Charlton game started when Len Millard, the West Brom captain, picked him up at Great Bridge. When they arrived at Birmingham Station a crowd of supporters travelling to the match spotted them.

Jackson reckons he was only five feet tall – he grew to about five six – and being unknown to most of the fans he was probably mistaken for Millard's son. When they found out he was in fact a player they all crowded around wanting his autograph.

On the train an incident revealed 'how illiterate I was in terms of my new surroundings'.

One of his new teammates went to buy a round of teas and coffees.

Jackson was used to drinking out of a big mug at home and when the teammate called out, 'How many sugars do you want, Jacko?', he replied, 'Oh, put me about six in.'

'The coffee cups were only this big,' he says, holding the tips of his thumb and index finger three inches apart, and whoever it was shouted back, 'Where the hell do you think you're going to put these six lumps then?'

When in London, the team went by coach to a hotel for lunch. 'I'd never seen anything like it. It was just across the road from … What do they call that park?'

'Hyde Park,' June says.

'That's it, Hyde Park. It was the Dorchester Hotel.'

When the players sat down for the meal, Jackson had a moment of panic. 'There were more knives and forks in front of me than we'd got in our house.'

Jim Sanders, the goalkeeper and a senior member of the team, came to his rescue. He put his hand on Jackson's shoulder and said, 'I'll sit right across from you and whichever tool you've got to use I'll give you the nod.'

'So every time I went for one he'd either shake or nod his head.'

On the coach to the ground, Jackson remembers sitting next to Ronnie Allen, an England international who would play more than 400 games for West Brom. 'Just imagine, five weeks and I'm sitting next to the bloke I'd idolised for years.'

'I'll put the laces in your boots for you,' Jackson told Allen.

'You put the laces in my boots for me! You're one of us now, you know,' Allen said.

His impact as a player could hardly have been more immediate. He scored within three minutes against Charlton to set up a 3–1 victory. 'All I can remember about the goal was that once I'd knocked the ball in they couldn't catch me,' he says. 'But the bigger memory was being with such great players as Ronnie Allen and Ray Barlow. The goal didn't really make any difference to me.'

Travelling by train was far less bewildering for Tommy Banks than it had been for the young Jackson. Banks was a seasoned traveller when he set off from London's Euston Station on the morning of Monday 5 May 1958. He had done his national service and been a full-time professional with Bolton Wanderers for nearly a decade.

With his Bolton teammates, Banks was bound for a triumphal return with the FA Cup to Lancashire, a journey he would not complete. By the time his teammates and the cup reached Bolton, Banks was nowhere to be seen.

But this was the London–Manchester train, not the Orient Express. And rather than being cloaked in international mystery, this particular traveller's tale was spun around a piece of Football Association genius by which they appointed the England manager but still did much of the managing, including selection, themselves.

Banks's conspicuous performance in Bolton's 2–0 Cup final win over Manchester United on the previous Saturday had persuaded the FA committee that chose international teams to consider picking Banks for the World Cup in Sweden in a month's time. As part of the build-up, a friendly against Portugal would take place at Wembley on the coming Wednesday.

Banks was put on standby but was told by Walter Winterbottom, the England manager, he could return to Bolton with his teammates. What did Walter know? By the time the FA countermanded his instruction, issuing an order to find Banks and bring him back to Wembley, the player was chugging north.

A guard on the train, unaware that the person he was looking for was a member of the victorious Bolton Wanderers team, moved from carriage to carriage calling out, 'Thomas Banks, Thomas Banks, I have an important message for you.'

When Banks heard the message he was mortified that he would not be part of the homecoming celebrations. As the train slowed to make an unscheduled stop to discharge him at Rugby, he pleaded with the Bolton manager to be allowed to stay aboard and travel back to London the next day. 'Sorry, Tommy,' Bill 'Nibbler' Ridding replied, 'you'll have to do what FA wants. They're the bosses.'

'So I returned to Euston,' Banks says, 'and by late that afternoon I was training with the England team at the Bank of England ground in west London.'

After all this he was not picked two days later against Portugal, but he did go to the World Cup where he played in all four of England's matches.

As contributors to football's road movie, Johnny Paton and his father, Johnny Paton Sr, who both played for Celtic, arguably have no equal.

Paton Jr, who was born in 1923, also played for three English Football League clubs, including Chelsea. And, among many other adventures along the way, he volunteered himself for a wartime fixture in New York that turned into a dark comedy.

When I visit him, he and Eileen, his wife of nearly seventy years, live in north London. Their home is as unremarkable as Alec Jackson's. Paton is ninety and, for a man of his age, leaves me just a little awe-struck by the exuberance and fine detail of his storytelling.

Paton Sr, his son says, was let go by Celtic in the early 1920s after the club decided to cut costs by disbanding the reserve team. Football was the only trade he knew and with little chance of making a living from it in Scotland, he took to the road.

First, Paton's father joined a number of other players – his brother-in-law Eddy Swann was one – who went to America. 'They thought the pavements there were covered with gold,' Paton Jr says. 'But my father got very, very homesick. My mother wouldn't go with him. She said she wouldn't leave Glasgow under any circumstances. In those days, going to America was probably like going to the moon.'

After one season Paton Sr came back to Scotland, had a brief spell with Aberdeen and then was off again. 'I think', his son says, 'he and another Celtic player, Johnny Donoghue, were the very first players to be transferred to the Continent. He played for the French club Roubaix just outside Paris and was very successful there.'

Once the older Paton finished with football – his last jobs in the game were as player-manager of Cork United and, briefly, being in charge of Celtic's reserves – he found searching for employment elsewhere 'a terrible shock'. From now on his travels were restricted to hunting for work around Glasgow. These were the '30s, the years of the Great Depression, and he was in no position to be fussy.

Paton Jr tells the story of his father turning up for one job where his employer was strangely reluctant to tell him what it involved. 'We'll tell you in due course,' he said. 'Just come with us.'

Next Paton Sr was presented with an axe. 'A great big axe and my dad said, "What's that for?"'

He was told not to worry what it was for but, again, 'to come with us'. So, carrying his axe, he tagged along until they arrived at the front door of a house in a Glasgow suburb. Only now was his task revealed.

'If the people inside won't open the door,' he was told, 'we need you to batter it down. Get it open with the axe.'

'This was an eviction,' the younger Paton says. 'So my father put the axe down and walked away. He'd only lasted one hour in the job.'

Johnny Paton Jr was born in Abercromby Street, Glasgow, 'a stone's throw away' from where the Celtic Football Club was born in St Mary's Catholic Church. He gained early recognition as a footballer of promise when, in 1937, he played in a schoolboy international for Scotland against the Republic of Ireland. It gave him a taste of the travel that would come to dominate his life in the '40s and '50s.

The schools team went over to Ireland by boat and, unknown to Paton, he was the reason the press photographers were gathered at the bottom of the gangplank.

During his time at Cork United, his father had been dubbed the King of Cork by the Irish press after the club won in the Irish Free State Cup. When sports editors heard that Paton's son was coming over with the Scotland schools team they dispatched their snappers to take photographs.

'Well, my image was completely different from my father's,' Paton says. 'He was shorter and stouter than me and the photographers were looking for someone in the wee Johnny Paton mould, which is why, I learnt later, I went straight past them. I didn't know it was me they were looking for so they missed me completely.'

Johnny Paton Jr signed for Celtic in 1942, aged nineteen. But, like so many other young men of his generation, he had his life yanked from its provincial orbit when he received his call-up papers. At that time this meant a summons to serve in the Second World War. He joined the RAF and was sent to St Andrews for flying training.

Soon, though, a much longer road opened out ahead of him. First he was transferred to a camp in Regent's Park in London and, from there, onwards to Canada to complete his training. By now his future in the RAF had been switched to being a navigator, and the skies over Britain were too dangerous for young aircrews to learn their skills at home.

While in Canada, with time on his hands and a free travel pass in his pocket – a perk available to servicemen and women – Paton took a fourteen-hour train ride to New York. He describes this as the best experience he had while in North America, even if the football match he fitted into his schedule bore little resemblance to what he was used to in Scotland.

'I was still very fit at that time,' he says, 'because I never stopped training. I had my spiked shoes in my kitbag and everywhere I went, it didn't matter where it was, any bit of spare ground, I'd go out and do my sprint training. I never neglected that. So when I arrived in New York, I decided to try to get a game of football.'

He knew from his father's experience in New York that they played what was known locally as soccer. In a phone box on Broadway, he looked up clubs in a directory and dialled a number.

Paton says he reckons the man who answered his call was thinking, 'I've got a nutcase here. I've got a man telling me he wants to play for us.'

'There are a lot of nutcases in America, as you know,' Paton adds.

Just in time, before the man could hang up on him, Paton said, 'Your accent – you're Scottish aren't you?'

'Yes – who are you?'

'I'm Johnny Paton, Glasgow Celtic.'

'I was connected with Glasgow Celtic, what a coincidence. Jimmy McGuire, the manager of the New York Rangers. Did you really play for Celtic?'

'Yes, course I did. Phone Jimmy McGrory up. He's the manager. He'll tell you.'

And so it was that Johnny Paton came to play for the New York Rangers in 'a terrible match'. It took place in front of about 1,000 fans – 'football was small-time in America then' – and against six-foot Italians who 'just ran into you as if they were charging a brick wall'.

A fight broke out towards the end after New York Rangers scored an equalising penalty. The opposition goalkeeper, who was dressed like a baseball player, reacted by running out and punching the scorer. At which point all hell broke loose.

'I ran straight off the field,' Paton says, 'remembering something my father used to say to me: "Johnny, never lift your hand in football, never. Only lift your hand and hit somebody if you're getting paid for it. Never get involved in a free fight."'

The match was abandoned with the result declared a 1–1 draw. Everyone then adjourned to the dressing rooms where the fight broke out again.

'It was terrible,' Paton says, 'but the only good thing was that I got $30, which was a lot of money for me – a month's RAF wages.'

The war ended before it was time for Paton to leave the services. If he was hoping the RAF might make it easy for him to resume his career with Celtic, he was mistaken. He was posted to Bentley Priory, the stately home on the northern fringes of London where Fighter Command had its headquarters.

The posting meant travel continued to play a big part in Paton's life.

Every Friday, after finishing his RAF duties, he took the night train to Glasgow to be in time to play for Celtic the next day. 'I was shattered,' he says, 'but I was under contract and I'd got to get my wages.'

Paton had a year's relief from this long-haul commute, when, after a chance meeting in the London suburbs, he negotiated a season playing for Chelsea. But he did not achieve a lifestyle of relative tranquillity until 1949, when he and his family settled in the capital after he transferred to Brentford.

For every mile old-time professional footballers spent playing cards on train journeys, they spent at least as many refining their brag and poker – mostly for stakes of no more than a few pennies – while travelling by coach.

In the very early days these coaches were charabancs, or charas, which had been horse-drawn vehicles before having motors fitted. During the week they carried industrial loads such as coal or scrap iron. Then at weekends they morphed into bone-shaking people carriers with bodywork bolted on and seats installed.

The charas then gave way to what is just about recognisable as the progenitor of the modern coach. These vehicles were updated gradually. Andrew Magowan of the family coach firm Ellisons Travel, conveyors of Liverpool teams for more than half a century, recalls his mother making curtains after Emlyn Hughes complained about the sun getting in his eyes.

Roy Wood, who is wonderfully self-deprecating about his goalkeeping for Leeds United – in fact he played a significant, ever-present role in their gaining promotion to the old First Division in 1956 – tells me a coach story that sends a shiver of transferred pain down the years. It concerns a journey in a vehicle of doubtful pedigree in the days when, as a very young man, Wood was making his way for Harrowby in the West Cheshire League.

On the Saturday before he was due to start his national service, he was keeping in a preliminary round of the FA Cup at Holywell Town. 'We got beat 16–0,' he says, 'but, having said that, I was carried off at half-time with three cracked ribs and one nearly broken.'

On the way home, Wood's teammates stuck him in the back of the coach. They then forgot about him as they cut and shuffled their decks of cards. Behind them Wood winced and grimaced as the coach bounced along on its ancient springs.

'When the doctor saw me, [after] the X-rays and one thing and another, he said if that coach had gone over a decent bump I wouldn't have been there to tell the tale. I thought, "Thank you very much."'

The story continues. On the Monday, Wood, swathed in strapping, missed his appointment with His Majesty's Armed Forces. Presumed to be skiving, he received visitors on the Tuesday. 'There was a loud knock on the door and there were two military policemen standing there. "Where is 'e?" they asked my mother. "Well, 'e's upstairs," she said. "You can 'ave him."'

'They took it all as a good joke. They had a couple of cups of tea before leaving and I went into the RAF six months later.'

As a serviceman in the RAF, Wood had grown very familiar with air travel by the time he signed for Leeds in 1952. When the Welshman Cliff Jones joined Swansea Town that same year, the nearest he had been to an aeroplane was when one occasionally flew over his hometown.

By the end of the decade, though, Jones had become used to flying as a member of Wales' international team, who reached the 1958 World

Cup finals, and as a player for Tottenham Hotspur, the north London club he had joined four months before those finals.

It was thanks to air travel that Jones made a trip he remembers more vividly than any other. 'Bill [Nicholson, the Spurs manager] took us on tour to Russia in 1959 and I'm telling you something, communism was rife. People were like queuing to go into the mausoleum to see Lenin and Stalin lying in state; they were very patriotic people … It was just unbelievable and we had three games against club sides and they were all battles.'

Jones describes the trip as 'a great bonding experience because we all really came together as a team, but it was such a difficult tour'.

Not least of Jones's personal difficulties was bonding with the no-nonsense Scotland player Dave Mackay. 'I roomed with Dave, a very unfortunate experience,' Jones says. 'For a start, he was so untidy, our room was a complete khazi, and I couldn't understand a word he said.'

When Jones asked if he could have an interpreter, Nicholson presumed he meant a Russian one. 'No, a Scottish one,' Jones told him. 'I don't know what Mackay's saying. Nay ou, ay ouze. Dear me.'

At the other end of the cultural spectrum from sharing a room with Dave Mackay was a night out at the Bolshoi Ballet, an experience Jones believes significantly influenced the way the great Spurs team of the 1960s played.

When Nicholson told Jones that was where they were going, Jones thought he was joking. 'No,' Nicholson repeated emphatically, 'we're going to the Bolshoi Ballet.'

'So we went there,' Jones says, 'and a young Nureyev was dancing. Can you believe that? It was an amazing experience. These ballet dancers, they were so fit and powerful. And of course Bill Nicholson was so taken with this he wanted to find out how they were so fit. And a lot of it was down to weight training.'

As a result, when Nicholson returned to London he sought out Bill Watson, who had been an Olympic weightlifter. Watson explained that everything came from the stomach; this was the core of a person's fitness and reactions.

'Watson got quite a lot of work after helping us,' Jones says, 'because our fitness definitely went up a gear. Bill's whole approach to football was that you will play the way you train. He said that if you train with method and if you train with effort you'll play exactly the same way, you'll take that out on the field. And it just worked for us.'

It took some years before professional footballers became masters of their own travel as car owners. In the first instance, only the wealthy businessmen who ran the clubs had cars. Players had to wait to be asked before being granted a lift in one of these modern wonders. It wasn't until well after the Second World War that every player had his own car as a matter of course.

Terry Neill, who joined Arsenal in 1959, remembers the slow advance of car ownership, started by the better-paid players, after the wage cap was lifted.

'When we got onto forty quid a week, we all started to acquire what we thought were fancy cars,' Neill says. 'I'm talking about a Sunbeam – second-hand, of course, knockdown price, a bit rusty.'

A car journey Terry Allcock experienced travelling as a passenger proved almost as blood-draining as Roy Wood's coach ride.

In the '50s Allcock was a good player in a very good Bolton side that contained three international inside-forwards. He scored for them in the early rounds of their triumphant 1958 FA Cup run. But then learnt he was superfluous to the club's needs.

How he found out, soon after moving into a house in Bolton, shocked him. Without any warning he was told when he arrived for training one morning that Norwich had made an offer for him. Bolton were keen to accept.

'Having got over my surprise,' he says, 'my first thought was, "Where the hell's Norwich?" I thought for a minute it was Northwich.'

Before agreeing to the move he was at least allowed to visit Norwich. This involved catching a train to Peterborough where he would be picked up by car. Allcock worried how he would recognise the driver but was told the driver would recognise him.

'And do you know,' he says, 'I was met by a midget. He worked for the chairman who was a friend of his. He was one of the famous circus acts.

'When we got in the car he said, "Do you mind if I drive fast, there's a match on at Carrow Road and we might catch the second half." They were playing Coventry. I was frightened to death. He had wooden things on the pedals and he couldn't see over the steering wheel. But we did make it for the second half.'

Another former Bolton player, Warwick Rimmer, was coming to the end of his fourteen years as a first-team player when the club drew the outstanding Manchester City side of Colin Bell, Franny Lee and Mike Summerbee in the third round of the League Cup in October 1971.

By now a professional footballer rich enough to own a car was no longer the improbability it had been a few years earlier. If he felt like it, he could even take his car on one of the new motorways, although there was a risk in this – encountering a motorway snarl-up.

So it was that Rimmer, having set out from his home in Blackrod for the short drive to Bolton's Burnden Park ground, ended up trapped on the M61. 'I wasn't on the motorway for two or three hundred yards when it was absolutely gridlocked,' Rimmer says.

His car was stationary for half an hour before he registered that the vehicle in front had a City sticker in the window. He quickly devised a plan, but it would work only if the woman passenger up ahead had a driving licence, which, as luck would have it, she did.

Rimmer apologised for asking rival fans to do such a thing, but would one of them drive his car to the ground? Legging it was his only chance of making the kick-off.

Rimmer told them that when they reached the ground the steward would recognise his car. He would arrange for them to be left a couple of tickets.

He reckons the only thing that kept him going as he jogged the three or four miles to the ground was trying to remember the registration of his brand-new car. 'I kept repeating it over and over in case I never saw it again.'

He reached Burnden Park with about three minutes to spare. The manager, Jimmy Armfield, was outside waiting for him. When Rimmer said he had been stuck in traffic and had to run the last bit, Armfield demanded to know how far. 'Oh, only round the corner, just back of the shops,' Rimmer fibbed.

'I dashed into the dressing room and stopped a young chap putting my shirt on. I didn't bother with any warm-up. So it just shows what you can do and that it's all in the mind.

'I got in a bit of trouble for being late but nobody bothered too much, particularly as we upset City 3–0 with a young Manchester boy called Garry Jones – he went on to do quite well at Bolton – scoring all the goals.'

Rimmer, who had made his debut for Bolton in 1960, was a member of the last generation who knew what it was like to play in the era of the maximum wage. By the time he completed his Football League career at Crewe Alexandra in the late '70s, it was thirty years since Frank O'Farrell had begun his.

When O'Farrell arrived at West Ham, a motorway snarl-up would have made it only into a sci-fi movie. Professional footballers truly were skint.

'After training,' O'Farrell says, 'West Ham would provide lunch for us at a restaurant about half a mile from the ground and because none of us had cars we'd get a trolleybus down there.'

Sometimes, O'Farrell remembers, the conductor would give the players free rides. 'That's all right,' he would say, 'leave it this time.'

CHAPTER TWO

SIGNING ON...

In which a punch thrown in anger leads to Bill Leivers becoming a professional footballer – a goalie makes his Football League debut to save the club money – Don Ratcliffe is indebted to a corner-shop owner's discerning eye – Mr Bushell delays Tony McNamara's Everton career because the evening institute's needs are greater.

A bright-eyed teenager tumbles out of the cinema one Saturday night in the late 1950s. A promising footballer, he is eager to know the press's verdict on his performance that afternoon.

He buys the sports newspaper *Ireland's Saturday Night* from the vendor strategically positioned in his usual place near the exit. The young man opens his paper at the centre pages and catches his breath. The headline over a story written by the trusted Malcolm Brodie is about him – and it is not a match report.

'TERRY NEILL FOR ARSENAL'

Almost from the day he first walked, playing football was Neill's passion. He had been born and spent his early childhood in east Belfast, in the same area where the families of Danny Blanchflower and George Best lived. Soon, though, the Neills moved out to Bangor, a seaside town in County Down. Here there was all the space a young lad and his mates needed to chase a football.

In time Neill passed the eleven-plus exam and went to Bangor Grammar School. His parents were thrilled by this achievement, but the young Neill shared their excitement only until he found out the school played rugby not football.

He says he received several beatings from the headmaster for refusing to represent the school in Saturday rugby matches. He preferred instead to turn out for the First Bangor Boys Brigade football team.

By the summer term, he was badgering his parents to let him go to Bangor Tech because he wanted to be an engineer. 'Of course it had nothing to do with engineering,' Neill says, 'it was simply because the tech had a good football team and a lot of my mates were there. I quite liked the grammar school but I wanted to play football.

'I must have broken my parents' hearts, but being the kind people they were they let me change schools.'

Playing for the technical college, as a wing-half as it was known then, Neill made a big impression and, aged thirteen, was picked to represent Northern Ireland schools.

He recalls a match in Belfast against England schoolboys: 'Their goalkeeper, Bob Wilson, would later become my colleague at the Arsenal and Norbert [Nobby] Stiles from Manchester was also in that England side, diminutive but already the dirtiest little so-and-so on the pitch.' Neill delivers this line with an approving smile, as he does most of the anecdotes that spill forth in an unstoppable flow. 'Nobby kicked lumps out of people even in those days and gave two-fingered salutes to the crowd.'

When he was fifteen, Neill signed for Bangor, whose ground was a few hundred yards from where his family lived on top of the hill.

'Those were the days of shamateurism,' he says, 'and I even got a few quid for signing on and a few quid in my boot every week.

'I was very happy with the way things were: a wonderful family life, great friends, a lovely place to grow up, serving an apprenticeship.'

At the time it would have seemed unbelievable to Neill, the boy from Bangor, to be told he would spend most of his working life in London, playing football full-time and then managing Spurs and Arsenal. And that then he would involve himself in business ventures in the capital – and still does, which is why, nearly sixty years from the day he first crossed the Irish Sea, we meet in a sports bar not far from where he began his Football League career.

He says that when he first saw the headline in *Ireland's Saturday Night* he did wonder whether moving to England was what he wanted, but he was soon persuaded.

These were the days before agents. The signing-on fee for players launching their Football League careers or switching clubs was so minimal and tightly controlled there were not even slim pickings for acquisitive go-betweens. Except, that is, when it came to the movement of players from Ireland – south and north – to English clubs, a trade that operated outside these controls, a kind of Irish dispensation.

In Neill's case, Bangor knew precisely what to do to exact maximum compensation. They upgraded Neill from amateur to professional, which meant they could now negotiate a transfer fee with Arsenal. The fee of £2,500 was a record for Bangor at the time.

And how much of this was passed on to the player usually depended on canny parents making sure their boy did not miss out, either. In Neill's case, his cut was about £800, an amount, he says, that Bangor did not need much persuading to hand over.

'They knew that if they didn't I only had to hold on for another three or four months and then I wouldn't re-sign for them as an amateur and just go to the Arsenal for nothing. Call it a bung if you like, or a private deal, but I suppose it's far enough removed now for the taxman not to be coming after me.'

As we shall see, this was fairly common practice in the many instances of players moving from the big Irish clubs to the Football League.

Neill's starting wage with Arsenal was £12, reduced to £10 in a closed season that was long and uncluttered enough for some footballers to play a summer's professional cricket. On his father's advice, Neill invested £2 of his wages each month on an insurance policy that would provide him with a modest benefit when he retired from the game.

One relatively modern aspect of Neill's transfer to Arsenal was the involvement of a scout who spotted him playing for Bangor. Others I talked to told stories of being introduced to their first Football League club in ways that were laughably unsophisticated.

In two instances a chance meeting with someone only loosely connected to a club led to a first break; in another a corner-shop owner talent-spotted a youngster who would have a fine professional career; and then there was the case of the player whose enthusiasm for football was nurtured by nuns.

I travel more than four hours by train to the heart of Cornwall to meet Bill Leivers, whose life changed as the result of an unexpected encounter with a groundsman.

Leivers, who was born in Clay Cross in Derbyshire, is best remembered as a stalwart defender for Manchester City in the 1950s and early '60s. Now into his eighties – he was born in 1932 – he still has a muscular presence that fills the front doorway of his home when he greets me on a peerless June morning. His build remains such that I worry he might give me a practical demonstration of one of the shoulder charges with which he once intimidated all but the hardiest attackers.

However much he likes his West Country retreat, in an area he grew to love on family holidays, Leivers, I can tell, retains a greater affinity with his roots. This is evident when he tells me: 'I come from Clay Lane – that's just outside Clay Cross.' It is a clarification that clearly means a great deal to Bill Leivers.

It was here that Leivers 'really got into football', as he puts it, playing with a group of village lads who did little else in their spare time.

One afternoon, despite the boys' closeness, the competitive tension that was never far from the surface erupted into an incident. 'This boy had been getting up my nose,' Leivers says. 'Although I'm a big lad, I wasn't very aggressive at that time, but after he kept on and on and on I turned round and smacked him. I gave him a good hiding.'

With that, Leivers picked up his things and headed home.

'As I was walking along I came across a man who I knew nothing about except his name because he went to the same church as me. As I walked past him he said, "He'd been asking for that, hadn't he?" I told him I wasn't proud of myself but, yes, he had been asking for it.'

Their conversation continued until the young Leivers, intrigued by the man's interest, asked him what he did. 'I'm the groundsman at Chesterfield Football Club,' he said.

Moments before starting this story, Leivers had told me his great ambition was to be a Chesterfield player: 'I wanted people to recognise me. I think that was what it was all about really.' And now here he was talking to the club's groundsman.

With barely a pause he said, 'Oh, are you? Well how do I get a trial?'

The groundsman was non-committal but did say, 'We have a practice match every Tuesday morning.' Which was all Leivers needed to hear.

'I used to go to school in the mornings on the same bus as Shirley,' he says. 'We were courting when we were fifteen. I'd get off at Tupton Hall [Grammar School] and she'd go on to college in Chesterfield.'

(Shirley is the lady who would soon become his wife and who has been feeding me tea and delicious Cornish cakes from the moment I arrived at their St Austell home.)

On the next Tuesday, Leivers took his football kit with him and, instead of going to school, stayed on the bus with Shirley. He carried on to Chesterfield where he made his way to the football club and watched the practice match.

After it was over, Bob Brocklebank, the Chesterfield manager, asked Leivers what he was doing. He had come for a trial, Leivers told him.

'Oh, have you? Well go and get your kit on then.'

Brocklebank was waiting for Leivers, ball in hand, when he emerged from the changing room; out on the pitch Ray Middleton, Chesterfield's first-team keeper, was standing in goal.

'Just get outside the penalty area there,' the manager said, before rolling the ball to Leivers with the instruction: 'Go on, smack that in.'

'So that's what I did. Whoomph!' Leivers says. 'Middleton thought it was a bit of luck, but by the sixth one he's desperate because he can't stop the ball going in the net.'

Brocklebank was impressed and asked whether he could do the same with his left foot. 'Being a bit cocky,' Leivers says, 'I told him of course I could and whacked half a dozen in with my left foot.'

Brocklebank asked Leivers where he lived and said, 'Right, I'll take you home. Will your father be there?' Leivers told him he probably would be.

'I can honestly say had it been a piece of toilet paper I still would have signed it,' Leivers admits. 'I was about fifteen and still at school. I played for the school in the morning and then in the afternoon for Chesterfield, starting in the fourth team, I think.

'The first match I played was out in the country on a pitch that had more cow muck on it than grass. We won 10–0.'

With his future as a professional footballer now virtually assured, although he would never earn more than a basic wage of £9 a week at Chesterfield, Leivers left school of his own accord. 'I shouldn't have done, really, but I was fed up with it and didn't bother to go. I don't think anyone missed me.'

He found himself a job at a tube works in Chesterfield, but it was dull and no one spoke to him. When Shirley told him there was a post going at the town hall, where she worked, he went there until starting his national service with the RAF, aged eighteen, on May Day 1950.

Roy Wood's Football League career also began with a chance meeting that was even more improbable than Leivers's given that the circumstances had nothing to do with football.

He had just finished his national service and come back to England.

'I went to get my identity card changed and met an old school-mate, Alfie Peers, who'd been in the army and was also having his card changed. His father was a director of New Brighton. Alfie said we could go and train down with the club and keep ourselves fit, which seemed a good idea.

'And that's how I came to play a couple of games for New Brighton in 1951 at the end of their last season in the Third Division North.'

Wood never actually signed for the club. As he tells it: 'I only played because they didn't want to bring their regular goalkeeper from a long way away, which would have meant them having to pay his expenses. They knew I was a keeper so they stuck me in because I cost them nothing.'

New Brighton, who had been members of the Football League since 1923, had been floundering for some time and were kicked out, never to return, when they finished bottom of the League.

Wood proved more buoyant, resurfacing two years later. A bit like the ugly duckling, he rose resplendently in new surroundings. As the goalkeeper for a major club, he would be unrecognisable from the gangling youth who filled in so briefly as New Brighton's stopgap stopper.

Harry Low owned a corner shop selling groceries in Castle Street, Newcastle-under-Lyme. He used to stand in the doorway, a model for Ronnie Barker's Arkwright, watching the boys play football in the street.

One in particular caught the shopkeeper's knowing eye. Don Ratcliffe was younger than the others, but Low soon recognised that the scrawny slip of a lad's speed and skills set him apart from the rest despite their age advantage.

Like so many of Ratcliffe's vintage – he was born in 1934 – a variety of aches and pains have pursued him into old age, the legacy of playing when a few dabs of the 'magic sponge' were deemed sufficient for most injuries.

His legs are now a mess and when I visit him he is in a nursing home in Crewe, not far from his home in the village of Hough. His wife, Barbara, has told me he is having a rest from the rigours of everyday living.

It is mid-morning but he is still in bed when a carer shows me to his room. 'It's my knee,' he says after a few moments. Then, unbidden, he pulls back the bedclothes with a flourish before rolling up his pyjama legs. A long vertical scar runs down and over the right knee. 'I've had that one replaced,' he says. 'It's this one that's giving me the trouble.'

Superfluously he points to his swollen left knee. His leg looks like a child's Christmas stocking that has had a rugby ball stuffed halfway down it. But his calves, ankles and feet are those of a much younger man, still slim and athletic.

'The legs that used to pass the ball to Stanley Matthews,' I say.

'Yeah,' he says, and smiles.

Another carer puts her head around the door: 'You all right, Don?'

'Yeah, fine,' he says.

'He used to be a good footballer,' I tell her.

'I know,' she says. 'He's told me all about it. You played with Stanley Matthews, didn't you?'

'That's right,' he says.

They talk about the Champions League match between Manchester United and Real Madrid at Old Trafford that will be on television that evening.

'I don't like Man United,' the carer says. 'You don't like them, do you, Don?'

'Yeah,' he says. A bright note in his voice conveys he does like them.

'Oh no,' the carer says. 'I like Everton.'

The carer leaves and Ratcliffe tells me about his days growing up in Newcastle-under-Lyme, the Staffordshire market town not far from Stoke-on-Trent. He was born in Castle Street where Harry Low had his grocery shop. Football was what dominated his life from a young age.

'I used to go into Harry's shop three or four times a day for my mother,' Ratcliffe says. 'The lads and I would play in the street there or we'd go down to Stubb's Walks, a big open space with a bandstand. There were no goalposts or anything. We just threw our clothes on the ground to make goals.

'I got on well with Harry, we talked a lot. I think some of this was because he knew I was good at football. He told my brother that, although I was young, I was good enough to play with him in the under-18s at Harpfield Youth Club.'

He says the other boys at the youth club were too old for him really. He was twelve and they were four or five years older, which was a lot at that age. But he was always very quick, he says.

'When I started playing in the Football League, the Liverpool hard-man Tommy Smith said to me before kick-off, "I hear you're quick." I told him I was and he said, "Not with one leg you're not." I didn't go near him after that.'

In time, Harry Low tipped off Stoke City about Ratcliffe – or 'Ratter' as he became known – and the club sent scouts to watch him play. They agreed with the shopkeeper's assessment and signed him as what Ratter calls a semi-pro.

'Waddo [Stoke's assistant manager Tony Waddington] knew other clubs were interested in signing me,' he says, 'that's why he got in first. Port Vale wanted me and so did Bury, there were quite a few.'

The only thing he remembers about his first football wage was that it was more than he got as an apprentice plumber. 'I still lived at home and my mum used to say to me, "You keep what you're paid for your plumbing work and I'll have your football wages."'

For nine years, from 1954, Ratter was a regular in the first team and a favourite with the Stoke crowd. Even in old age, lying in a nursing home bed, he communicates a roguish charm. It is easy to imagine why he was so liked on the terraces.

Just about the only person he says he did not get on with at Stoke was Norman Tapken.

'He was the trainer when I arrived at the club. I didn't like him and he didn't like me. He said I was a dirty devil because I didn't wear any underwear. I used to tell him it was because I was that hard I didn't need any. But he kept on at me. One day he caught me cleaning my shoes and said I shouldn't bother with them, because I was a plumber, I should be cleaning my blowlamp instead.

'When Waddo got rid of him I looked him out and said, "Who's got to clean their blow torch now!" That made him mad.'

Before Terry Allcock's alarming car journey with the chauffeur who had a problem reaching the pedals, there were the nuns. And to tell me these stories he suggests we meet in a funeral parlour.

The headquarters of Allcock Family Funeral Services was once a pub on Norwich's City Road. The *Good Funeral Guide* rates these services very highly: 'Allcocks is staffed almost entirely by family members. They are a notably impressive lot, warm, friendly and unhurried – of a far higher calibre than most funeral home personnel.'

The guide is as good as its word. My meeting with the business's affable patriarch, arguably the best striker Norwich City have ever had, contradicts the idea that an undertaker has to be an old misery guts.

Not all the credit can go to the nuns for what Allcock achieved as a professional footballer after signing on for Bolton Wanderers. He was one of those naturally blessed athletes who excelled at a number of games.

At one point in his nascent sporting career, Allcock represented Yorkshire schoolboys at football and cricket – he remembers having cricket nets at Headingley with two future Test captains, Brian Close and Ray Illingworth, and the celebrated umpire Dickie Bird. He also played rugby league for Leeds.

But it was certainly the nuns at St Anthony's, a Catholic comprehensive in Leeds, who made sure Allcock's love of sport was nurtured from his early school years.

'They showed a great interest in sport,' Allcock says, 'which was good because the school didn't have a sports master as such and sport wasn't very highly organised. If it hadn't been for the nuns and their enthusiasm we'd have been in the hands of this one male teacher, an elderly gentleman. He was more or less a do-it-yourself job. He wasn't particularly interested but, despite everything, we were very successful.'

Within the space of a few years, Allcock had progressed from the protégé of nuns to claiming a place in the England schoolboys football team against the Rest. Along with most of the boys who were in that England side, Allcock was automatically filtered, as he says, into a top Football League club. He and Ray Parry joined Bolton; two of the others, Duncan Edwards and David Pegg, went to Manchester United.

'We weren't old enough to sign as professionals straightaway,' he says, 'and there weren't apprentices as such in those days. I signed as soon as I was seventeen for a weekly wage of £5 in the summer and £7 in the winter.'

The new signing was still seventeen when he made his debut for the Bolton first team in a home game against Manchester City in October 1953. He remembers his great excitement at being picked and playing in front of 50,000 people in what was a local derby, City being just five miles up the road. 'The crowd was big,' he says, 'but we'd been playing regularly in front of 10,000 to 15,000 in the reserves, so it wasn't too much of a shock.'

Allcock would score twice – a goal with each foot – as Bolton beat City 3–2. 'This was quite normal for me,' he says. 'I naturally worked the ball with my left foot but I felt equally adequate with either foot. Not like present players who can use only one foot.'

But before the '50s were out, Allcock had been transferred to Norwich City. He would spend the rest of his football career at the Norfolk club playing in the lower divisions. For such a talented player still in his prime – he was only twenty-three – it seems a nonsensical move. It was very much of its time, though, as will shortly be explained.

Howard Riley's only recollection of joining his first club, Leicester City, in 1955 was being paid his signing-on fee in ten-shilling notes; while Cliff Jones recalls his father's insistence that he learnt a trade in addition to signing on as a professional footballer.

'I recall walking out clutching all these notes,' Riley says. 'I was also issued with what was called a player's ticket, which I was supposed to show whenever I entered the ground, and a copy of the club rules.

'What my wage was I'm not sure. I didn't think of it too much. I was more interested in the big honour of signing for Leicester City than the money I got.'

Cliff Jones signed pro for Swansea in 1952, when he was seventeen, with the words of his father fresh in his memory. He says, 'At this particular time my father, who had himself been a very successful professional footballer, but had no other skill whatsoever when he packed up playing, was doing a crap job in a local steelworks.'

Because of his experience, Jones Sr understood as well as anyone that a playing career was, at the very most, only half a working life. Earning enough to retire to the golf course straight afterwards was unimaginable. And he was going to make sure his son did not make the same mistake. 'Listen, son,' he said, 'learn yourself a trade.'

Which is why, at the same time as going pro with Swansea, Cliff Jones signed up to serve a five-year apprenticeship as a sheet-metal worker in the Prince of Wales Dry Dock, clocking on at half past seven and off at five o'clock.

He is in no doubt about the benefit of having done this.

'It shaped me, if you like. It meant that when I did become a full-time professional footballer, I knew what working life was about. The majority of footballers today don't really know what working life is – all they know is football.

'I say football is not work; it's a pastime, even if it is a very highly paid pastime. When I was playing it wasn't so highly paid. But it was still a pastime.'

A number of other clubs wanted to sign Jones, which is why he started on £15 a week and £12 a week in the summer. 'I was also getting a bit of money, £2 10s I think it was, for doing my apprenticeship,' he says, 'so compared to my mates I was doing OK.'

When Terry Neill signed for Arsenal, he became merely the latest player from Ireland or with close Irish connections to be recruited by top English clubs. Those who had come over before Neill and whose Football League careers overlapped with his included George Eastham, Frank O'Farrell and Peter McParland.

Eastham had, in fact, criss-crossed the Irish Sea. Born in Blackpool, he was an only child whose parents moved to Newtownards in Northern Ireland in 1953 when his father was appointed player-manager of the semi-professional club Ards. Three years later he returned to England to play for Newcastle United. He made his Football League debut two weeks after his twentieth birthday.

Eastham's father, also George, was a decent player whose clubs included Bolton, Brentford and Blackpool. His one international appearance was England's first ever match against Holland in May 1935, an away friendly that England won 1–0.

Eastham had just finished school when the family settled in Newtownards. At Arnold School in Blackpool he had encountered the same problem as Neill: having to play rugby when his heart was in the round-ball game. But he did enjoy rugby sufficiently not to resort to Neill's guerrilla tactics to avoid playing it.

The young Eastham divided his Saturdays between representing the school at rugby in the mornings – his selection in the key position of fly-half was a sure sign he was a skilful player – and playing football for Highfield Youth in the afternoons.

Once out of school, Eastham says he fiddled around with a few apprenticeships, first as a joiner and then as a fitter and turner. All he really wanted, though, was to be a full-time footballer – and, unlike Cliff Jones's father, Eastham's did not insist he stuck with learning a trade.

No one could have guessed the effect of his not having a second job would soon have – not only on his career, but on the game in England.

To keep his son occupied, Eastham Sr started taking him to the Ards training ground. 'I was with my father virtually all the time,' Eastham says. 'I trained on my own in the mornings and afternoons and then I trained in the evenings when the rest of the players came to the ground. It was the only time I got to see other people.'

Bit by bit he worked his way into the Ards first team until landing a regular place.

'The nice part was that I got to play with my father. He was a very good inside-forward but I'd only ever watched him play. Then all of a sudden I was in the same side as him and we even won cups together, which not too many fathers and sons can have done.'

Eastham's performances for Ards gained him selection for the Irish League, which brought him to the attention of English clubs. The next thing he knew he had been bought by Newcastle and made his debut in the Football League against Luton in October 1956, two weeks after his twentieth birthday.

Eastham gives the familiar response to my question about his starting wage: he is not entirely sure what it was, but thinks it was £10 a week. Other things are more firmly lodged in his memory.

These include the sharp reprimand he received from Jimmy Scoular, the Newcastle captain. As far as Scoular was concerned, football was, first and foremost, a physical-contact sport and, second, a profession in which seniority meant something. He was well known for his tackling abilities and having no truck with young players.

Eastham recalls an early Scoular reprimand:

'I had the ball and I tried to beat somebody. They took it off me and Scoular said, "Who the hell do you think you are – Ernie Taylor?" Ernie was a very good player at that time, not one, Scoular reckoned, I should be trying to imitate. He told me to get rid of the ball as quickly as possible while I was learning my trade. You were supposed to know your place.'

Peter McParland's passion for football was also conflicted – although in his case rugby was not the other party in his love affair with sport. At the Christian Brothers St Joseph's school in Newry, County Down, which is in Northern Ireland, close to the border with the Republic, McParland played Gaelic football, which remains a potent symbol of Irish identity.

The school would not countenance any association with what it called soccer. And this was why McParland, who was captain of the school's Gaelic football team, found himself barred on one occasion from the Ulster schools final. 'You were playing soccer yesterday,' a Christian Brother told him, 'so you're not playing in the Gaelic final on Saturday.'

McParland liked the Gaelic form of football – 'It's a catch-and-kick game, which I enjoyed,' he says. 'It's rough and tumble' – but he preferred soccer. This was the game he played with his mates as soon as he left the school premises. When a summer league started these friends formed a team called Shamrock United.

It was while playing for Shamrock that McParland, aged sixteen, was spotted and, in 1950, joined Dundalk, who competed in the League of Ireland in the Republic. He soon established himself as a goalscorer.

He is mildly incensed when I tell him that Wikipedia has him down as scoring only two goals in fourteen appearances for Dundalk's first team. He points out that he scored two on his debut against Bohemians.

'I know this,' he says, 'because I was made the sports star of the week by the *Irish Independent*. When I went into work the next day the boys had pinned it up on the wall. So I was the big star in the workshop. They were all proud of what I was doing.'

In 1952, a trip with his summer league side to Birmingham included a visit to Villa Park. The highlight for McParland was a summons to play in a practice match with Villa's first-team players. These players then advised George Martin, Villa's manager, to 'sign the wee number ten who gave us so much trouble'.

McParland's transfer to Villa had marked similarities with Neill's move a few years later. As with Neill, McParland's amateur status was rescinded immediately before the signing so that money could change hands. 'At two minutes to three I signed professional for Dundalk and at two minutes past three I signed for the Villa,' McParland says.

Protracted negotiations over the transfer fee involved the owner of Dundalk and the chairman of Aston Villa, Fred Normansell, with McParland's father also having a say. 'I know that Dundalk were looking for £5,000 for me,' McParland says. 'In the end it was agreed that the fee would be £3,800 and I would get £1,400 out of it.

'It was a normal thing then with fellas who were transferred from Ireland to England to get a cut.'

According to McParland, his father 'then got a bit greedy'. After settling things with Dundalk, he went to George Martin and said, 'Now, what's the signing-on fee?' And Martin said, 'There's nothing other than the £10 signing-on fee when you sign for Villa.'

'So that was me signed for life – for a tenner,' McParland says. 'As things stood, Villa could decide what to do with me from then on.'

While Neill's professional playing career in England overlapped with Frank O'Farrell's, it did so by very little. When, in 1948, O'Farrell abandoned his idea of becoming a train driver to join West Ham United, Neill was only six.

Like McParland, O'Farrell was playing in the League of Ireland, for Cork United, when he came to the notice of West Ham. And, like McParland and Neill, he received a tidy backhander, in his case £1,000, when he was transferred for £3,000.

'Although I never quite made it to being an engine driver,' O'Farrell says, 'the new trains came in soon after I went to West Ham, replacing the steam engines, which is what I really wanted to drive, so I think I made the right decision.'

O'Farrell's move to London in January 1948 might have been a difficult transition for a young man from rural Ireland who, by his own admission, was not an instant success at West Ham. As it was, he settled down quickly in digs in Nigel Road, Forest Gate.

'Mr and Mrs Davy used to take in footballers,' he says. 'Mr Davy was a cooper by trade, making barrels, and a great West Ham fan. He used to tell me all about the old West Ham days. Sometimes I'd irritate him because he'd be telling me these things and I'd be deep in a book, but he was a lovely person so I never really got homesick. And quite often West Ham got knocked out of the FA Cup early on in January and then the club would let me go home to Cork for a week.'

O'Farrell's playing fortunes changed on the Monday night he went to Upton Park to watch the first team play a testimonial match against Arsenal. He was still in the reserves, struggling to justify his signing, when he was drafted into the side just before kick-off. 'Somebody had dropped out of the West Ham side,' he says, 'and I was available so they grabbed me.'

Arsenal had just won the Football League First Division (1948) and FA Cup (1950) and O'Farrell worried that playing against such powerful opponents might undermine his reputation still further. 'But as it turned out I had a good game and not long after Ted Fenton picked me for my first first-team game against Notts County. We lost the match 4–1 but he kept me in the team and I held onto my place for the best part of six seasons.'

Many of the Irish players and those with Irish connections who played in the Football League ended up signing for clubs in the north-west, so often the first landfall for those arriving from Ireland. Dave Whelan and Tony McNamara both had forebears from across the water.

'My grandfather was born in Tipperary,' Whelan tells me. 'He was a Catholic, his family had a farm, and he married my grandma who was a Protestant and they wouldn't allow them to marry in Ireland. So they came over and settled in Wigan. My father, who became a brilliant, brilliant singer, was born here and that's how I came to be part and parcel of Wigan.'

More accurately, Wigan came to be part and parcel of Dave Whelan after he purchased the football club, Wigan Athletic FC, in 1995.

In the 1950s, though, when Whelan was an ambitious young footballer, Wigan were not in the Football League – they joined in 1978 – and the young Whelan would end up signing for Blackburn Rovers, the Lancashire club who had been founder members of the League in 1888.

It was Whelan Sr's firm response to young Dave's acts of petty criminality that played a significant role in his developing into a highly effective player.

'My dad was serving abroad during the war and when he came home in 1946 I was nearly ten and not behaving myself – stealing things, usual stuff youngsters get up to,' Whelan says. 'He immediately grabbed me, marched me off to Wigan Boys' Club, which was only quarter of a mile away in Wallgate, and from there I just developed because of what they did for me.'

Of the variety of distractions the boys' club laid on for the young ne'er-do-wells – ranging from joining the brass band to honing snooker skills – football and rugby were what attracted Whelan. He was outstanding at both and went on to captain Wigan schoolboys at football and rugby league.

He was picked to represent the National Association of Boys' Clubs football team at Wembley, which in turn brought him to the attention of Football League managers. Johnny Carey, once a star performer for Manchester United and now manager of Blackburn, noted the young lad from Wigan with the combative attitude.

'One day,' Whelan says, 'Johnny Carey knocked on the door of our house and said he wanted to sign me. Him turning up like that amazed me because I was only just coming up to seventeen. To think that someone like Johnny Carey, with his record in football, came and knocked on our door, that did it for me.'

If Whelan's father had firm ideas about what was good for Dave, they were no firmer than those of his mother, who thought the same way as Cliff Jones's father. 'If you don't make it in football, love, you've got to have a trade,' she told him. Which is why young Dave's first employment was with Mellings, a company that manufactured winding gear for coal pits.

Whelan's determination to play football professionally could not be resisted for long, however. While he was still in his teens, the man who would go on to make millions in business signed for Blackburn for what even then was not much more than small change.

Tony McNamara's Irish ancestors farmed near Ballina in County Mayo. His father's father was the one who came to Liverpool, a city he made his home and where Tony, his grandson, would make his name as a footballer. A spring-heeled winger, McNamara, who was born in 1929, would play for both Everton and Liverpool.

A good young player for St Matthew's, his school in the Walton area of Liverpool, McNamara continued his football education in the Liverpool CYMS (Catholic Young Men's Society) League. 'It must have been while I was playing in that league for an evening institute side that I got spotted by Everton,' he says. 'And the reason I was spotted was that the team were playing in a match at Goodison in a final of some sort in which we beat a team from Crosby 11–1 – after they scored first.'

To say that Everton, having spotted McNamara, pursued their man doggedly would be overstating it. 'There was a player on the Everton books who didn't live far from us and the club asked him to go to visit this fella McNamara to ask if he'd play for Everton,' McNamara says. 'So he came along to the house and that's how it started.

'But Mr Bushell, who was the manager at the evening institute side, wouldn't let them have me straightaway because we were still in the running to win the league and cup. I joined Everton as an amateur at the start of the 1947–48 season.'

McNamara's elevation to being on the books of a Football League club received a mixed reaction from his parents. 'My father was a betting man who was too interested in following the horses to bother too much about my football career,' he says. 'My mother was the supportive one. I have this memory of her shouting from the stands, "Be quick, Tony; be quick."'

McNamara's future in-laws were happy enough that their daughter Doreen was courting a young man who was about to sign on as a professional footballer. But at a time when footballers were skint, their worth as breadwinners was not necessarily what mattered most.

Doreen tells me she was reluctant to talk to her parents about the gentle-natured young man she was dating. She kept it from them for as long as she could that her husband-to-be was a Catholic.

THE FIRST PROFESSIONAL

Fergie Suter, a Scottish stonemason, visited England for the first time in the mid-winter of 1875.

The slightly built eighteen-year-old with a limp moustache that looked like an attempt to establish his manliness was travelling by train with the Partick football team. They were on a London-bound express but going only as far as the textile heartland of east Lancashire – also a hotbed of football – for a fixture against Darwen FC.

Their sortie south was an indication of the extent to which football was on the move. It was a mobility that would lead to Britain's version of kicking a round leather ball about achieving a wider appeal than any other game.

Partick – not to be confused with Partick Thistle, a team that came later – were at the forefront of developing the so-called passing game. This had created a far more free-flowing spectacle than when the accepted procedure was for one player to dribble the ball until dispossessed.

Darwen FC were made aware of Partick's credentials by W. H. Kirkham, a former Darwen player. He had worked in the cotton industry before moving north to Glasgow where he became one of the leaders of this new style of play.

Now a Partick player, Kirkham had written to Darwen proposing a friendly fixture. His idea was swiftly taken up by the Lancashire club's progressive owners.

These far-sighted owners, who had established the Darwen club in 1870, were the sons of Nathaniel Walsh, an industrialist who, with his brother Ralph, ran power looms for weaving cotton at Orchard Mill.

Nathaniel's wealth derived from the coal that fortuitously lay beneath the family's smallholding in Darwen. It meant the Walsh boys – James and Charles and, almost certainly, George, the third son, too – had enjoyed a privileged upbringing. This included an education at Harrow, the public school in north London, much favoured by those with new money as somewhere to give their male offspring a leg up in life.

Over the years Harrow, along with Rugby and most other public schools, had cultivated games' playing, particularly cricket in the summer and various forms of football in the winter.

These games, so the theory went, encouraged team spirit in a competitive environment and promoted an ideal of conduct and character. Also, they exhausted the energies of young men who might otherwise have found less wholesome ways of doing so.

At Harrow, the Walshes loved their football to the point that when they finished their education and returned to Lancashire, they set about establishing Darwen FC. It would be a pioneering force in the game that was rapidly gaining popularity across Britain.

Crucially for the story of football's development, the Walshes and others like them did not entirely buy into the high-minded Corinthian ideal of amateurism and gentlemanly behaviour that had been preached to them at their public schools. They were receptive to any ideas or practices – even playing a team from Scotland of unknown pedigree – that would enhance football's appeal.

So it was that, on New Year's Day 1876, Darwen met Partick in a friendly football match at Barley Bank, a walled ground overlooked by Orchard Mill that was shared by the town's cricket and football teams. The grandstand, for wealthier spectators, consisted of seats perched on brewery wagons.

The Scots, with their superior passing game, won 7–0, but the fixture was judged such a success that a return contest took place in Scotland. This time Partick won only 5–0.

It turned out that the gap between the two teams was closing faster than the first two scorelines suggested. When the teams met for a third time, two years after the original fixture, Darwen won 4–2 in front of a crowd of 3,000 crammed into Barley Bank.

Despite this loss, it was Fergie Suter's contributions over the three games that had made the greatest impression.

He had celebrated his twentieth birthday on 21 November 1877 and his upper lip now sported a proper-looking moustache. On the pitch he combined stamina and determination with notable dribbling, or dodging as it was known, skills and the ability to consistently deliver precise passes.

When, on his return to Scotland, Suter not only suffered the disappointment of being rejected by Glasgow Rangers, but also faced the consequence of Britain's industrial decline, he knew exactly what to do: go south. This was where his services as a stonemason and footballer would be better appreciated.

This time he left Glasgow with a one-way train ticket in his pocket. His journey was not simply a personal milestone, it was a small piece of a wider body of evidence that football's status was undergoing a profound change.

Kicking a ball about was no longer just another form of recreation; it could now persuade a man to pull up his roots in search of a better life. And as the game progressed as a spectacle that people would pay to watch, clubs inevitably devised ways of holding onto their good players.

Still, though, the future into which Suter stepped was an uncertain one. It offered no more than the vague possibility that he might become slightly less poor than he was already.

Another Scot, Archie Hunter, who went on to captain Aston Villa to victory over West Bromwich Albion in the 1887 FA Cup final, said that he and Suter both came to England in 1878, 'and we two led the Scotch Exodus, as it has been called'.

Hunter, who has been described as one of Victorian football's first household names, also said in his book *Triumphs of the Football Field* – an unrecognisable forebear of the kiss 'n' tell memoir – that when Suter went to Darwen he 'practically taught that club the game'.

At first everything seemed harmless enough as Suter settled into his new life in east Lancashire. But, such was the fevered atmosphere now enveloping competitive football in the area that neighbourliness had come to mean jealously watching how other clubs conducted their business.

The question of the reprehensible practice of paying players for their services was growing particularly sensitive. So it was no surprise that a rumour spread rapidly after an official of the Blackburn side Turton was overheard being told to pay Suter out of prize money for his performance in a cup tie.

A dastardly deed had taken place that meant the footballing community of the north-west had a Scottish mercenary in their midst.

This may not have been strictly against the letter of the law; professionalism would not be officially banned – and then only briefly – until 1882, but it did grievously offend its publicly proclaimed spirit.

More accusatory murmurings followed when Suter, having been poached by Darwen, gave up his day job but still managed to live quite comfortably. The obvious conclusion was that he was being paid for doing something other than chipping away at lumps of rock.

He had pursued stonemasonry with enthusiasm in Scotland,

moving from Blythswood to Partick to be near new building sites. Now, though, he offered the unlikely claim that he was abandoning it because the stubbornness of the local Lancashire stone made his arms and hands swell. What sort of granite, people wondered, had he been happily chiselling into shape in Glasgow?

A letter to the editor of the *Football Field* accused Tom Hindle, the secretary of Darwen FC, of being 'one of the first to introduce so-called professionals into Lancashire' and asked darkly, 'Can Mr Hindle explain the circumstances attending Suter's first appearance for Darwen?'

The furore caused Hindle, an accountant from a respectable middle-class family, a great deal of discomfort. Keeping professionalism and sport apart was a shibboleth of his social circle – 'a sordid grasping after easy money' was the typical view of one opponent of professional football – but Hindle also found himself pulled in the opposite direction by his allegiance to Darwen FC.

Hindle would never admit the club paid Suter – or any other player. But the evidence was as conclusive as it could be that the Glaswegian now received payments and other favours for playing for Darwen.

Suter's own view of the consternation caused by what the new-moneyed classes regarded as the tawdry practice of footballers receiving remuneration for their services seems to have been fairly relaxed.

He probably knew enough of history to be aware that other sports, usually under the influence of an aristocracy who had long regarded sporting competition as little more than a gambling medium, stood aloof from worrying about moral implications of professionalism.

For example, Thomas Waymark, whose patron was the Duke of Richmond, was a paid cricketer, and openly so, more than 100 years before Suter was born.

What Suter would certainly have known was that some of his contemporaries who played cricket were being paid – a match between the Gentlemen (amateurs) and Players (professionals) had been an annual fixture for years. And an old football adversary, Tommy Marshall, openly received prize money for winning sprint races.

Suter was quite sharp enough to reason that the idea that footballers should not be similarly rewarded was untenable.

The journalist J. H. Catton wrote some years later that members of the Darwen club contributed a little each week 'to keep Suter in the necessaries'. In time he would be proclaimed – by Archie Hunter, among others – as the first professional to set foot on a football pitch.

CHAPTER THREE

MOVING ON...

In which George Eastham gives up playing for Newcastle to sell cork – a judge called Wilberforce puts an end to football's slavery rule – the Black Prince's goals are not enough to keep him at Old Trafford – Stan Anderson is persuaded to do the unthinkable and join Sunderland's great rivals.

M y long-distance call is answered by a cheery voice. It belongs to George Eastham.

He is quietly retired now in Cape Town where he settled in 1978. He considers the climate nicer there than in his native Lancashire.

It is a very long way removed in time and place from the '60s front-page drama featuring Eastham that rocked English football to its fossilised foundations.

When Eastham expressed a wish to top up his wage-capped earnings as a Newcastle United player, he unwittingly started a process that would expose and then bring down a major injustice enshrined in the game's outdated rulebook.

The year was 1960, by which time Eastham was a veteran of more than 100 first-team appearances for Newcastle in four years.

'When you think about it,' he says over the airwaves, 'it was a silly sort of situation. All I was looking for was a job in the afternoons because footballers did nothing in those days. You finished at lunchtime and then the rest of the day you became a good snooker player or whatever, a good golfer – but you didn't have anything to do.'

Eastham was approaching his twenty-fourth birthday. His wedding was coming up. It struck him that rather than potting snooker balls all afternoon it would make more sense to find a second job and save some money.

'In those days, when you married they gave you a club house to reside in, you paid your rent and that was how it worked. There was no buying your own house because you couldn't afford it.'

The house he had been given was on the shabby side. If he could earn a little more, he might be able to do something about it.

'But I couldn't get a job and I couldn't come to any agreement with Newcastle,' he says. 'They told me, "Oh, we'll get you a job, no problem, no problem." But nobody ever did anything.'

So one day he told them, 'I'm off to London to find work.'

In London he went to see Ernie Clay, an army friend of his father's, who had a firm in Reigate, Surrey. Thanks to Clay, later the chairman of Fulham Football Club, Eastham started work as a cork salesman. His career as a footballer was placed on hold because Newcastle had withheld his registration.

The club were entitled to do this under football's retain and transfer rule – aka the slavery rule – despite Eastham's contract with them having come to an end. What is more, in accordance with the rule, Newcastle stopped paying him and refused to release him to play for anyone else.

The upside for Eastham was that everyone wanted to buy cork off the man whose photograph and story were all over the front pages. 'Everywhere I went was an open door,' Eastham says, 'nobody said they didn't want to see me because I was in the newspapers. So I sold a bit of cork and I was getting more money selling it than I was playing football.'

Eastham hung on for seven months before Newcastle relented in October 1960 and allowed his transfer to Arsenal. For the moment, this ended one of the most acrimonious 'moving on' stories in English professional football. He repaid Arsenal with six productive years after starting off true to form: two goals on his debut and an early skirmish over his wages.

He fondly remembers his Highbury days: 'I did well at Arsenal,' he says. 'It was a good club for me' – and evidently the fans liked him, too. An approving profile on the Arsenal website says that Eastham was 'blessed with a left foot which wouldn't have looked out of place on the end of Liam Brady's leg'.

He is touched when I tell him this: 'Well, that's good enough for me.'

Something else was happening in the autumn of 1960. Professional footballers generally were on the march and their leader, Jimmy Hill, would soon threaten the strike that ended the maximum wage.

Emboldened by their victory on pay, the Professional Football-ers' Association resolved to press further for reform and remove the scourge of the slavery rule.

'Newcastle were probably hoping that after I eventually signed for Arsenal the dispute over the retain and transfer system would fall away,' Eastham says. 'But the PFA were looking to me to be the man to take the fight forward, to bring an end to the system.

'They were coming to the end of their resources – they weren't a big PFA in those days, they were a small PFA, the money wasn't coming in like it does now – but they offered to pay my expenses if I carried on.

'I said "Yes, let's do it. Let's go the whole hog." I wasn't happy with the way things had gone with my transfer. So the case went to High Court and that broke the retain and transfer system.'

It was a historic triumph that could hardly have been concluded by a more appropriate figure. The judge appointed to try the case in 1963 was Mr Justice Wilberforce, whose great-great-grandfather, William Wilberforce, had led the movement that resulted in the Abolition of the Slave Trade Act of 1807.

It seems almost too neat to be a mere coincidence that, 156 years on, Richard Wilberforce would be the one to abolish football's so-called slavery rule.

Little could Wilberforce or anyone else have known that his land-mark decision, even though loudly hailed at the time, would eventually transform the game by quite such a multiple.

The end of the maximum wage followed by the collapse of the clubs' feudal hold over the dressing room did not bring immediate major changes.

These came much later when television cash turned from a trickle to a torrent and the riches spilled over into the pockets of the players.

For the time being, things remained pretty much as they were. With still no significant financial inducement for players to move on, most were reluctant to uproot from areas where, in many cases, they had grown up and were now raising families of their own.

As we have seen, Terry Allcock was a reluctant mover in 1958. But his dilemma would have been no different had he been confronted with it five or even ten years later – clubs carried on being as tight-fisted as ever. The nation's economy running out of puff towards the end of the '60s removed the possibility that football directors might start to err on the side of generosity.

Allcock's club Bolton had an embarrassment of good attacking players and jumped at Norwich City's offer to buy him.

The club stood to make a profit but there was absolutely no financial incentive for Allcock to move from the First Division to the Third Division South. On the other hand, there was no financial downside. He would earn as much at Norwich as he had earned playing in the top division. Should he stay in the north-west, where he felt so at home, or should he go?

The clincher, Allcock says, was that 'I fell in love with the beauty of Norfolk' – a remark that prompts the unlikely thought that Adam Lallana, for example, chose Liverpool in 2014 because of the exquisite landscape of the Wirral.

Alex Dawson was another unhappy decamper. Like Allcock, he was forced to move on against his will for only a fistful of small change while his club, Manchester United, made thousands of pounds out of him.

Dawson, a tank of a man who would become known as the Black Prince, made his first-team debut for United in 1957, aged seventeen. He developed into an uncompromising finisher whose sixteen League goals in 1960–61 included hat-tricks against Chelsea and Manchester City in successive matches. The last thing he expected was the heave-ho from Old Trafford.

But United's manager Matt Busby had just paid Arsenal £35,000 for David Herd and needed to balance the books.

'Soon after Busby signed Herd, he asked me to report to his office,' Dawson says. 'I thought it was strange that he wanted to see me at this time, but I went along and he always started the same, by asking me how I thought I was playing.'

Dawson told him he felt he was doing OK, particularly as it had taken him two years to settle into the team after the distress of the 1958 Munich plane crash, which had claimed the lives of eight United players. 'It was hard on a youngster to be put in the first team after that,' he says. Although only young, he had played for the first team by the time of the disaster and was friendly with a number of those who were killed.

'Busby then asked me whether I was fit, and when I said I was, he told me the reason he had sent for me was that Preston had been in touch. Not only did they want me, he said, the directors had given him permission to sell me.

'I was stunned. It wasn't a bad move – I had six good years at Preston – but I couldn't believe it. But I suppose if you've got a young lad who someone's prepared to pay £20,000 for of course you're going to take it.'

Twenty grand for United, ten quid for Dawson: take it and leave us. That's the way it was. And the theory put about at the time was that Busby did these deals only with clubs where he felt the exiting player, particularly if he was much good, was unlikely to do any harm to United. Although Preston had some success in the '50s, their glory years were in the nineteenth century.

As George Eastham showed, there were other reasons for a player moving on when to do so profited him nothing. Eastham's was far from being an isolated case of someone wanting to leave because of a breakdown in his relationship with his club.

The great Stanley Matthews moved on twice in his marathon career

– once before and once after the end of the maximum wage. Both moves were precipitated by bust-ups with managers and neither did him the slightest good financially.

Although Matthews was impeccably behaved on the pitch, he was no paragon off it. He feuded with three of the five men he served under at club level.

In 1947, he left Stoke City, the club with which it was reckoned he had an unbreakable tie, for Blackpool after developing a dislike for his manager Bob McGrory that was entirely mutual. 'Get them off bighead,' McGrory advised a friend of Matthews's who asked him for FA Cup tickets.

Matthews returned to Stoke in 1961, nine months after the maximum wage had been scrapped. This time it was a row too many with the Blackpool manager, Ron Suart, that caused him to move on – or rather move back – to his old club.

The reason? Suart wanted Matthews to play as he was told; Matthews countered by asking whether all the other managers he had played under who allowed him to roam as he wished had been wrong.

Matthews's one falling-out with a manager that did involve money came right at the end of his playing career in 1965.

While Matthews accepted that as a footballer he was always likely to be skint, he felt that as a national celebrity, which he undoubtedly was, he deserved a few perks.

This led to a sour end to his friendship with Tony Waddington, the manager who had brought him back to the Potteries. Waddington told a friend that he was weary of 'the business of Stanley always wanting that little bit extra'. Only with the greatest difficulty did this friend dissuade Waddington from selling the story of 'the real Stanley Matthews' to a Sunday tabloid.

Stan Anderson was another highly regarded player who shocked his friends and, particularly, his family – along with the supporters of Sunderland – by moving on. As with Matthews, it was the manager who was the third party who caused the seemingly rock-solid marriage to fail with no post-nuptials for Anderson to ease the parting.

Certainly Anderson never thought he would leave Sunderland, the club to which he had been devoted since boyhood, even for a whacking financial inducement. But the course of Anderson's life changed when he fell out with Alan Brown. 'I didn't get on with the manager,' he says. 'It was a well-known fact. He probably didn't like my style of play, that was fine. I had no argument with him on that score.'

Anderson left Sunderland twelve years after that day in 1951 when, as a timid teenager, he had received instruction from Tommy Urwin about negotiating his signing-on deal. By now he had played 400 first-team games, represented his country and was one of the game's most polished midfielders, a master of the measured pass.

An incident in a League match brought the animosity between Anderson and Brown into the open, with the manager blaming Anderson for a long-range goal scored by John Charles for Cardiff City.

'I allowed big John Charles to hit it from thirty-five yards out,' Anderson says. 'I stood there and thought, "You're not going past me," and he had a shot. Young Jimmy Montgomery should have saved it; he had the ball in his hands but fumbled it and it went in the net.'

Anderson says he understood why Brown publicly faulted him to protect Montgomery's morale; Montgomery was at the start of what would become a long Sunderland career. His prodigious double save in the 1973 FA Cup final against Leeds would go down in club history.

What riled Anderson – and still does – was that Brown used this as a pretext to drop him. Not only that, rather than play Anderson in the reserves, which he wouldn't have minded so much, Brown selected him as a first-team travelling reserve. In those days before substitutes the reserve very rarely played.

'When I saw the team sheet for an away match at Plymouth and I was twelfth man I was bloody fuming,' Anderson says. 'I said, "Come on, boss. You're taking me all the bloody way to Plymouth! You could take anybody. Give a young lad the chance."'

Brown was unmoved.

It was the great Len Shackleton, formerly a Sunderland player now working as a journalist, who put the unthinkable thought in Anderson's Sunderland-for-life head: 'Stan, you ought to ask for a transfer.'

Anderson was told by Brown and Syd Collings, the club chairman, he would never be allowed to leave the club. But when Shackleton wrote a story in *The People* about Anderson's unrest, the story accelerated towards an improbable conclusion.

It was a Thursday night and Anderson was on his own at home, his wife having gone ten-pin bowling. There was a knock at the door.

'I want a word with you, Stan,' Alan Brown said.

Having been ushered to an armchair, the manager continued: 'You've been a fantastic servant to Sunderland, Stan, but because you want to play for another club we've accepted a transfer offer for you.'

'Oh, that's quite a change from telling me I'd never leave. Who wants me?'

'Actually, I've got the manager sitting in the car outside.'

'You're telling me that you've left the manager sitting outside in a bloody car all this time? What's going on?'

'Well, I wanted to agree something with you first, Stan.'

'Bring him in and let's have a look at who it is.'

Anderson says he just started laughing when the man who walked in was Joe Harvey, the Newcastle manager.

'You must be mad,' Anderson told Brown. 'Newcastle is the last bloody team I would ever go to. My family, from my father and mother down to my brothers and my cousins, they're all bloody Sunderland supporters. How the hell do you think I'm going to go to Newcastle?'

While he continued to argue with Brown, Harvey was killing himself laughing, Anderson says.

'Ah, you'll be all reet, man. You'll luv it up there.'

'Joe, I'm sorry but there's no way I can play for Newcastle, no way.'

Harvey did at least persuade Anderson to go to Newcastle to talk to Wilf Taylor, a Newcastle director, who would prove every bit as dogged as Anderson. 'Why you silly bugger, Stan,' Taylor said. 'Sign for us, man, you'll have a luvly time. Here, get the bloody pen in your hand and sign it.'

An hour later, Anderson, having rung his wife, Madge, to talk to her about it, went ahead and signed. But he knew the hard bit lay ahead – telling his father.

'I called him,' Anderson says, and recalls the telephone conversation:

'Dad, I've signed for another team.'

'Well, well, if that's what you want to do. Who is it then?'

'Newcastle.'

[Sound of the phone being slammed down.]

'He put the bloody phone down. Put the phone down,' Anderson says.

'Later I spoke to my mother who said, "He'll not speak to you." And for a couple of weeks I played my matches with only the wife there to watch me until we managed a couple of wins and I said to my mother she should try to get Dad to come along. Eventually he said he would – and he never stayed away after that.'

Anderson says that something happened: 'Joe Harvey probably had a hand in it, but my mother and father got invited into the boardroom at Newcastle and they never stopped going up there. They were always in the bloody boardroom. Other players' wives and mothers and fathers didn't go there, they were all in some other room.'

And so it was that Stan Anderson, a player of real substance, moved to a club that he had always imagined no amount of persuading would get him to join. And he did so for no more than 'a few extra pounds', even though the lid had just been lifted from how much players could earn.

CHAPTER FOUR

FOR BETTER, FOR WORSE

In which Cliff Jones takes a Tube ride to glory – Liverpool fans bounce the Milne family car out of a spot of bother – Chelsea shut the door in the face of an FA Cup finalist – a chance meeting in the street leads to Johnny Paton getting a First Division contract.

'Look, Cliff, do yourself a favour, son, you sign for Tottenham. They'll suit your style of play.'

Not all transfers in football's austerity years were to the accompaniment of one or other of the parties grinding their teeth.

The fatherly words of Ronnie Burgess, Swansea Town's manager, to Cliff Jones in 1958 were full of genuine goodwill towards a young man who ached to join one of the great English clubs. A deal was done and Jones, at the age of twenty-three, left Swansea for Tottenham Hotspur.

Jones never moved back to his hometown, even though he remains the proudest of Welshmen. In happy retirement, he lives in rural Hertfordshire, just north of White Hart Lane.

After visiting him on a bright spring morning, too beautiful for me to resist the two-mile walk from Cuffley Station to Jones's house, I am in no doubt that while Wales may be the land of his fathers, The Lane will for ever be his spiritual home.

The lure of the big club is nothing new. Names such as Manchester United, Liverpool, Newcastle, Arsenal and Tottenham resonated with players six decades ago just as they do today, even if joining one of them back then came with no discernible change in bank balance or lifestyle.

In Jones's case he saw next to nothing of the £35,000 that Swansea Town – they changed the Town in their name to City in 1969 – banked for selling him to Spurs.

'When I signed for Swansea as a seventeen-year-old,' he says, 'they gave me a £10 signing-on fee and when they sold me to Tottenham for all that money I got virtually nothing for six years' service.'

Jones was inspired to seek a transfer by the experience of a former teammate, Terry Medwin.

'Swansea were a very good Second Division side,' he says. 'The crowds wanted to see us because we played attractive football. But we weren't getting anywhere. I was ambitious and I wanted to play at a higher level, something I'd seen Terry, who was another Swansea boy, do at Tottenham.'

A number of clubs had shown an interest in Jones, who in time would be seen as among the best left-wingers in the world.

When word reached Burgess, the Swansea manager, that two of the front-runners for Jones's signature were Tottenham and Arsenal, he did not stand in the player's way. He did, however, tell him that on no account should he sign for Arsenal.

As a former Tottenham player himself, Burgess could not stand the thought of Spurs' north London rivals burgling a player of Jones's quality. He took Jones aside and advised him to do himself favour: White Hart Lane was the place for him.

If Jones's memory is correct and Burgess also told him Spurs would suit his style of play, it was a prescient piece of advice. At the time Jones signed, early in 1958, Spurs were struggling under manager Jimmy Anderson. It was not until later in the year, when Bill Nicholson was plucked from the coaching staff to replace Anderson, that the club's future was entrusted to the man who would bring the very best out of Jones.

Jones remembers well his debut for Tottenham, and not just because it was against Arsenal at Highbury a week after he signed. He was still doing national service and travelled to the game by Tube from St John's Wood. He had not so much as trained with his teammates since signing.

'When I arrived at Highbury, the commissionaire in the marbled halls – a big old bombardier sort, all uniformed up – wouldn't let me in.'

'What's up, son?' the bombardier asked.

'Cliff Jones, I'm playing today.'

'I've heard that one before.'

Nicholson, who was the first-team coach and had told Jones to arrive by 1.30 p.m., had to be called.

'That's him,' Nicholson said. He then shook Jones's hand and added, 'By the way, you're late.'

The match ended 4–4 with Jones having what he says was 'a very good game'. But what he recalls most clearly is something that happened shortly before kick-off.

Nicholson looked at his boots and said they were no good, particularly the studs. 'In those days you didn't have screw-ins or blades, you had them knocked in,' Jones says.

'So anyway, about ten minutes before half-time, I've picked the ball up and they had this big full-back Jim Fotheringham. My plan was to go at him at pace with the intention of stepping inside, which I managed to do. Jack Kelsey was the goalkeeper and I'm just on the edge of the box and I can see myself slotting the ball just inside the far post. But just as I'm about to do it I slipped, didn't I?

'Of course, as soon as I came in at half-time, Bill said, "What did I tell you about those boots?" He paid great attention to detail did, Bill. "In future, son," he said, "we're looking after them boots." That was it, then, the boots were sorted out for me.'

Gordon Milne was someone else who found the appeal of an illustrious name irresistible when he moved to Liverpool from Preston North End in 1960. In his case, he had just come out of the army.

'I'd played eighty-odd games for Preston in the late '50s, so I must have done something right in that period,' Milne says, 'and I'd also played for the army team, which in those days was a good strong side.'

First Arsenal made an approach for the newly demobbed Milne, before Bill Shankly, a former Preston stalwart who had recently been made Liverpool manager, expressed an interest. 'You don't want to go to London, son,' Shankly, a Scot who specialised in succinct advice, told Milne after making a special trip to see him.

He also told him, 'We're a sleeping giant' – a reference to the fact that Liverpool, who had won their fifth League title in 1947, were now in the Second Division and still looking to win the FA Cup for the first time.

'I'd read about Shanks,' Milne says. 'He was just an enthusiast. His passion was for football and he believed in Liverpool. He knew what he wanted and he knew how the game should be played – simple and straightforward. He always emphasised the team, players complementing one another.

'But at the time it worried me whether I'd made the right decision by turning down Arsenal, who were in the First Division. It was only in the long term it turned out to be the best move I ever made.'

Liverpool paid £16,000 for Milne with the player receiving the statutory tenner as a signing-on fee.

'Shanks had started building at that time and I was the first one of that team he signed,' Milne says. 'Afterwards he signed Willie Stevenson, Big Ron [Yeats], Ian St John and Peter Thompson. This group joined what they'd already got there: Tommy Lawrence, Chris Lawler, Gerry Byrne, Ian Callaghan and Roger Hunt.'

Milne did not start well. His first-team debut in August 1960 was a 1–0 home defeat against Southampton.

'I always remember Joe Fagan, who was number three behind Shanks and Bob Paisley, coming to me. Joe had a different nature from the other two, a softer nature. Joe said, "The manager thinks it'd probably be better if you had a little spell in the reserves. Moving clubs is a big thing."

'In those days you didn't challenge things. There wasn't the arrogance among players there is now.'

The match against Southampton has a number of memories for Milne, including the fact that he was driven to Anfield by his dad. His mum and Edith, his wife-to-be, also came along. 'There was no meeting at a hotel or anything like that. You just turned up at the ground. It was a wet night, we parked in a side street and walked to the ground.'

When they went back to the car after the game, they found it jammed in by other parked vehicles.

'Now I'd just signed for Liverpool and we're standing there wondering what to do. Some fans came by who recognised me. "Oh, there's Gordon Milne. Let's go and help." And they bounced the car out. They bounced it so my dad could get the front of the car out. "Don't worry about the game," they said. "It's only your first game." All this sort of stuff. Typical Scousers.'

Grateful for their kindness, Milne was not convinced by the fans' encouraging words:

'The fact was I was very ordinary. We lost the match to Southampton and I was like a little boy lost, partly because I didn't know anybody. Things changed when Shanks started to bring in other new players and build a new team. So I wasn't the new boy anymore and it clicked from that.

'Sometimes players have different styles and they have to adapt to each other, but with Shanks it was square pegs in square holes. There were no oddballs.'

During the time he spent in the reserves, Milne worked at justifying his first-team selection in midfield ahead of Johnny Wheeler, who was coming to the end of his career. Also during this period he married Edith.

'Having to find a house was one of the reasons it took me time to settle as a player,' he says. 'The house we eventually found was a place in Kenyons Lane in Lydiate on the road to Ormskirk. It was £2,600.'

It was not uncommon for a female – usually the wife or future wife – to be the most influential figure in determining a player's next move. And it was for entirely different anthropological reasons, many too many to mention, that the heroines of the 21st-century TV series *Footballers' Wives* wielded such influence.

Straight after the war, Johnny Paton looked forward to settling back in Glasgow once he completed his national service at the RAF base at Bentley Priory on the outskirts of London. He was fed up with the weekend commutes to and from Scotland to play for Celtic.

All this changed when he met Eileen at a dance at Watford Town Hall and 'things started to get a wee bit serious between the two of us'.

Initially, Eileen, who lived with her family in north London, had been unsure about going out with the young Glaswegian. 'She asked me what I did for a living,' Paton says. 'I told her I played football for Glasgow Celtic up in Scotland, which meant nothing to her. I could tell her mind was going round wondering how being a footballer was going to pay the rent and other bills.'

The moment he knew she had overcome these misgivings was when she invited him to her home in Greenford. 'The family want to meet you, Johnny,' she said. 'Can you come for a roast dinner on Sunday?'

'I wasn't going to miss that,' Paton says. 'A roast dinner. Never heard of it up in Scotland. We got mince and potatoes for Sunday dinner up there.' It goes without saying, of course, that a bigger reason for accepting the invitation was Eileen.

At this point, Paton says, fate took over.

Walking from Sudbury Town Tube station to keep his lunch date with Eileen's family, he noticed another man coming briskly down the road towards him. 'There were only the two of us,' he says. 'There was no traffic on the roads in those days.'

To his surprise, the other man stopped and – to his even greater surprise – said, 'I know you, you're Johnny Paton, aren't you? Glasgow Celtic?'

Paton took a closer look and saw it was Johnny Harris, the captain of Chelsea. 'He was much better known than I was.'

'Yeah,' Harris said, 'what are you doing down here in London?'

Paton explained he was waiting for his demob and travelling up to Scotland every Friday night to play for Celtic on the Saturday. 'I'm under contract to them. I've got to get my wages.'

Harris had a better idea: 'Why don't you come and play for us?'

And that extraordinary chance meeting was how Paton came to play for Chelsea during the 1946–47 season. 'It was a unique one-season transfer,' he says. 'It wasn't a loan, it was a complete transfer and a complete transfer back. It was because I wanted to be here in London with Eileen.'

In his season with Chelsea, Paton played eighteen times and scored three goals, but it was many years later, in old age, that he had more of an influence on a Chelsea match than he ever did as a player.

In December 2013, eight months after his ninetieth birthday – he was by now the oldest surviving Chelsea player – the club invited him to watch a Sunday match against Southampton at Stamford Bridge. And once there he was invited to go on the pitch at half-time to address the crowd. He agreed because there was something he badly wanted to say.

He remembered that in his Chelsea playing days he thought the home support was pretty pathetic compared to what he was used to at Celtic. And now, nearly seventy years later, he felt the same. Chelsea were losing 1–0 to Southampton at half-time and the crowd were not giving the team the lift they badly needed.

So he took the microphone: 'I've waited a long time to say this. I'm ninety years old but I'm very, very proud to have worn the Chelsea jersey, sixty-seven years ago, on the left wing, when we beat the Arsenal in an FA Cup tie.'

The stadium, which had been quiet, erupted, and the noise rose to a crescendo as Paton asked twice: 'Do you really want Chelsea to win this game?'

He now had a captive audience. 'Well,' he told them, 'I want to hear the Chelsea roar. The players on the field, in my opinion, won't win this game – you will.'

'The place went mad,' Paton says. And down in the Chelsea dressing room, John Terry told Paton later, the players were aware of a buzz going on and wondered what it was.

After the match, Chelsea having won 3–1 after scoring within minutes of the restart, a message reached Paton that José Mourinho, the Chelsea manager, wanted to see him.

'I'd never met him,' Paton says. 'And you know what he said? I couldn't believe it. He said, "Johnny, I want to thank you. You helped us to win this match."' Paton told him that he had merely done what came naturally.

In 1947, after his season with Chelsea, Paton went back to Scotland. He would probably have stayed there had it not been for two things: one, he fell out with Celtic; and two – and more importantly – his London fiancée, Eileen, was now his wife.

His row with Celtic was all about money. He earned only £8 a week from which the club deducted £1.50 in rent. After other deductions had been taken into account he took home just £5.

'I was constantly asked by people for my autograph,' he says, 'and I would tell them, "Actually I should be asking you for your autograph. I only earn a fiver a week."'

When, in 1949, Celtic said they would drop his wages by £2 if he was injured, he had had enough and headed south to be close to Eileen's family. Through a contact he fixed up a move to play for the west London club Brentford.

Brentford was the same club Bill Slater would join two years later – and, as with Paton, the lady in his life proved a big influence. 'In 1951, I met my wife-to-be,' Slater says, reminiscing at his home in Ealing. 'She was teaching in London, she was from around here, and because I wanted to see her at weekends I decided to see if a London club would have me.'

Such was the limit on footballers' earnings that Slater, who was studying at Carnegie Physical Training College in Leeds, preferred to carry on as an amateur when he first played for Blackpool in the Football League in 1949. Two years later he was running parallel lives, lecturing in PE at Birmingham University while still turning out for Blackpool for no pay.

Meeting the London girl who would become his wife put an end to this arrangement. As their romance flourished, Slater decided to move to a club in the capital that might sign him. With his future bride at his side, he went first to Chelsea.

'We don't take on people like that. You have to be a good player,' the man at the Stamford Bridge door said.

'I think I am a good player,' Slater replied, which was a fair point considering he played for Blackpool in the '51 FA Cup final alongside Stanley Matthews. 'Will you speak to someone in the club for me?'

'No – no, no. Don't waste my time,' the man said, and closed the door.

'So, a bit disappointed,' Slater says, 'we set off round to Brentford where they at least said they would have a look at me.' Jackie Gibbons, the manager who took on Paton, was still in charge and liked what he saw.

Slater began playing in the Brentford reserves but was soon promoted to the first team. 'Jimmy Hill was the other wing-half and Ron Greenwood was the centre-half, so I was in good company.'

When Slater made it into Brentford's first team the club agreed to pay his travelling expenses, which was the only remuneration he received. He still did not want to commit himself as a pro, having just landed a post as a lecturer.

He played only one season at Brentford before, now as a married man, he moved with his wife to the Midlands to be close to his university job.

Wolverhampton Wanderers signed him and he became an indispensable member of the mighty Wolves sides of the 1950s. 'I played my first two years or so with Wolves as an amateur,' he says.

'I never became a full-time professional, but the club told me they were keen to pay me something. I'd never really thought about it, I just didn't think it would be possible, but I checked at the university with my head of department. I suggested that if I received payments from Wolves I would acknowledge in my contract that my teaching duties at the university had priority.'

It was as unique an arrangement as the one that took Paton to Chelsea.

Not everyone moved on. Remaining a one-club player was more common then than it is today, even if some of the old, tempting advantages for staying put still apply: chiefly, the possibility of being awarded a benefit or testimonial match and being cherished by fans, who gave players high marks for loyalty.

The saintly Tom Finney was the exemplar of the faithful player. He signed for Preston North End during the Second World War and stayed there until 1960, supplementing his football income by working as a plumber. Preston fans adored him.

But even Finney was prepared to move on if the price was right. In 1952, the Italian club Palermo offered him a package that included a £10,000 signing-on fee, a monthly wage of £130 before bonuses, a villa and a sports car. Finney, into his thirty-first year, was eager to say, 'Yes, please.'

But the player and the sweet-talking Italians had reckoned without the straight-talking Nat Buck. The Preston chairman had made his wealth out of building houses and calling a cement mixer a cement mixer.

When Finney told Buck about the offer he wanted to accept, he received a blunt reply: 'Listen to me, Tom,' Buck said, 'if tha' doesn't play for Preston then tha' doesn't play for anybody.'

End of conversation.

CHAPTER FIVE

YOUR COUNTRY NEEDS YOU

In which illness rescues the Preston conscript's playing career – a wartime recruit finds out what 'flying by the seat of your pants' really means – Colin Collindridge sits in a Lancaster bomber expecting to be blown up – a member of the army football team decides to desert.

G ordon Milne clearly remembers the day when, at the age of twenty-one, he thought, 'That's my football career ended.'

The year was 1958, when Milne was an eager prospect playing for Preston North End.

At that time, beyond Milne's narrow existence, the world was stuck fast in the permafrost of the so-called Cold War, which was in fact a long, dangerous peace that followed the Second World War. It meant that, until 1960, young men continued to be called up to do national service in the armed forces.

Many hundreds of professional footballers were among them.

In Milne's case he was conscripted into the East Lancashire Regiment, whose fairly recent history included a heroic role defending the Dunkirk beaches during the evacuation of British forces from France in 1940.

After basic training Milne would be posted locally so he could continue to play football. Or so he imagined.

A pattern has emerged since I started to gather material for this book. Nearly all my veteran interviewees have been contentedly married for many years. It is tempting to think of this fact as an essential difference between now and the old days. Could it be that making do on small wages created a more lasting marital bond?

The wives are invariably the ones who answer my phone call and, always very obligingly, pass me on to their husbands. Edith Milne is no exception. Gordon Milne says he would be happy for me to come to see them.

The Milne house is in a neat crescent in a suburb of Hinckley in Leicestershire. It is no mansion but is probably the poshest of all the homes I visit. I imagine this is not unconnected to Milne's long career as a manager – at home and overseas – after he stopped playing. Christmas is coming and some elaborate decorations are in place.

We chat in a spacious, meticulously housekept living room. David Peace's book *Red or Dead*, which is about Milne's old club Liverpool, is on a table next to where he sits. The book has been a big success, but Milne says he is finding it hard going.

Milne was showing early signs of the player he would become when his call-up papers dropped on the doormat. As he picked up the envelope, military service was the last thing on his mind. He had recently made his first-team debut for Preston, the club for which his father, Jimmy, had played and where he was now trainer. The family lived a goal-kick away from Preston's Deepdale ground.

Milne's debut match was a First Division fixture at Portsmouth, but all he really remembers about it was that he was playing in the same team as Tom Finney. Given that Milne found it awe-inspiring to be in the same room as Finney, to be on the same pitch was almost overwhelming.

'And then I got called into the army,' he says. For the first six weeks he and his fellow recruits did basic training, 'a six-week void', as he calls it, 'when I lost contact with Preston, dropping off the perch as far as the club was concerned'.

Even so, at this point Milne had reasons to be confident his football career would not be badly affected. His regiment was based at the Ful-wood Barracks in Preston and the colonel-in-chief, a Colonel Knight, was keen on sport and knew the chairman of Preston North End. Between them, the two men – the colonel and the chairman – would secure Milne a local posting.

After two weeks' leave, the recruits returned to the barracks. 'There were big boards up on the walls with our names on them in alphabet-ical order and where we were going to be posted,' Milne says. 'And my name was on the list to go to Malaysia.'

The moment Milne saw this his heart sank. His world was about to be shattered. He raced home, got in touch with the club, but was told, 'Sorry, we can't do anything about it. If your name's on the board there's no way we can shift that now.'

Milne was desolate: 'Two years away, I'd be twenty-three when I got back. God knows what would happen then.'

He spent the next ten days being kitted out for the Far East – uniforms including jungle greens, weaponry and various medications. Then there was a week's leave to say his farewells before setting sail.

It was during this week that providence rescued his football career.

'I was still living at home with my mum and dad in their terraced house,' he says, 'and during that week I developed a throat infection that turned into quinsy. It might have been the shock of being posted to Malaysia, but for two weeks I was out of it, I was genuinely gone, and in that two weeks my army group left.'

When he returned to Fulwood, he presented the regiment with a problem: what do we do with this guy? There's no one left here, what do we do with him?

The solution, Milne says, was so lucky it was hardly true. Colonel Knight's batman was finishing at that time. So the colonel had a word, the club had a word, and eventually Milne got the job as the CO's batman.

'For the rest of my national service I was living at home, jumping on the bike at half past six in the morning, up to the CO's house, put the kettle on and made sure all his kit was ready for parade: boots clean, trousers pressed, hoovered his house, which was on the Fulwood campus, made up the fire. This was like paradise. No drills, no guard duty, no anything: just the CO's batman. I was fireproof.'

Milne resumed part-time training, which included joining up again with his Preston teammates. In time he played his way back into the first team.

And it was because of this outcome, wholly the result of Milne's attack of quinsy, that he came to the attention of Bill Shankly and was one of the great Liverpool manager's earliest recruits.

It was a propitious time to become an honorary Liverpudlian. The Beatles had just been formed in that city and Shankly was about to give the name Liverpool FC a lustre that has survived, still bearing his imprint. Milne, with his poster-boy looks and unruffled presence in the Liverpool midfield, might have been supplied by central casting.

Like Milne, Bill Slater played football regularly during his national service after missing out at the last minute on being posted to Asia. In his case, though, with the Second World War not quite yet over, the circumstances were very different.

'I was starting to get established in Blackpool's wartime team,' Slater says, 'when, at eighteen, I was called up into the forces.

'Although the war in Europe was more or less finished, there was still action in the Far East and I was on a draft to go out there – by then I was in the army Physical Training Corps – but almost the day before I was due to leave the Americans dropped the atomic bomb on Hiroshima and everything changed.'

Slater was sent to Germany and, with the war coming to an end, the only action he saw was at the physical training centre where he was posted and on the football field.

'Wherever I happened to be,' he says, 'there was usually a football team and I played quite a bit. I was still an inside-forward then and we had matches against other army teams or German teams.'

Even those who served a little earlier than Slater, when the Second World War was at its height, had opportunities to carry on playing, particularly if they spent extended periods based in Britain.

After Prime Minister Neville Chamberlain's solemn declaration of Britain being at war with Germany in September 1939, his government quickly decided that suspending professional football indefinitely would be a self-inflicted wound to national morale. Within a week, a list was drawn up of those regions where matches that admitted ticket-buying spectators could take place.

Areas thought to be at risk of heavy bombing by the Luftwaffe were excluded.

Johnny Paton was one of those footballers-turned-servicemen who played on during the war – until the RAF sent him overseas. He still has a newspaper cutting with the headline: 'CELTIC'S FLYING WINGER SCORES FOUR GOALS IN A WEEK AFTER DOING HIS FIRST SOLO FLIGHT'.

Paton had been conscripted in 1943, the year after he signed for Celtic. He had long wanted to be a pilot if he were called up and by joining the Air Training Corps had already received rudimentary instruction in navigation, air spotting and gunnery. As a result he was accepted for flying training and packed off to St Andrews.

Within days he grasped why aviators often talked about flying by the seat of their pants. After only seven lessons in a Tiger Moth biplane he received what he says was the shock of his life when his instructor told him, 'Go on, Paton, take it up.'

'What do you mean, take it up?'

'Take it up.'

He says he trembled with fright as he walked over to the Tiger Moth. He had difficulty keeping his footing as he climbed into the open cockpit. But thanks to his determination and the resilience of the seat of his pants, he survived the ordeal.

With a wistful shake of the head, he marvels now at how he managed it. 'When you're young, circumstances prevail, things happen and that's it,' he says.

Not long afterwards, the RAF transferred him to Regent's Park in London as a prelude to his being posted. While he and his fellow conscripts waited to hear their fate, Paton says they just marched up and down every day until they were sick of it. But there was also the considerable consolation of being let out to play football.

He guested for a number of clubs, Celtic's permission having to be sought before each game. Among others, he turned out for Arsenal, appearing on the left wing with Stan Mortensen [of Blackpool and later of England] as his inside-forward. 'Like myself,' he says, 'Stanley was in the RAF.'

To his dismay, though, Paton received word that while he had been accepted for flying duties he had not been accepted as a pilot. He complained without success.

'I told them I wanted to be a pilot and I didn't want to be anything else. I'd flown a plane – not very well – but at least I'd done it. But they wouldn't budge and told me I was going to be trained as a navigator. We were known as sprog navigators, which was just about the lowest you could get.'

Navigators, along with other aircrew members, were sent either to Africa or Canada to do their training, the skies over Britain being too dangerous for non-operational flying.

Paton went to Canada where he spent a year and half at Mountain View in New Brunswick and then nine months on Prince Edward Island in the Gulf of St Lawrence. It was from here that he did his main navigational training all over Canada.

'I was trained as a bomb aimer as well,' he says, 'although the only bombs I dropped were in Lake Ontario. They had big targets and if your bomb landed within half a mile of one it was recorded as a hit.'

While Paton was in Canada, the war finished, and he never did aim a bomb in anger.

Colin Collindridge, on the other hand, was involved in the RAF's bombing operations against Germany after being conscripted in 1941. But his job as a bomb armourer meant he did not leave the British Isles, and the most danger he was ever in was when he nearly blew himself up.

As well as serving his country as a bomb armourer, he played for a number of football clubs competing in the wartime leagues. Taking advantage of the freedom to turn out for whoever wanted him, he wore the colours of Sheffield United, his peacetime club; Notts County, which was close to his RAF posting; Lincoln City; and Oldham Athletic.

Collindridge was nonplussed when told he was to be trained as an armourer. 'I didn't know what it meant,' he says. 'They said it concerned either bombs or guns and I didn't know anything about either. I did roughly ten weeks training as a gun armourer near Penrhos in North Wales.'

As Collindridge tells it, he did not have a good war in Wales, which in his very personal view was tantamount to being sent abroad. He says he has never been back there since, except to play football, and he has no intention of returning.

'It's not the fact that the Welsh people aren't nice people – but I didn't like anything about Wales.

'The beer for one thing. The length and breadth of England I've made a point generally of having a pint in every town I've been to. Glenice, my wife, reckons the best pint is in Nottingham, but for someone used to Barnsley bitter the Nottingham beer is like home brewery, like drinking shandy. In Wales the beer was lousy, like vinegar.

'There was another thing, too. If I went in a pub with one or two pals the people in there would be talking in English, but as soon as we rolled in in uniform they'd start talking in Welsh. Bloody Welsh rubbish, so bang [he punches the palm of his hand], there were punch-ups. And I was a useful boxer.'

Having trained as a gun armourer in Wales, Collindridge was sent on another course, this time to learn to arm planes with bombs. 'This is how I ended up at Syerston near Newark,' he says, 'staying fit by winding bomb loads onto Lancasters.'

He reels off the makeup of one of these loads: 'It involved a cookie and cans; a cookie being a 4,000-pounder with a lot of explosive – it would blow a whole street up – and a can being an incendiary case about four times as long as a cookie but much thinner. There were fourteen bomb outings for the cans on a Lancaster but you didn't put any either side of the cookie.'

The idea was that these bombs were then released over Germany. But one day things did not quite work out as planned.

'There were four in a bomb crew,' Collindridge says, 'two upstairs winding the bomb on and two downstairs guiding it up to fit where it should.

'On this particular day we'd just put the cookie on, it had clicked into the safety position, and me and a mate, Johnny Kirkby, were sitting in the kite [the Lancaster] having a rest. I was sitting in the wireless op's seat and, suddenly, the kite went up a couple of feet.

'We looked at one another and ran to the front, down the dip into where the bomb aimer operated and I said, "What was that then?" Johnny couldn't talk. He pointed. "The cookie, the cookie," he said, eventually, "it's dropped off."

'I couldn't talk either for about five minutes. We thought it might have gone off. You never knew your luck with those bombs because so often they used to go off when they shouldn't have. I wanted to run away from the aircraft but my pride wouldn't let me – and it was not long before they had sent somebody to take us to the next kite that wanted bombing up.'

No one reported the incident to the authorities, although, Collindridge says, 'the authorities weren't our main concern. It was the aircrews who took the kites out we thought about. I had one or two friends who were aircrew and I always respected them.'

Although he admits to some resentment that the war coincided with what would probably have been his best footballing years, he counts himself lucky.

'A local lad, Ernest England, was captured by the Germans at Dunkirk. He'd worked down the coalmine at Woolley and when he was taken prisoner they stuck him down a coalmine in Germany. He came home and he'd been back for a week when he died. I'm not sure what he died of, but what happened to me was nothing compared to that.'

A number of professional footballers lost their lives actually fighting in the war, although far fewer than in the 1914–18 conflict. Two Bolton players, Harry Goslin, a defender who represented England against Scotland at the start of the Second World War, and Walter Sidebottom were among those who died.

Goslin, the Bolton captain, told a crowd of more than 20,000 at Burnden Park in April 1939 that after the match against Sunderland he would lead his teammates to the local Territorial Army hall to sign up. He was killed in action in Italy in 1943, when a mortar exploded in a tree under which he had set up an observation post.

Sidebottom, aged twenty-two, died the same year, drowned when his ship was torpedoed in the English Channel.

The war also threw up instances of grim humour. Just before a match at Preston's Deepdale ground, an air-raid siren sounded. As the players hurried to the nearest shelter, one of them remembered he had left his top set of false teeth in the dressing room. He had to be forcefully persuaded not to go back to retrieve them.

Other players' wartime experiences were as children and adolescents, their national service coming later. The most vivid memories belong to those who recall the blitzes. These were not confined to London and the south-east. They included cities across the land, from Bristol and Plymouth in the south-west, Cardiff and Swansea in Wales, Birmingham and Coventry in the Midlands, and Liverpool, Manchester and Newcastle-upon-Tyne in the north.

Tony McNamara, who would represent Liverpool's two great clubs, remembers intense bombing raids, notably the Christmas Blitz of 1940. The school he attended was hit on one occasion and parents opened their homes so lessons could continue. The school football team hardly played because of the disruption.

McNamara says quite a bit of bombing took place around where he lived in Sandyville Road. He and his three sisters and brother used to take cover in the Anderson shelters set up in the road outside their home. 'Most nights during the Liverpool Blitz we'd go into the shelters at around seven o'clock and often stay there until as late as midnight.'

McNamara's father eventually tired of the routine. 'He got fed up and took to staying indoors,' McNamara says. 'When we came back into the house one night, the windows had been blown in and my father was lying there in bed with glass splinters all around him. It didn't seem to worry him.'

In fact not much seemed to worry the McNamara patriarch. On another occasion a landmine attached to a parachute went off at the bottom of the road and blew the soot from the chimney all over his wife. McNamara recalls that his father just sat there laughing and told her she looked like Eugene Stratton, a music-hall artist who used to black his face for a singing routine.'

But the luckiest escape McNamara's father had was when the road in which he managed a bakery shop was hit in an air raid. Fortunately for him he had been called to another of Scott's bakeries a couple of miles away to sort out a problem.

'While he was away a landmine struck a building in Durning Road and this building collapsed on the air-raid shelter where my father would have been. More than 100 people were killed.'

During the course of my conversation with Roy Wood, who was born in Wallasey on the Mersey, he produces a photograph of a wrecked building. 'This is the house I used to live in,' he tells me, 'which gives you some idea of what happened when it got bombed and burnt out on the twelfth of March 1941. Buxton House it was called, my grandfather's house, and it was in Wallasey village.'

Wood, his grandfather and parents, his sister and a brother – two more brothers would arrive in due course – were taking shelter in the cellar when the bomb struck. 'When I saw it four or five weeks later, when we came back to the area – we'd been at my mother's sister's in Sale near Manchester – there was a great big dent in a girder above the cellar, so I'm surmising that the bomb had hit that.'

Others were less fortunate. An incendiary bomb coming down by parachute had, blown by the wind, hit a row of old people's houses 200 yards from the Woods' house. 'It landed in School Lane and wiped them all out,' Wood says. 'They all got it, every one of them. At that stage my father was upstairs and got blown back into the house by the blast.'

Not far away from Wallasey, George Eastham was growing up

with his family in Blackpool. He has slightly less fraught memories of bombing raids.

'My father was in the Desert Rats in Africa with Montgomery,' he says, 'so it was the war that dominated our lives, not football. It was a case of: "Here we go into the shelters. The bombs are coming over."

'Nothing very serious ever happened, but you had to go to the shelters to keep out of the way. It was just a precaution. I think they might have flown over Blackpool on the way to somewhere else. Nothing fell on Blackpool. They must have known it was a holiday resort.'

For Dave Whelan, who not only went on to play professional football but to own a Football League club, the privations of war are what stick in his mind. These included basic essentials such as food and also being without a father after he joined up in 1939.

Whelan was three and living in Wigan when his father was sent off to Iceland, part of a force tasked with denying the Germans bases for their submarines in the North Atlantic. 'I never saw my father for four years.'

'Like everybody else I was hungry throughout the war,' Whelan says. 'All we used to live on was chips and pea wet, which was the water the mushy peas had been boiled in.

'You'd buy fish, chips and peas if you could afford it. We couldn't because my mum had four of us and was living on nineteen shillings and sixpence [97p] a week. So we used to go and ask for threepence worth of chips with some pea wet on it. You used to get that in a basin. And that was basically your best meal of the day.'

Nearly every player who was too young to serve in the Second World War but was old enough to play professionally before the end of the maximum wage had eventually to submit to national service.

Milne was probably the only one whose service consisted of making the colonel's tea and pressing his trousers before heading for the training ground but, still, most were surprised by the amount of football they were able to play.

In McNamara's case, his club Everton actually saw to it that he was posted close to home so he was available for Football League matches.

'Everton reckoned I had a future in football,' he says, 'and I wouldn't have been much use to them if I'd been sent abroad, which was where most of the other recruits went. So they arranged with the RAF that I got sent to the Liver Building in the centre of Liverpool. I was given a desk job, paperwork and so on, distributing kit and other equipment to members of the armed forces going overseas.'

Sunderland did not indulge Stan Anderson to quite the same extent. But he was not sent far and, like a number of others, admits to quite enjoying national service simply because of the amount of football he played.

Based at Catterick with the 7th Royal Tank Regiment, he says he played football all the time. 'In two years I don't think I did army training for more than a couple of days because I was playing football three or four times a week.' As well as still turning out for Sunderland, Anderson represented the British Army, which he captained for a while, his regiment and the Northern Command team.

The army team in the '50s was more than just a random selection of good players. It contained several Football League players and had a fixture list that included trips to Germany and France. Anderson reels off a list of contemporaries who played for the army that includes Duncan Edwards, Graham Shaw, Jimmy Armfield, Alan Hodgkinson and Phil Woosnam.

Tommy Banks, on the other hand, is quite scornful about the impact national service had on his career as a professional footballer. He could not step out of uniform quickly enough and get back to playing for Bolton Wanderers.

Initially, while he was working underground as a miner, Banks was exempt from being called up. After he surfaced to start as a full-time pro with Bolton, he lasted only a few weeks before His Majesty's Armed Forces – George VI was still on the throne in 1950 – sought him out.

He was packed off to Aldershot to be drilled in the ways of army life with the 17th Training Regiment Royal Artillery, after which he volunteered to join the Parachute Regiment.

The Paras were also stationed at the Hampshire base and Banks, never scared of a bit of hard physical toil, watched admiringly as the men in the maroon berets were put through rigorous routines. 'They were always running, running, running,' he says. 'They never stopped. Carrying heavy kit as well.' He pauses before adding with a beaming smile, 'It were terrible.'

But his ambition to join the Paras was thwarted, because the army had other ideas for him. As a professional footballer he was barred from joining the rugby-playing paratroopers. 'You're stopping with us, Banks,' he was told. He was kept on to be a physical training instructor and play in the regimental football team.

Banks thought it was a very poor substitute for playing in the Football League. When the army offered him an extra twelve months' service so he could attain the rank of sergeant – and play a bit more football – he was horrified.

As soon as his two years were up he caught the first train home to continue his quest for the one thing he wanted in life, permanent ownership of the left-back's No. 3 shirt in the Bolton first team.

One man for whom the course of national service definitely did not run smoothly was Alec Jackson. It did not suit him at all.

'I went into the Royal Artillery and was based here, there and everywhere,' he says. 'First of all I got fitted out and then they sent me off to a base in Wales and then I went to another one. What actually happened was I got fed up with travelling and I decided to go home – and you know what that means?'

He pauses and looks at me quizzically. He is waiting for me to give an answer. So I do: 'You deserted.'

'Correct.'

He explains how, while based in London, he had been picked to play for the army in Scotland. 'I hadn't been in the army very long and they said, "Jackson, you're going up to Scotland. You're playing for the army against the Scottish FA." And that's when I bolted.'

He was given three days to travel up to Scotland and back. 'I was never off the train,' he says.

'I was bored stiff. I played in the match and then on the way back down, when the train got to Wolverhampton, I said to myself, "That's as far as I'm going. I'm getting off. I'm going home." Three days, I'd had enough of travelling.

'The policeman sent to fetch me knew who I was. He just came to the door and said, "I know you're there. Let's have you back." – and that was it.'

Jackson says the army did not really bother with him after that. 'I got lost. I played a couple of games of rugby; I had the [boxing] gloves on…'

And he drew his army pay, for what it was worth. In the mid-1950s the daily pay for a national serviceman – stellar footballer or not – was four shillings.

CHAPTER SIX

THE MAJOR AND
OTHER OFFICERS

In which Major Buckley sets football abuzz with talk of monkey glands –
Shankly tells his team, 'You're the worst I've effing seen in my life' – Brian
Clough fails to disguise the truth about spying on an old mate – a knight of
the realm upsets Frank O'Farrell by calling him 'an independent sod'.

Last glimpsed, Roy Wood was making a demoralising start to his
Football League career, a couple of games for New Brighton before
they were booted out of the League for ever. Wood described how he
played as a stand-in goalie, free of charge, so that the club could save
money it did not have.

Wood likes telling stories and specialises in those of the self-deprecating
variety. The way he delivers them, from a deep armchair in his home in
the coastal town of Bridlington, not far north of Hull, makes you wonder
whether he would have been just as well off as a music hall act.

In fact, his name is Royden Wood, he says. 'The story goes that my
mother did a bit of professional ballroom dancing at one time and
taught Lord Royden [who lived on the Wirral and became chairman
of Cunard] to dance.

'Because she liked the name Royden, I got it when I was born. I call it my Sunday name. Sometimes when people call me Roy I put on a bit of an accent and say, "I'm actually Royden."'

Wood says, with calculated drollness, that he disappeared into obscurity after New Brighton dispensed with him. He took what he calls 'little bits of jobs', one of them working for a man in Wallasey called Broadbent. 'He had a handcart and ladders, a tin of paint and some putty and was repairing all the damage that had been done in the war.'

Next he found work in Oxton, a suburb of Birkenhead. It was a job crushing brick and loading lorries with lime for the building trade.

One night when he came home from work 'there was a big, posh car outside the house we'd rented in Grasmere Drive and I thought something must have happened'.

The visitors were two representatives from Clitheroe FC of the Lancashire Combination League wanting him to sign for the upcoming season.

Wood says his immediate reaction was, 'How the heck will I get there? It's quite a long way for me.' He came round to the idea, though, when the visitors assured him they would pay his expenses.

He describes his journey from work to play midweek matches for Clitheroe: first he had to travel from Oxton to Woodside Ferry in Birkenhead, then cross the Mersey on the ferry, walk up to Central Station, go to Preston and finally get picked up at Preston by taxi to take him to Clitheroe. 'So you can imagine what time I got home at night.'

He got a few quid out of it, he says, but the reason he is telling me this story is because of the event that occurred during his time at Clitheroe that changed his life. It happened when he was playing against Darwen in the Lancashire Combination at the end of one season, April time.

Not only was the Clitheroe pitch a terrible one, Wood says, laid out on a pronounced slope, on this particular night in the early '50s, the weather was awful.

'Anyway,' he continues, 'there was just one chap behind the goal and it was still banging it down with rain. He'd got a trilby on and a military mac and was soaked to the skin.'

Wood told him he was going to catch a death of cold. 'Don't worry about me,' the man replied.

Before leaving at half-time, the stranger approached Wood. 'I'd like you to sign for Leeds United,' he said. 'You don't have to make up your mind now. You've got until the end of June. When you make up your mind, ring this number and we'll do the rest, your travel and everything like that.'

The man was Major Buckley.

Major Frank Buckley is someone whose name may largely have disappeared into the mists of long ago, but he was a substantial figure in football's post-war development.

Player after player mentions his name. Not all liked him, quite the reverse in one case, but the impression that emerges is of a character who would have stamped his personality and ideas on whatever profession he had chosen in whatever era.

Buckley was born in Urmston, Lancashire, in 1882. Photographs of him in middle age show a strong face with a slightly wry expression. A physiognomist would almost certainly have concentrated on the well-set chin. Had he been a Hollywood actor in the 1940s and '50s he would have been much in demand as a gunslinger. Gary Cooper might not have got the *High Noon* part.

Given this and what he would achieve in the long run, Buckley's CV when he was a player has a surprising impermanence. An aggressive half-back, he served eight clubs between 1902 and 1920 and although he was capped by England, it was only once in a shock 3–0 home defeat by Ireland. Maybe it would have been more had he not spent four of these years fighting with some distinction in the First World War.

Buckley had been in the army briefly from 1900. He advanced rapidly through the ranks before buying himself out to play football. He was a Bradford City player, the seventh of his eight clubs, when on 15 December 1914 he travelled to London where he was among the first to sign up for the Footballers' Battalion, officially known as the 17th Battalion of the Middlesex Regiment.

Sir William Joynson-Hicks, Conservative MP for Brentford, made what was reported as 'a splendid speech' when he addressed Buckley and his fellow recruits at Fulham Town Hall, where they had enlisted.

He told those preparing to swap football kit for battledress, 'I am inviting you to no picnic. It is no easy game against a second-rate team. It is a game of games against one of the finest teams in the world.' None of these 'games' was more hideously fought than the Battle of the Somme where Buckley received lung and shoulder wounds.

Generally, despite the wounds, he had a good war and given his previous military experience he was awarded a commission, rising to the rank of major. Although intended only as a temporary title, Buckley chose to keep it. It chimed so perfectly with his character as an unbending disciplinarian and organiser that even his wife took to calling him the major.

When he finished playing, Buckley was almost as ubiquitous as a manager. His seven clubs included Norwich City, Notts County and Leeds United, but it was during seventeen years at Wolverhampton

Wanderers, 1927–44, that he made his name as the most innovative manager of his time. Some of his ideas and methods survive to this day.

His shrewd deals, such as acquiring the unproven Roy Wood while at Leeds, went largely unnoticed but were the sort of thing that could transform a club's finances. At a time when even the big clubs were relatively small businesses, Buckley made Wolves a six-figure profit in transfers in a single year.

He also came up with numbering on shirts, the first structured scouting system and developed a youth policy complete with a nursery club in Yorkshire: Wath Wanderers.

Above all, though, it was his attention to coaching that singled him out, his one regret being that the nearest Wolves came to winning the League title during his time was finishing second in 1938 and '39.

Coaching hardly existed before the Second World War and sports psychology was a distant whisper. Buckley engaged with both. In particular, he was at the forefront of introducing routines with a wider purpose than simply keeping players fit.

For a start he challenged the quaint notion that practising with a ball was unnecessary because players saw quite enough of it on Saturday afternoons. Buckley put practice matches at the centre of his coaching and demanded a direct style of play rather than excessive elaboration.

He developed a contraption that shot out balls in no particular pattern to sharpen players' close control and stressed the importance of being able to kick with either foot. He even encouraged players to do ballroom dancing, foreshadowing Bill Nicholson's ideas, to improve their poise and balance.

Rowing machines were also introduced so that fitness sessions were not simply a case of running up and down the stadium terracing.

Some of his other ideas were downright strange, according to Jackie Sewell, an earlier Major Buckley 'find' than Roy Wood. Sewell, a born goalscorer from the mining community of Kells in Cumberland, had started a job at the local pit when Buckley, having moved to Notts County in 1944, took him on as a seventeen-year-old amateur.

The strangest idea that Sewell remembered was Buckley's opposition to players marrying. He thought it suited neither partner: the wife being a distraction to the husband and the threat of a career-ending injury to the husband being a constant worry to the wife.

An even wackier idea associated with Buckley had run its course by the time Sewell moved to Notts County: the use of monkey glands.

The story went, and maybe or probably it was just a story, that Buckley was persuaded that monkey gland implantations helped with stamina levels, recovery and improved mental performance. It was said he tried them on himself and the Wolves players.

For a while the football world was abuzz with the possible advantages conferred by these glands. The fact that celebrities such as the playwright Noël Coward and the author Somerset Maugham were entertaining this treatment as a possible elixir of life gives some credence to the likelihood that Buckley was experimenting with it, too.

Nothing was conclusively proved, and after Wolves lost by three goals to Portsmouth in the 1939 FA Cup final – sometimes referred to as the Monkey Glands Final because Portsmouth were also said to be sampling the treatment – the whole episode was consigned to being one of Buckley's more bonkers ideas.

Roy Wood had heard all the talk about Buckley's plans 'to plant monkey glands into footballers to give them a boost' but was offered nothing more stimulating than a bog-standard contract. It carried with it the promise, maybe, of a slightly better life than his current one.

Buckley's journey to Clitheroe and decision to sign Wood on the flimsiest of evidence demonstrated a keen intuition, although the early signs were not promising. Wood took time to settle after making his debut for Leeds in the 1953–54 season, when the regular goalkeeper, John Scott, was injured. He played in ten games that season, letting in twenty goals, including five at Nottingham Forest on Christmas Day.

As things turned out, though, Buckley's judgement proved flawless. In the three seasons from 1955 to '58, which included the season, 1955–56, when Leeds gained promotion to the First Division, Wood played 125 out of 126 League games. In all, he appeared in 196 League games for Leeds and played in seven FA Cup ties.

If Roy Wood did not always get the credit he deserved, it was not his fault or Major Buckley's – it was Ray Wood's.

'It was a funny thing,' Roy Wood says, 'that when I had a right good game the papers confused me with Ray Wood, which was the name of the old Manchester United keeper, and when I had a bad game I was always Roy Wood.'

He cites an FA Cup tie against Aston Villa in which he played a blinder even though Leeds lost. 'RAY WOOD THE LEEDS HERO', announced one newspaper headline.

Buckley's restless search for young talent knew no bounds of place or time, as the Paton family discovered one winter's night in Glasgow.

Darkness had fallen when there was a knock at the door. The Patons were not accustomed to having visitors at this hour, especially unsolicited ones. Paton Sr decided he should go to see who was there.

'I'm a football scout,' the man on the doorstep said. 'My club are interested in signing your boy.'

'Which club are you from?' Paton Sr asked, expecting the answer to be a Scottish club keen to beat Celtic to the fifteen-year-old Johnny Paton's signature.

'Wolverhampton Wanderers,' the man said.

It turned out the caller was one of Major Buckley's army of scouts who had been sent forth across the British Isles to watch all junior international teams with a view to creaming off the best young talent.

On this occasion, Major Buckley would be thwarted by that redoubtable individual, the young footballer's mother. 'My mother nearly had a fit,' Johnny Paton says. '"My son going to England, to Wolverhampton? No. Leave home? Oh no." So I never, ever went.'

Paton does recall the limited success Major Buckley's Wolves team achieved before his experiment was rudely interrupted by the outbreak of war. He says the papers were full of Major Buckley's Babes, some years before Manchester United's Busby Babes appeared on the scene. He remembers particularly the Monkey Glands Cup Final in 1939.

'The idea was,' he says, 'that these young players of Major Buckley's would run Portsmouth off the field. But Pompey had a lot of older players and Wolves got beat 4–1. That burst the bubble of thinking you could win anything with young players.'

Someone as forthright as Buckley was bound to collect enemies just as someone such as Colin Collindridge, a Yorkshireman with an amplified capacity to take a deep dislike to certain people, was never destined to be drawn to a figure as overbearing as the major.

Collindridge, born in 1920, goes back further than anyone else I interviewed. Time, though, has done little to impair what he remembers, particularly where those who caused him grief are concerned.

After secondary school, Collindridge went to play for Wombwell Main, a strong team in the Barnsley Association League, who were once good enough to compete in the FA Cup. 'There was one League match,' Collindridge says, 'where we played a team from Hoyland who were useless and we beat them 22–0 – and I scored eight.'

As a result he was given a trial with Wolverhampton Wanderers at the Cadbury chocolate ground near Birmingham. He scored a couple of goals and thought, 'I've done all right here.'

'The main reason I'll always remember Wolverhampton Wanderers, though, is not because they signed me on the ground staff but because of a fellow called Major Buckley who managed the team.'

Anyone introduced by Collindridge as 'a fellow called' is not being lined up for an accolade. 'Buckley got his name major from the army when he was in the war, which was fair enough,' Collindridge says. 'He may have been a brave man, I don't know. But that's beside the point because the reason I remember him is that he didn't come to tell me that I'd got the push. One of the trainers said to me, "Oh you've got to pick your cards up."

'I said: "Pick my cards up? Well that means I've got the sack then." I thought this was funny because I hadn't played for the first team, second team or third team. I'd just been on the ground staff.'

On three occasions after he had sacked Collindridge, Buckley tried to shake the player's hand and speak to him. Each time, Collindridge ignored him. 'And I intended ignoring him,' he says. 'If he'd come to me and just said, "Colin, you're not good enough," I'd have shaken his hand.

'Maybe I wasn't good enough, but what Buckley did was a poor way of showing respect. I wasn't brought up like that. My father had brought me up that "if anybody uses bad manners, son, or swears badly in front of your mother, give 'em that [he raises his right fist], and, if you can't, give 'em that [he raises his left boot]. And you're not bad with the left clog."'

Collindridge says what Buckley did was a faux pas, a most un-Barnsley phrase almost certainly archly chosen to match the grandness of Buckley's crime. He backs the charge by quoting something that journalist Fred Walters wrote about his playing ability. The article appeared in the *Green 'Un* sports paper when Collindridge was playing for Sheffield United, which he did either side of the Second World War.

'Walters was the ace, king, queen and jack of football as a journalist in Sheffield,' Collindridge says, 'and he said I should be playing for England.'

Major Frank Buckley: a man ahead of his time – or just another ruthless megalomaniac? A pinch of both, probably.

With limited funds at their disposal, managers of Major Buckley's generation had to rely far more than they do now on their wits and wiles. It may explain why there were so many genuine eccentrics who held managerial posts and, without TV cameras following their every move, fewer of the posturing variety who have become so familiar today.

Like Major Buckley, Bill Shankly, who took idiosyncrasy to the extreme, built hugely successful teams by cleverly husbanding his resources and refining a highly effective, homespun form of player psychology.

The Liverpool teams he assembled over fifteen years as manager from 1959 to '74 surpassed all their predecessors. His legacy is such that the club's stature has endured despite the efforts of lesser managers.

Gordon Milne observed Shankly from a front-row seat. Milne, you may recall, left First Division Preston in 1960, turned down Arsenal, also of the First Division, and chose instead to go down a division to join Shankly's Liverpool.

This was partly because Milne was a northern lad who didn't fancy moving to a London club, but mostly, he says, because there was 'something about Shanks, his enthusiasm and all the other things'.

'Shanks was never particularly approachable,' Milne says. 'He kind of spoke to everybody the same. He'd talk collectively to you as against picking someone out.

'I never remember him saying to someone in the dressing room, "You did that today" or "That was your fault" or "Come to the office, I want to see you." He talked generally: "Why did we do that?"

'He'd talk third party; he'd talk to us through Bob [Paisley] sometimes. He'd talk to Bob after a game and say things like, "Well, Bob, that's the worst effing team I've seen in my life. They will not win another game, Bob. They'll not win another game." And we're all sitting there in the dressing room listening to it. He'd walk past everybody. That's how he did it.

'Then, after we'd won five-nothing, he'd say, "Bob, that's not a bad team, you know. That's not a bad team. They won't go down, Bob. They will not go down. They've just beaten a great team."'

Milne describes another of Shankly's ruses: 'The old Anfield dressing rooms were terrible. We used to come in the side way, which they still do, go through a little door and then down this narrow corridor, turn right and then walk towards the dressing rooms.

'To get to their dressing room the visitors had to pass Liverpool's on the left, and on this particular day West Ham were the visitors. Shanks, as he did quite regularly, was standing just inside our dressing room, with the door open a bit.

'As he looked out he'd say things like, "Och, Bob, here's Martin Peters coming. Martin Peters. He's pasty-faced. He's pasty-faced, Bob. His face is white." Or he'd say, "They're frightened to death. Their faces are blank, Bob. Blank. They're frightened to death."

'This was Shanks's way of motivating us as we sat there rubbing our legs – we didn't go on the pitch to warm up in those days, we just went straight out – or combing our hair or whatever. But he always did it through somebody else.'

Milne has no idea why, but points out it was a mark of Shankly's teams that they suffered very few injuries. He says he was reminded recently that in the 1961–62 season, when Liverpool won the Second Division by eight points with a goal difference of fifty-six, and in the season that followed, he did not miss a game.

'And a lot of that team – and there were forty-two League games, never mind the cups – had played forty games, forty-one games, thirty-eight games. Nobody seemed to get injured. I don't know how the hell this happened, but they didn't get hurt.'

It became a ritual that journalists would ask Shankly, 'What's the team at the weekend, Bill?' And he would say, 'The same as last year, son.'

Also, Shankly would express or feign surprise when rival teams asked for tickets for the directors' box at Anfield. Milne recalls him saying to Paisley things like, 'Bob, they're getting tickets for the directors' box, they're sending three people to watch us play. What a waste of money. They know the team and everybody knows how we play.'

Milne returns to the theme of Shankly's gift for choosing players who complemented one another:

'There were no egos, there was nobody character-wise who dominated the group. Big Ron [Yeats], the captain, might have dominated physically but he was a softie, [a] great guy. It was a mixture.

'You had your lads with plenty of confidence – Ian St John had his aggression, Ian would fight the world, and his personality was something that maybe none of the other ones had – and then there were others that were quiet. The two full-backs, Chris Lawler and Gerry Byrne, never said boo to a goose.'

In Milne's view, because of the care with which Shankly chose players his teams almost managed themselves. 'Though I say it myself, we were an easy group to handle. As players we were all capable in different ways of winning a game or saving a game. There were strengths that were complemented and we protected one another.'

Brian Clough came after Shankly as a player and manager. He too, though, was raised in those years of austerity that hardened certain types to strive for success with an almost psychotic intensity.

But as personalities, Shankly and Clough were very different. Shankly was more guarded, canny, a man whose *mots* had to be dragged from him; Clough was exuberant, someone who liked to shock often and unbidden.

Stan Anderson knew Clough as a player and a friend. They appeared together for Sunderland in the early '60s and later their managerial careers coincided. 'He used to make me laugh,' Anderson says, 'but eventually things would get to the point where I'd say, "Now look, Brian, don't try to kid me because I know you."'

When they were players together, the kidding was just that:

inconsequential. It was when they were managers with opposing interests that Anderson was glad to be forewarned of the kind of antics in which Clough specialised.

When manager of the Fourth Division club Doncaster in the mid-'70s, Anderson had in his charge a young player called Terry Curran. He describes Curran as a good footballer but one who had difficulty doing what his manager wanted despite being told this was the only way he'd make the most of his talent.

'Then one day,' Anderson says, 'this lad John Quigley, who was my coach, said, "Guess who I've seen coming into the ground? Peter Taylor [Brian Clough's assistant at Nottingham Forest]. He was wearing a big scarf, a hat and dark glasses."'

'How do you know it was Peter Taylor?' Anderson asked.

'I know Peter Taylor,' Quigley replied.

Anderson already knew that Clough and Taylor were interested in buying Terry Curran and had been manoeuvring to get him as cheaply as possible. It was no surprise when, not long after the poorly disguised Taylor had been spotted by Quigley, Anderson took a call from Clough.

'Hi Stan, how are you keeping?'

'Fine, Brian. Kept them out of the bottom four and we're pushing for promotion.'

'They tell me you've got a lad called Curran there.'

'Well you should know because Peter Taylor was here on Saturday.'

'No he wasn't.'

'Brian,' Anderson said, 'he was here on Saturday because two or three people saw him. Don't kid me, because that's what you're doing.'

Caught out by Anderson, Clough pressed on, unabashed.

'Well,' he said, 'I'd heard of him before and I think that I'd like to sign him.'

'OK,' Anderson said, 'but he'll cost you quite a bit of money because he's only young.'

'Aye,' Clough said, 'come down and we'll talk.'

Anderson had planned to go down to Nottingham on his own, but Ben Rayner, the Doncaster chairman, insisted on coming too. Anderson was not happy: 'I knew Cloughie would tie Rayner around his little finger.'

After they arrived at Forest's City Ground there was a brief exchange of pleasantries before Clough came straight to the point: 'How much do you want for him, Stan?'

'Seventy-five grand.'

'A bit high that.'

'How about this, Brian: would you sell me Ian Miller and Dennis Peacock as part of the deal?'

'Aye, thirty grand.'

'Come on,' Anderson said. 'For a start neither of them is playing in your first team.'

'Look,' Clough said, 'we'll make it fifty-five grand for Curran plus you get Miller and Peacock.'

The two managers shook hands on it, before Rayner piped up: 'Oh no, we want sixty grand. I can't go back to the board and say we've only got fifty-five grand for him.'

Anderson pointed out: 'You've got two other players as well, Mr Rayner. The deal is seventy-five grand and I've knocked him down to twenty grand for Miller and Peacock.'

He wouldn't listen, Anderson says, and in the revised deal Clough confused Rayner by agreeing to pay more for Curran but wanting more in return for Miller and Peacock.

'Going back in the car,' Anderson says, 'Rayner said to me, "Good deal that. Good deal." I said, "Do you realise you've just cost the club thousands?"'

'After I'd explained it to him he didn't know what to say. Cloughie had pulled a fast one on him. He was brilliant.'

Frank O'Farrell's football career seemed to be ebbing to a peaceful conclusion in 1961. He had played for thirteen years in the Football League, first with West Ham and then Preston North End, and was approaching his thirty-fourth birthday. A second cartilage had recently been removed.

'It was then that Weymouth came in for me to be player-manager,' O'Farrell says, and the image is, irresistibly, of a life slowing down to a soundtrack of distant seagulls and the gentle wash of surf.

'I asked one or two people about Weymouth and they said it was a good club,' he says. 'It was a non-League side, of course, but they always did well and got decent gates. So I went down for an interview and was given the job.'

Apart from anything else, the economics made sense. 'I was on £20 a week at Preston as a First Division player,' O'Farrell says. 'I went down to Weymouth where I got £25 a week and, being the manager, a club car and a club house. So I was better off in Southern League football than being a First Division player. That's the way it was.'

And that's the way O'Farrell himself thought it would stay. 'I wasn't seeking after things,' he says.

But he had not reckoned on others seeking him out, which is what happened after O'Farrell, within a year of joining Weymouth, guided the Dorset club to the fourth round of the FA Cup for the first time.

Weymouth actually went into the fifth-round draw after their tie at O'Farrell's old club Preston was abandoned after fourteen minutes because of bad weather and rescheduled for two days later. With the prospect of playing Liverpool in the next round as an incentive, Weymouth failed to respond and lost the delayed match 2–0. But their Cup run had reflected well on their young manager.

'It meant that journalists from London were now ringing me up for stories,' O'Farrell says, 'and I was getting talked about in the national papers.'

In 1965 he took his first manager's job in the Football League at Fourth Division Torquay. 'I brought a lot of First Division players down from London,' he says, 'which was easier then because the difference in wages between the divisions wasn't as great as it is now.'

Specifically, he raided West Ham's larder of veterans with whom he had once played. Players such as John Bond and Ken Brown would travel down to the Devon resort at weekends while continuing to live and train in London.

The arrangement worked well. Torquay won promotion straightway and O'Farrell, again a target for larger clubs, moved to Leicester City in December 1968.

His stay at Leicester started eventfully. In the space of a few days at the end of his first season Leicester were relegated and appeared in the FA Cup final, which they lost 1–0 to Manchester City. But they were only briefly in the Second Division, O'Farrell taking them back up in 1971.

'Once again this got me noticed,' he says. 'Next thing Matt Busby came and asked me if I'd go to Manchester United.'

At the time Busby was a towering figure in English football. He had been Manchester United's manager from 1945 to '69 and was badly injured in the 1958 Munich plane crash. Since December 1970 he had been temporarily in charge while United sought a new manager.

O'Farrell's version of his eighteen months – June 1971 to December 1972 – at Old Trafford goes like this: 'It was a difficult time to go there because the club needed rebuilding and Matt hadn't done anything. He was very loyal to his players, including those who came through Munich with him, and I could understand that. But it meant it was a job that whoever it was who succeeded him was going to have to do. I happened to be the first one and then there were three more after me before things kind of settled down.

'It was a difficult job, changing players, dropping someone like Bobby Charlton who then went around with a long face, but these are things you have to do as a manager.

'And, yes, it did upset me when they got rid of me. Matt had admitted that he'd let things go and that it might take me a while to sort things out and, no, I don't think they gave me that time.

'One time I had a bit of an altercation with him. The club used to have an annual function, a dinner, which the players and directors went to. Ann and I went while we were there and, coming back in the car, Ann said to me that Matt had a word with her.

'She said he had told her: "Your husband is an independent sod, Ann. Why don't you get him to come and talk to me?"

'I was bloody angry really. I saw him most days if he wanted to see me. He could come into my office; he knew where I was. But to go through my wife, involve my wife, when it was nothing to do with her…

'So I waited deliberately until he was in after the weekend. I invited him into my office and said, "Matt, Ann says you told her I was an independent sod and that she should get me to come and talk to you. Here I am. What have you got to say?"

'So he said, "I don't think you should have dropped Bobby Charlton."

'He was interfering now, telling Bobby Charlton he wouldn't have dropped him and finding fault with Martin Buchan [an O'Farrell signing], who was settling into the club and who turned out to be a great player for United for many years after that.

'I stated my case and he went away.

'But then, in December 1972, we lost heavily at Crystal Palace [5–0] and the club had a board meeting on the Tuesday and they called me in. They sacked Malcolm Musgrove, my coach, as well as me and also John Aston, the chief scout. I don't know what he had to do with the team getting beaten. He'd been a player there and came through the Munich disaster.

'I said: "What reason are you sacking me for?"

'The chairman, Louis Edwards, used to mumble a bit although he was all right really. Matt had him in his pocket. He said, "W... w... we're bottom of the League."

'I said: "Well, we're not bottom actually, we're third from bottom."

'But that was the reason they gave, which I needed to know because I had to go to see a solicitor now and hire him because they were awkward. And they were awkward – they didn't pay me for nine months. They stopped my money and they wouldn't give me the remainder of my contract that I was entitled to.

'A very good solicitor recommended that I went to this QC, Ben Hytner. So I went to him and I said: "Mr Hytner, you may think I'm out of order and I shouldn't say it, but what happens if my case comes to court and I get one of the judges on the circuit who I see in the boardroom of Man United trying my case?"

'He said: "I shouldn't worry about it, Frank, I'll get Matt Busby in the witness box and he won't be able to escape from me."

'Things dragged on and on and on and then eventually, before it came to court, they settled. About £17,000 I think I got. But nine months they made me wait. I had no money. They were just bloody nasty people. Busby was the nasty one really. He had the influence over the chairman. Not a very nice man.

'When they sacked me they should have said, "We're sacking you for these reasons, thank you for your service, here's your money." At least they would have done the decent thing by doing it that way. But they didn't. They made me fight for what they owed me.'

Other versions of this story exist with Matt Busby, or Sir Matt as he had been since United won the European Cup in 1968, emerging with the high esteem in which so many people held him – and still hold him.

But whichever version is correct – or nearest to the truth – does not alter the fact that O'Farrell's experience shows us that in the days when footballers were skint, managers were not particularly well-off, either. Just as today's big-club players are extravagantly rewarded, no manager separating from a club of United's stature in the twenty-first century would do so without an ample pay-off.

'Then when it got settled,' O'Farrell says, 'I went down to Cardiff City for a while, before Iran came in for me to manage the national team. I enjoyed that. Then it was back to Torquay.'

And this is where he and his wife, Ann, still are when I visit them. His quiet, courteous manner and contented air place him as a stereotypical

Torquay retiree. The stories he has to tell, though, instantly place him outside the circle of pensioned-off bank managers and accountants who are his neighbours in the clifftop homes overlooking the English Channel.

The rancour of the manner of his parting from Old Trafford has clearly survived, but loses much of its venom when delivered in Frank O'Farrell's *sotto voce* Irish brogue.

CHAPTER SEVEN

A MAN'S GAME

In which miners find a healthier alternative to digging coal – 'Crunch' Whelan clogs the star player who asked him not to – the 'wild bull' breaks the wrong player's leg – Frank Barson warns: 'Them O levels won't do you a bit of good against some great big, dirty centre-forward.'

The taxi driver wonders why anyone would want to travel from London to Newark-on-Trent on a mission to visit New Balderton. 'It's just a new housing estate,' he says. 'Not much of a place at all.'

His cynicism may prove justified, but Colin Collindridge, one of the oldest surviving Football League players, lives here – an invaluable source given his direct link with professional football's pioneering days.

Collindridge was born in November 1920, only four years after Fergie Suter, the man widely regarded as the game's first professional player, died in middle age. As a young man Collindridge mixed with many of the figures – Major Frank Buckley was just one – who contributed to the game's formative years.

The taxi driver is right. The estate he has just turned into is a regimented assembly of what the Americans call cookie-cutter houses.

Maybe he was right, too, in implying that there could be nothing or no one of interest in surroundings of such overbearing conformity.

Collindridge is in the kitchen brushing leaves away from the back door when his wife, Glenice, lets me in. It is only when he sits down in his armchair in the front room that I register his complexion, which is pink, glowing and without any blemishes. Glenice, sitting opposite him, suggests he spends far more time than is necessary maintaining it.

His clothes are neat and look carefully chosen, particularly the brown corduroy trousers.

Is this really the sturdy competitor who played for three Football League clubs when a bit of clogging was mandatory, and if you could not play with freezing mud filling your big leather boots you should be doing summat else?

Collindridge starts by telling me he was born at Cawthorne Basin. In case I should wonder where exactly this is, which I do, he adds that it's down the bottom of the hill a quarter of a mile from Barugh Green, the first village out of Barnsley on the Huddersfield road.

'Half the relations of mine lived in Barugh Green and there were about forty of them. I still love that place and Barugh Greeners, though I was quite young when we moved to Wombwell, on the other side of Barnsley, where my dad got a council house.

'I couldn't have been born any better really. I was working-class Yorkshire, south Yorkshire, where most people were skint. Some of them had got work at the colliery and some hadn't and it was the mine owners who ruled – only the one thing they didn't do was dare fight my dad.'

A patriarchal home life when he was a lad and a tightly knit mining community forged what I soon learn is an uncomplicated set of values.

Throughout my two interviews with Collindridge – the second was partly to clear up some things he had said during the first and partly to convince myself I had not dreamed him up – I am constantly reminded, in various ways, that where he came from near Barnsley, a man was nothing without his manhood and a footballer was nothing if he was not prepared to settle something behind the stands with his jacket off and sleeves rolled up – and then share a pint of bitter and a laugh.

These are things that obsess him over and above the considerable success and popularity he achieved at his three League clubs – Sheffield United, Nottingham Forest and Coventry City – as a speedy left-winger, and occasional centre-forward, with a bullet-like shot.

He and Glenice are as attentive and hospitable hosts as you could find, but even today, seated and leaning back, his face softened by a disarming smile and never wasting an opportunity to extol the singing voice of Bing Crosby, Collindridge makes me feel ever so slightly uneasy.

In fact there is one tense moment when his face clouds and he stiffens just a little. He wants to know whether, since I keep glancing at the clock, I would prefer to be on my way. I tell him – and, thankfully, he accepts my explanation – it is the family photographs on the mantelpiece that are distracting me, not the time.

But I get the sense that in common with most men who regard their masculinity as the ultimate badge of worth, he holds women in the highest regard, even fears them a little. Of the two other people in the room with him, I suspect he would pick a scrap with me if he wanted the easier victory.

'I've met hundreds of nice females,' he says, 'including my missus, who's a good Nottingham girl who puts me in my place.'

Glenice rolls her eyes wearily at having to listen to a familiar script. Collindridge keeps going: 'You've heard of Jock McAvoy, the boxer, a Lancashire lad who fought for the world light-heavyweight title? Well, my missus is a better scrapper than Jock was.

'And you've heard of Betty Grable? Well, she paid a million dollars to insure her legs, and they were great legs, and my missus had legs that were as good as Betty Grable's. But she doesn't believe me, because she doesn't believe anything I say...'

He returns to his father: 'He worked in the mines after he left school. He'd got one or two mates who stuck up for miners and he could use his tongue, my dad, but he could also use these [he holds up his fists]. So if the coal mine owners had one or two rough tough guys, my dad used to sort them out generally with that [he holds up his right fist], although I think he were a southpaw, actually.

'He taught me nicely, but the only thing was, at school I was always in scraps because someone wanted to fight me. And, of course, generally I showed them that one [he holds up his left fist] and banged them with it, because I was southpaw. So that was part of my upbringing.'

Physicality will be one of the most popular reference points for the former players I visit and nowhere will this be more evident than in Collindridge's home. The fact he is from rugged mining stock, and mighty proud of it, is particularly relevant, a hefty strand in what differentiates football either side of the Second World War from what it has become today.

At a time when English football was very narrowly defined – rooted firmly in working-class communities and almost purely domestic in terms of its labour force – coal mining was an industrial powerhouse that churned out black gold and fit young men by the score.

Numerous collieries had football teams and it followed that men whose day jobs involved great physical toil should take with them onto the pitch the same muscular approach that was part of their everyday lives underground.

In the 1930s, professional football was chock-full of former miners. As an alternative to working deep down in cramped conditions, making a living above ground playing a game they loved and that still allowed them – encouraged them even – to celebrate their manly strength must have seemed too good to be true.

The fact that hundreds of them went back to mining once they were no longer fit to kick, chase and head a ball is an indication of how little they prospered financially from football.

Tommy Banks even suggests he would have been better off had he not left his job at Mosley Common Colliery in the Lancashire coalfield to play professional football.

Banks, Bolton Wanderers' left-back for much of the 1950s, says, 'If I'd have stayed in the pit I'd have been on a lot more money once I'd have come up to the [coal]face. Footballers' pay didn't keep up with the times.'

Typically, but not exclusively, the miners made excellent defenders. They might have had a reputation for possessing the nimbleness and turning circle of a horse-drawn dustcart – a description that Banks, noted for his speed, objects to in his case – but were mightily effective at stopping opposition forwards.

Gradually, a shift took place. The ethos of the mining community and its approach to playing football survived for some time. But fathers, particularly those who knew the realities of working down a mine, steered sons who might have a future as a professional footballer towards the less hazardous opportunities provided by the expanding jobs market.

'My dad worked as a miner,' Bill Leivers says, 'where the mine was two-foot high, lying on his stomach getting coal. From where I come from most of the people in work there at that time were miners, but my dad threatened me if I ever showed any inclination to join them.'

Not all heeded such warnings, though. Banks, for example, still saw going down a pit as part of his heritage.

Old man Banks had not wanted Tommy, the youngest of his seven children, to be a 'pitmon'. But on a bright summer's morning sitting in his front room in Farnworth, Banks remembers his time underground almost as fondly as he does his days playing football.

At eighty-eight, Banks, who played six times for England, remains a cult figure, and not just in the Bolton area. His wife, Rita, points out two envelopes on the table beside his armchair. Both contain requests for his autograph; one is from Germany. His appeal is conveyed in the answer he gives to my question about what it was like to be a miner. 'Just normal,' he says.

As a hard but fair defender, Banks's manifest enjoyment of the physical life endeared him to those from the same background who watched him play. He had all the banter, too. He used it to turn a stern rebuke from a ref or a glare from a victim of one of his heavy tackles into a moment of shared laughter. 'Every time I see Tommy I try to think of something funny to say,' Bobby Charlton once said, 'but he always beats me to it.'

Banks gives a glimpse of his 'just normal' life underground when he describes how each working day began: 'You had to be there at seven o'clock sharp. If you missed the cage they wouldn't let you go down and you'd be docked a day's wages.

'And when you did get down there, very quickly you couldn't see a thing. It was all the dust thrown up by the men breaking up the slabs that had been cut overnight from the coalface.'

'It sounds a hellish existence to me,' I say.

'Not for people from around here, it weren't,' he says, grinning.

He had told his mother that, despite his father's disapproval, he saw coal mining as his only chance of steady employment while he tried to convince Bolton Wanderers he was good enough to be signed by them.

He made his first descent into the mine at Mosley Common soon after his sixteenth birthday. He continued to work there 'on the haulage' – hard, dangerous drudgery making sure the tubs that carried the coal ran smoothly – while playing part-time for Bolton.

It was not until November 1950, when he was twenty-one, that he could finally call himself a full-time pro and wash off the coal dust for the last time.

Like Banks, Collindridge spent time underground maintaining the flow of tubs to and from the coalface. 'I was lucky, though,' he says, 'because there were better players than me about, even in our village, but things didn't work out for them. One lad was a brilliant footballer before he went down the coal mine. Afterwards he couldn't run 100 yards, you see, because of the dust in his chest.'

To start with, Collindridge avoided the ordeal of a pit life. The young, quicksilver forward might not have been to Major Buckley's taste, but Sheffield United liked what they saw of the promising teenager and gave him a contract. 'My mother couldn't believe it,' he says. 'They signed me on for £3 a week, which I reckon was more than my dad got for hacking coal at Wombwell Main colliery.'

Collindridge made his first-team debut for Sheffield United in October 1939. By then, though, war had broken out and the match just down the road against Huddersfield that launched Collindridge's football career was only a friendly. The Football League had been suspended while wartime leagues were organised.

Although Collindridge continued playing football, it was no longer a paid job and he was forced to make a decision: join up and go to war or find employment in a job that exempted him from doing this – down a coal mine, in other words.

'I could have gone into the services, but I didn't want to,' he says. 'I didn't want a uniform and be made to wear narrow trousers. It was a vogue then that we all wore wide trousers like sailors, which is by the way.

'Instead, my Uncle Harry got me work at Woolley Colliery on the Monday and I worked there until I fell out with someone.'

'He could fall out with himself, that one,' Glenice says, pointing energetically at her husband.

'That's by the by,' he says. 'I moved on to Dodworth Colliery and left there after a coal fall deep underground. After that I took a labouring job of sorts down the road in Huddersfield.

'It was a job where you could get enlisted into the services, which is what happened. I must have been a fair worker because when I was called up my boss said, "You should have told me [you were liable to be called up], I could have got you another six months off."

'I said, "Well, I'll have to go some time." Which was fair enough. With that I went into the RAF at the back end of 1941.'

Even though, as the war years receded, fewer and fewer men who had worked down the mines or had a direct link with mining came into the professional game, the idea that British football was a gritty occupation for 'real men' lasted well into the 1960s.

Few can have embodied this idea more emphatically than Dave Whelan. He positively revelled in it.

Throughout his career he was widely known as 'Crunch' Whelan, a nickname that stuck following his switch from playing at wing-half for Blackburn in the 1950s to full-back.

'When they were short of a full-back,' he says, 'Johnny Carey, the manager, picked me there for the first team after I'd done all right in a practice match. That's when I got the Crunch name.'

He confesses he quite liked it and enjoyed people calling out, 'Hello Crunch' when he walked about Blackburn.

'The style of play then was the full-backs couldn't go over the half-way line. You had to stay in your own half. That was the unwritten rule – a mad, mad rule – but that was how it was. Your job was to defend. And, not like today, you could really clog people. I broke my leg by somebody coming over the top to me. It was a ruthless, ruthless game then, but still great.'

Every player remembers matches in which he played well, which in Whelan's case was a match in which he clogged well. He cites a reserve game for Blackburn against Liverpool: 'They had a winger who was unbelievably famous at the time, Billy Liddell.

'It was a night match at Anfield and Liddell, who had been injured, was trying his leg out. So he came over to me before the match and said, "Hello, David, nice to see you." I was still a teenager and in awe of this man.

'He said, "I'm coming back and I may only play half a game. I'm just seeing if I'm fit, so do your best not to tackle me too hard or to kick me." And I thought, "I'll kick you up in the air as soon as I can."

'Sure enough he got the ball, I saw my chance and I clogged him.

Which I would. He got up, looked at me, shook his head and said, "I asked you not to do that." I just ran off. I thought, "Piss off." He was a great player. He played three-quarters of the game and then went off.'

I suspect many of those who did business with Whelan in later life – and business was the world in which he really shone – walked away from the experience feeling similarly clogged.

But Whelan's clogging on the football field did not work on everyone: John Dick of West Ham for example. 'I really clogged him,' Whelan says, 'and he took no notice whatsoever. He totally disregarded me. It was like, "Go away."

'When you went up against a big, strong fella like he was, and he didn't even look at you when you clogged, just walked away as if you were non-existent, that made you feel very small. Players these days should sometimes turn their backs and just walk away from some of these lads who are having a go at them. When Dick did that to me it taught me a lesson.'

Bill Leivers shared Whelan's attitude to tackling: 'If you're going to tackle,' he says, 'you might as well let the bloke know that you're there. Nowadays you can't get near anybody.'

Such was Leivers's reputation that his manager Les McDowall once sent him onto the pitch for Manchester City specifically to exact retribution for a foul committed by an opponent.

It was on a close-season tour of Germany, a country City visited frequently because having former German paratrooper Bert Trautmann in the team meant 'we got more money', Leivers says (before making a slight adjustment, 'the club got more money', in case there was any doubt where the profits went).

Given the packed fixture list on the short tour, McDowall rotated his players. Leivers was sitting out one match but then City's centre half Jackie Plenderleith got injured.

'This player went deliberately right over the top at Jackie,' Leivers says. 'I'm not supposed to be playing, but Les says to me, "Go on, get changed, get him sorted out." I thought he was joking, but he said again, "Go on, go on."

'I'm out there a couple of minutes and what did this player do – he was coming over the top. So I thought, "Right, mate." So I went over the top at him and they carried him off.'

Leivers says it would be wrong to think that only defenders clogged. 'In my day forwards used to tackle just as hard as defenders. Nat Lofthouse, for instance, the centre-forward who played for England.'

He recalls the day he clattered Bolton's ace attacker and knew what was coming next. 'About ten minutes later the ball's coming down the middle and Nat's about fifteen yards away. Although by the time he reached me the ball had gone, he ran straight into me and absolutely flattened me. He knocked me back about five yards flat on my back.'

Jimmy Jinks of Millwall was another centre-forward who not only could look after himself, but acted as minder for the rest of the team. 'He had been a sailor,' Johnny Paton, who played for Millwall as a wartime guest, says. 'He used to walk around the park swaying from side to side as if he was still on a ship. You couldn't make up these characters today.'

It was Jinks that Paton turned to when he was threatened one day by an opposing defender. 'Every team was noted in those days for having a killer in their team, usually a defender,' Paton says, 'the guy who would say, "I'll get yer if you do anything to me." It was not like the passing game of today.

'And playing against Millwall one day was this big right-back who said to me, "Paton, I'll break both your legs next time you come near me." So I reported him to Jimmy, who said, "Leave him to me, Johnny."'

As an aside, Paton notes that in his day centre-forwards such as Jimmy Jinks were all big, bustling six-footers. 'Not like today,' he adds. 'Barcelona haven't even got a centre-forward.'

A combination of Jinks's size, his running shoulder charge and the low wall that separated the crowd from the pitch at Millwall's old Den ground meant Paton's tormentor was summarily dispatched.

'When Jimmy smacked into the back of this guy at a throw-in, he hit the brick wall, did a half somersault, landed on the concrete and was carried off on a stretcher. He came back with this bandage on his head and was running around like a wild bull.

'I reckon he was looking for me but I don't think he quite knew where he was and it wasn't my legs he broke, it was the leg of the left-half behind me, Len Tyler. It nearly finished Len's footballing career.'

Paton finishes his story with a postscript: 'Len was a good-looking bloke and worked part-time as a film extra. There was an actor called Robert Donat, who was the star of *The 39 Steps*, and Len worked as Donat's double while playing for Millwall. Because wages were so low, we all did extra things to make money.'

Fred Hall was the 'killer' defender who played for Sunderland when Stan Anderson signed for the club. Hall was a centre-half who did score for Sunderland in 215 appearances for the first team in eight years – but only once. Scoring goals was not part of his brief.

'Fred called me "kid", he never called me Stan,' Anderson says. 'He was a huge fella. I mean he had a big gut on him. I used to look at him and think, "How can you play as big as you are?" He was enormous. You wouldn't get away with it now.'

In those days players were weighed at the end of the season and then again at pre-season training after a break of nearly two months. 'I always remember Fred finishing the season weighing thirteen stone something and coming back weighing fifteen stone something – fifteen stone! I mean I was nine stone wet through.'

Anderson gives a snapshot of Hall in action: 'We were playing Wolves and I had the ball when Billy Wright, who was a left-half then, came through. As I played a one-two he whacked me and left me lying on the floor.

'Fred came across, looked at me and said, "Get your bloody self up." When I told him I was injured, he said, "Don't you show them that you're hurt. Get up on your feet."

'And then he said that if Wright came through again, I was to let him go past me and he, Fred, would be waiting.'

Not long afterwards, Wright came through and Anderson did as instructed. Moments later he heard 'this horrendous crunch' followed by a scream and he turned round to see Wright lying on his back with Hall standing over him saying, 'Bloody told you, didn't I?'

'Billy Wright went back to left-half and I never saw him again,' Anderson says. 'That was the way the game was played then and no one took any notice. I mean nowadays they'd be carried off. It was a hard league.'

'My own feeling of the present generation is that they're fairies, quite honestly,' Terry Allcock says. 'When I played injuries were accepted. I broke both legs – and I played on for seventy-five minutes after breaking one of them in a League Cup game – broke my collarbone, broke my ribs, I broke both ankles, broke my nose four times and I had three metatarsal injuries – and all they did with those was take you to the hospital, gave you an injection and you played. You didn't have three or four months off.'

Arguably the hardest man to play in the Football League was the half-back Frank Barson. Born in Grimesthorpe, Sheffield, in 1891, he began his long League career at Barnsley in 1911 and made 140 appearances for Manchester United between 1922 and '28.

He was once handed a seven-month ban, which was deemed a bit harsh for the actual offence but was almost certainly a case of previous misdemeanours being taken into consideration. *The Times* once reported that on 'frequent occasions Barson was escorted out of grounds by policemen to protect him from groups of angry opposition fans'.

Once he stopped playing, Barson took to preaching what he had practised.

Cliff Jones encountered Barson the footballer turned coach-cum-trainer in the early 1950s. 'When I signed for Swansea on leaving school,' Jones says, 'I'll never forget meeting this character called Frank Barson, the first-team trainer. He was just one big hard nut.'

Jones's most abiding memory of Barson is when he and three other ground staff boys reported for their first training session on the old Vetch Field. 'Barson came out. He was about 6 ft 2 in. and sixteen stone, he had a broken nose and was covered in scar tissue and he just looked like one tough, mean bloke.'

In particular, Jones recalls an exchange Barson had with Gerald Griffiths, another of the Swansea new boys:

'OK, you lads, if you listen to me you'll learn everything there is to know about football. Now tell me, lads, have any of you got any qualifications?'

'Yes, Mr Barson, I've got four O levels – maths, English, history and geography.'

'Is that right, son? Now what position do you play in?'

'I play centre-half, Mr Barson.'

'I'm going to tell you something now, son. When you've got some great big, dirty six-foot centre-forward bearing down on you, he's going to kick you right in your bollocks. See them O levels? They won't do you a bit of good, but you listen to me and you'll be able to do something about it.'

'What we got from Frank Barson was total commitment to the game of football,' Jones says. 'He was a very controversial character. We had some hard boys down at Swansea then. This was 1950 and the war had finished five years ago and a few of these lads had gone through the military and seen a different type of action in the Second World War.'

'But they never messed with Frank Barson, I'm telling you.'

Several of the old-timers make the point that what makes clogging different from what happens today is that, in their day, it was accepted all round – by the clogged as much as the cloggers. It is no longer even called clogging. Its modern counterpart tends to be more subtle, more deceitful and, the biggest difference, those on the receiving end squeal regardless of whether or not they are hurt.

Bill Leivers, in completing his story about tangling with Nat Lofthouse, quoted the unwritten etiquette of how a player used to react to a heavy tackle, particularly a retaliatory one: 'You got up and grinned about it, you didn't roll about on the ground for ten minutes.'

The nimble-footed Stanley Matthews had to deal with being clogged more often than most. But Matthews neither grinned nor whimpered.

He developed a response straight out of the Al Capone handbook: he turned a stony face on all who assaulted him and, if the attack was bad enough to qualify for physical retribution, he deployed a hitman to do his dirty work for him.

Over his long career he had two minders he regarded as special. One was Jock Dodds, an energetic Scot who was a teammate in Blackpool's formidable wartime side. Dodds was particularly effective at sorting out those who caused Matthews aggravation in a way that referees accepted. But not always.

On one occasion he overdid it when giving the Oldham full-back Tommy Shipman his comeuppance for harassing Matthews. He knew he had taken things too far when he saw the look on the referee's face, at which point he feigned injury himself, falling to the ground, to try to win the official's sympathy.

'Are you OK to walk?' the ref asked Dodds in a kindly tone.

'Yes, I think I can, ref,' Dodds replied.

'Then you can walk off down the tunnel,' the official said, pointing to the tunnel in the days before red cards.

Late in his career, when Matthews was nearer fifty than forty and back at Stoke, Eddie Clamp was responsible for protecting the club's ageing asset. Clamp had been passed on to Stoke by Arsenal, whose manager Billy Wright was looking for more finesse from his players than Clamp offered.

Clamp's finest moment was in the battle of the Choppers, a nickname he shared with Ron Harris of Chelsea. From the first minute of a Second Division promotion match at Stamford Bridge, Harris had been hacking away at Matthews until the referee finally intervened with a warning Clamp considered insufficient for the crimes that had been committed.

When the opportunity presented itself, Clamp took Harris by the shirt, called him a little sod and warned him that he would be well advised to pick on someone other than Matthews for the remainder of the match. Harris ignored this advice and soon afterwards Clamp delivered a tackle the likes of which, Matthews said, he had not seen in thirty years of football. 'I never had a spot of bother from Chopper Harris for the remainder of the match,' Matthews said.

Tom Finney was another skilful player who was more sinned against than sinning. In fact, hardly anyone could remember an instance of his ever having sinned. And Preston's seriously gifted forward regarded being battered as an excuse neither for complaining nor for retaliation. He wore his bruises as some warriors do campaign medals.

Gordon Milne tells a story about Finney when they were team-mates at Preston. It was the Friday evening before a home game. 'I went down to the ground and Tom was having treatment,' Milne says. 'His fitness was vital to Preston because when he didn't play the gates went down considerably.

'Tom was sitting on a table under a heat lamp. That was it. No electronic gadgets or anything like that. He was bruised black and blue – his thighs, his legs – and he was having a bit of a massage.

'Much later, when Tom was in his sixties, we used to talk about our playing days and I would say, "I remember seeing you when you were covered in bruises, Tom." And he'd say, "Ah, it was all right. It didn't bother me." He was on six quid a week, but he still didn't complain about having to take so much punishment. "Those were great days," he would say. He wouldn't have changed them.'

Collindridge has now reached the point in his life story where his time as a Sheffield United player is coming to an end. The year was 1950, and although Collindridge had been with the club for more than a decade, the war years meant he had made only 142 appearances, scoring fifty-two goals.

In his version of why he left, Collindridge suggests it followed on from Jimmy Hagan being stripped of the captaincy after falling out with the directors. He, Collindridge, was then offered the captain's role but says he turned it down out of loyalty to Hagan, whom he regarded 'as the classiest footballer I ever played with or against. And I was lucky because he made me look a good footballer.'

Glenice had appeared not to be paying any attention, but the idea that it was Hagan's sacking that led to her husband's departure from the club is something she clearly feels needs correcting.

'No,' she says, 'he left because he was courting a Nottingham girl.'

For the only time in my several hours talking to him, Collindridge falters. He hesitates, but it's only for a couple of seconds. 'Ah, maybe so,' he says slowly. 'Could have been. I'm not trying to evade anything. I think I may have finished up marrying her.' (Glenice is his third wife.)

Another brief pause and he is ready to go again with a new theory for his departure: 'No, the real reason I left Sheffield United was because I was getting to a stage where I thought I wasn't quite good enough.'

His first inclination was to go to see the people at Notts County he knew from his wartime days. But they were all on holiday so he made the short journey across the River Trent to Nottingham Forest. And it just so happened that Forest were looking for a left-winger to replace Gordon Kaile.

'Gordon was a nice lad,' Collindridge says, 'but sadly for him I pushed him out. He was only slight and didn't have a good shot on him – and also he wasn't a clogger, you know, dirty. I'd got that south Yorkshire style – Sheffielders have it to an extent – of getting stuck in.

'It was like at school, if there was someone who wanted to bully me they got a fist or a clog, simple as that. You're not supposed to do that but I wasn't supposed to do a lot of things on this planet and I've never changed my style.'

He is making me feel uneasy again.

CHAPTER EIGHT

WHEN THE CUP WAS KING

In which Peter McParland causes an outcry by 'shaking up' the goalie – the 'hotchpotch' team rises from the ashes of Munich – players suffer the agonies of the Wembley hoodoo – Bill Slater, a losing Cup finalist, travels home the same day in the same train as the winners' triumphant fans.

More than half a century later, my memories of a few fleeting moments on the afternoon of Saturday 4 May 1957 remain clear: schoolboy cricket match, master in charge, knowing my interest in football, comes over to tell me something.

There has been an incident early on in the big match at Wembley. A forward and goalkeeper have collided resulting in the badly injured goalie being carried off on a stretcher.

Now, on a midwinter's morning, my reason for travelling from London to Bournemouth is to meet that forward, Peter McParland.

The weather is mild but, given the time of year, it is still a surprise when McParland comes to the door wearing a pair of shorts – long shorts, mind you, but still shorts. 'I always wear them indoors,' he says. Could it be a last, nostalgic association with playing football?

We sit talking across a small kitchen table. He recalls the collision and analyses it with frame-by-frame precision.

And when the goalkeeper recovered how did he react?

'He wasn't happy,' McParland says. 'But I wouldn't have been either.'

The reason the collision was a defining event in McParland's career and is lodged so firmly in my memory is that these were the days when the Cup was king – and it was in an FA Cup final in front of a huge audience that McParland, playing for Aston Villa, crashed into Ray Wood, the Manchester United goalie.

Had it been a League match it would hardly have registered.

In 1957, the Cup final was still the major event in the football calendar. It dwarfed any other match, home or away, in the English public's consciousness, including the World Cup final.

The FA Cup, first played in 1871–72, is the world's oldest – and, for many years, its most popular – football competition. The World Cup followed nearly sixty years later, only to be ignored by the English for its first three stagings. The FA finally deigned to enter the national team in 1950, but very few in England took much notice.

It was not until towards the end of the twentieth century that the FA Cup started to lose its lofty place in public esteem. The really steep decline in its popularity came after 1992 when massive investment saw the First Division repackaged, rebranded and reborn as the Premiership.

Having been the fancy dan of the English game, the FA Cup suddenly found itself being pushed aside by a hustler not afraid to flex its commercial independence to exploit football's popularity like never before. Players' wages surged as clubs fought for the considerable financial rewards, made possible by TV money, for success in the new league.

The FA Cup was now a distraction viewed, increasingly, with condescension by the top clubs. Infamously, the FA themselves did not help by backing the disrespectful idea that Manchester United, the holders, skip the 1999–2000 competition to play in the world club championship.

There had been a steady improvement in what players earned since the upper limit had been removed, but this was hardly surprising given the low base from which this improvement began.

For the last Cup final before the demolition of the wage ceiling, Wolves v. Blackburn in 1960, Dave Whelan recalls the Blackburn players each received a princely six quid from a Milk Marketing Board advertisement of the team drinking the board's product. This bumped up Whelan's Cup final extras to eight pounds. He cannot recall the source of the other two pounds.

With his £20 weekly wage and with Blackburn's defeat meaning he was denied a win bonus, Whelan made £28. It was the most he ever earned from football in a single week.

Howard Riley was on the losing side a year later when Tottenham completed the Double with their 2–0 win over Leicester City. 'The maximum wage had ended shortly before the final,' Riley says, 'but I think we were still probably on twenty quid a week or not much more – and I'm not sure we were on a win bonus even if we had won, in front of 100,000 spectators.'

The improvement in pay would continue, but the relentless upward mobility of the Premier League means the Cup is unlikely ever again to achieve the status it enjoyed when footballers were paid buttons.

Today, McParland's collision with Wood would be noticed only if it occurred in a top league fixture.

The 1957 FA Cup final and the one a year later score highly for the sort of dramatic content that was accentuated at the time by the competition's royal status.

The two matches had much in common: both were played on gentle May afternoons in front of seam-bursting attendances; both were lost by Manchester United; and both times the winning teams featured a striker who not only scored his side's two goals, but gave the opposition goalie a bit of a crack.

At the same time the 1958 final was a match apart not just from its immediate predecessor but from all previous finals and all that have succeeded it. The clue to its unique separateness was sewn into the shirts of the Manchester United team: specially designed badges depicting a phoenix rising from the ashes.

In the Villa dressing room before the 1957 final, centre-half Jimmy Dugdale, sick with nerves, threw up just before kick-off. With the match due to start, the referee Frank Coultas waited for a signal from the Royal Box, where the 31-year-old Queen Elizabeth had just taken her seat, before blowing his whistle.

Although Villa were the underdogs, they had two or three players of outstanding quality. Peter McParland was one of these – combative but creative and clever, the sort of player any manager would crave. He had scored twice against Wales on his debut for Northern Ireland and would be their best player at the 1958 World Cup finals.

McParland starts his own story of the 1957 Cup final in the build-up to the match. He had made a mental note of something that his team-mate Jackie Sewell mentioned to him. 'Jackie said to me two or three weeks before the final that he had met Tommy Lawton at a wedding in Nottingham and Tommy said, "Remember to shake the goalkeeper up." That was something you did then.

'And Jackie told Tommy, "Yeah, we've got a fella who might go and give him a bit of a shake."'

McParland says he was already aware Ray Wood reacted badly to physical contact – 'He went for people, Ray did' – and recalls an example of his petulance.

Not long before the final, he was with the Villa team when they stopped at a pub on the way home from a midweek League game at Burnley. Highlights of a European Cup semi-final between Manchester United and Real Madrid were on TV. 'And I remember [Paco] Gento came flying through the middle and Woody ran out, picked the ball up and whacked Gento. Put him on the deck. So he was prepared to hit people at the time.'

Like Gento, McParland played on the left wing and did so with gusto.

At Wembley, six minutes had passed when he clattered into Wood. 'Jackie Sewell had the ball on the edge of the box in the inside-right position,' McParland says, 'and I'm out here on the left and I'm coming in.

'Jackie played a nice ball in and when it was in flight I said to myself, "This is going back into the far post. It's in the back of the net."'

McParland's version of what happened next goes like this: 'So I came in and I banged it with my head but I banged it straight into Ray Wood's arms as he was coming off his line.

'He'd come running towards me and I was running in just in case there was a drop and I turned my shoulder then to shoulder-charge him. He turned to me to shoulder-charge and then turned away at the last minute, last seconds. As we clashed, the side of my head hit Ray here on the cheek. It was through not getting the shoulder to shoulder [that the injuries occurred].

'I was lying on the deck and 100,000 people were spinning round me. I thought, "Oh, I'm finished. This is me out."

'I got myself together again, though, and when the trainer came on he made me feel better. But Ray had a problem and went off by stretcher before coming back on just before half-time.'

Wood was posted at outside right with the time-honoured instruction to the walking wounded: if nothing else, cause problems. Wood did this to such effect that McParland felt he was sufficiently recovered to go back in goal, which was what in fact he did for the last few minutes. But McParland's irrepressible performance – not only did he clash with Wood but scored two excellent goals – would prove enough for Villa to win 2–1.

The BBC TV commentator Kenneth Wolstenholme said immediately that what happened between McParland and Wood, which left Wood with concussion and a broken cheekbone, was a pure accident. He called it a fair challenge, 'but unfortunately their heads collided'. Although this was not the universal view, there was a far greater acceptance then of the fairness of such collisions.

McParland apologised to Wood after the match and says he has no argument with his not being happy. 'He wouldn't have been happy; I wouldn't have been happy if I had been taken off. He reacted in a sporting way to my apology but you always had the feeling that he felt he was hard done by.'

The press criticism McParland received did not really bother him, he says. 'I was glad because we had won the Cup. It was part and parcel [of being in an incident like that] that they were going to slam me and some of them did. I just had to take the flak.'

Despite this criticism and Wood's obvious resentment, McParland remembers suffering no backlash from other opposition players. The United defender Bill Foulkes even told him that 'Woody should have got out of my way – and he didn't because he liked having a bash at people.'

'The next season,' McParland says, 'before all the games I played early on, the goalkeepers said, "You wouldn't have done that to me in the final because I'd have sidestepped and let you run into the back of the net." All of them said that.'

Fifty years later, when the BBC made a documentary comparing the 1957 and 2007 finals, the verdict was very different, reflecting how views on what constituted a fair challenge had diverged since Wolstenholme made his comments.

The documentary described the 1957 final as infamous because of McParland's 'shocking challenge' on Wood. The football writer Henry Winter, interviewed for the programme, said, had it happened today, McParland would have been sent off and heckled as he left the pitch.

By the 1958 Cup final, Wood's and Manchester United's fortunes had changed harrowingly. Wood had returned to the first team at the start of the 1957–58 season but lost his place after United bought the Northern Irishman Harry Gregg in December for £23,000 from Doncaster Rovers.

On Thursday 6 February 1958, Gregg and Wood were on the British European Airways flight that crashed attempting to take off from Munich airport. Twenty-three of the forty-four people on board, including eight of the Manchester United players who were returning from a European Cup tie in Belgrade, were killed or mortally wounded. Gregg and Wood survived. Although Gregg received a terrible crack on the skull, he was in better condition than Wood, who suffered wounds to his head, leg and hip.

Despite being hurt, Gregg refused to leave the crash site, staying to help the rescue effort. Among those he pulled clear of the wreckage were his teammates Bobby Charlton and Dennis Viollet. And then thirteen days later, he and Bill Foulkes, who also survived the crash, were in the United team who ran out for the club's first fixture since the disaster.

One newspaper described the side that won this game, a fifth-round home FA Cup tie against Sheffield Wednesday, as 'an incredible hotchpotch of Munich survivors, Central League youngsters and imported stars'.

The hotchpotch fought through five matches – two of them replays – to reach the final, a remarkable run that attracted intense national interest. Whoever the team were who were attempting to impede their progress were regarded by the vast majority of the population as the bad guys taking on the good guys.

Alex Dawson was one of the youngsters drafted into the United side. He had been issued with a visa to travel to Belgrade but at the last minute was not included in the party.

Dawson's first foreboding of the tragedy he had avoided and that would change so many lives was the sound of running feet. 'We were playing snooker at the club,' he says, 'when we heard people running in the passageway.' It was an unusual sound that immediately put Dawson on edge. 'When they came in I joked that someone must have been chasing them. But they said, "No, the plane's been in a crash." There was a reporter there who confirmed this.'

Dawson scored in the 3–0 win over Sheffield Wednesday, a match that was more emotionally charged than any other of the post-Munich fixtures given its proximity to the crash.

There was huge fascination, too, in seeing how the hotchpotch team put together by assistant manager Jimmy Murphy would measure up. Murphy had taken temporary charge in place of Matt Busby, who was so badly injured in the crash that he twice received the last rites. He would eventually pull through to reoccupy the manager's office for the season that followed and for ten more after that.

Dawson attests to the brilliance of Murphy's leadership that, together with the passionate support from the terraces, helped to yield performances that a makeshift team would never have achieved in normal circumstances.

'Jimmy helped us,' Dawson says. 'He was fantastic. His team talks…' The upward nod of the head tells me that the content of these talks are better left behind the dressing-room door (and later substantiates this by relating one wholly unsuitable lavatorial anecdote). 'Jimmy didn't get the praise that he should have done.'

Once brought into the side, Dawson remained in it for the rest of the Cup run, including the final. Although he established himself as a natural finisher during this run – notably when scoring a hat-trick in the semi-final replay against Fulham – his clearest recollections are not about his own achievements, but about the emotions that surrounded those surreal weeks leading up to the final.

'The atmosphere was fantastic,' he says. 'The crowds really got behind us. They wouldn't have liked it if we had got beat.

'United already had big crowds, they were the team really, but there were sixty-odd thousand every week. It didn't matter who we played. For the Cup tie against Wednesday it was packed inside and there must have been another sixty-odd thousand outside.

'The noise was such that you felt you had to win for the players who had died. And we always thought of them when we were playing.

'That team, the one involved in the crash, had always been very supportive of the other players. You couldn't get a better bunch of lads to help the younger ones. Duncan Edwards, he was smashing; Harry Gregg, he was great with the youngsters. They all used to come to watch the reserve games. And they'd talk to you about the match the next morning. And we remembered that when we took their places.'

The one group who did not wish Manchester United well on that audacious march to Wembley were the eleven who opposed them in each of the matches. Without bitterness, Dawson says, 'They didn't care who we were, they wanted to beat us.'

And no one wanted to beat them more than Bolton, United's opponents in the final who were renowned in their own right for being the £10 team. No member of their side had cost more than the £10 signing-on fee.

Once again the match was blessed with beautiful spring sunshine but, while the context of the match ensured it was infused with drama, as a spectacle, it fell short of the hopes invested in it. It was as if United were climbers who stumbled just short of the summit of Everest having exhausted their supply of enriched oxygen.

Dawson, still only eighteen, was picked on the right wing, up against Bolton's 28-year-old left-back, Tommy Banks. Never short of a quip, Banks exerted a little gentle pressure on his young rival: 'Imagine putting out a little baby to play against me.' After the game a grinning Banks would tell Dawson, 'For a kid you're not bad.'

The more vigorous and telling pressure came from Bolton's captain and centre-forward, Nat Lofthouse. His typically hard-edged performance over the full ninety minutes brought him both goals in the one-sided 2–0 victory.

Like McParland, though, Lofthouse emerged from the match a controversial figure, his second goal having had distinct echoes of the previous year's final. A no-nonsense shoulder charge in the fiftieth minute laid out Gregg in the United goal and sent the ball spinning into the net. This time it was the Pathé News commentator who pronounced it a fair challenge, but the goal would almost certainly have been disallowed today and Lofthouse brought to book.

Later it became clear that the effect of Lofthouse's shoulder charge, within minutes of which Gregg was back in action, might have been so much worse. He had started to develop headaches soon after Munich and it was only when he visited a neurosurgeon that he found out the knock to his head when the plane crashed had fractured his skull.

For the second time in the 1950s, Bolton's cheap-as-chips team had found themselves in a Wembley final supported by virtually no one bar their own loyal supporters.

Five years earlier the nation had sided with Blackpool as Stanley Matthews, a 38-year-old national celebrity, attempted to win his first Cup winner's medal having been on the losing side in the 1948 and 1951 finals.

Matthews played a blinder. Blackpool won 4–3 from being 3–1 down with barely twenty minutes to go and the whole country, except Boltonians, celebrated.

Now, in 1958, the cheering inside the stadium by Bolton fans was loud enough, but the wider response was a collective groan that Manchester United had lost out to a team who refused to stick to the Hollywood script.

By the 1950s, the Wembley sports complex had been a hub of sporting events for a number of years, for professional sports as well as amateur.

In 1937, Fred Perry, by now a professional tennis player, contested matches at Wembley's indoor arena, earning an estimated £4,000 for less than a week's work in front of crowds of 8,000. Boxers Henry Cooper and Cassius Clay, soon to be Muhammad Ali, would be paid a percentage of the gate when, in June 1963, they fought a memorable heavyweight bout in a ring erected over the Cup final pitch. Cooper was reckoned to have received £25,000 and Clay double that.

But the Cup final itself was by far Wembley's greatest attraction and yet the wages of the players who took part in the 1957 and 1958 finals were still pegged at a weekly £17 maximum.

Looking back, it is now possible to see that such was the competitive urge to win the Cup final that players were not only short-changed in terms of what they were paid for entertaining a vast audience. It would not have been outrageous if they had claimed danger money.

Because of the great fixture's special status sixty years ago, players almost certainly strove that little bit harder, causing a disproportionate number of injuries compared to other matches. Things became so bad in the 1950s that the epithet 'the Wembley hoodoo' was born.

Mostly it was outfield players who suffered, but, as we have seen, goalies copped it, too. Harry Gregg was in fact the third keeper in successive finals to be unceremoniously clobbered. There had been Ray Wood before him and, in 1956, Bert Trautmann of Manchester City had been the unfortunate victim of a very nasty collision.

Trautmann, who had settled in Lancashire after being captured and imprisoned by the British towards the end of the Second World War, was knocked unconscious when he launched himself at the feet of the Birmingham City inside-forward Peter Murphy. It would turn out that this was much more than just a nasty blow on the head.

Bill Leivers, Manchester City's right-back, was a few yards from Trautmann when the incident happened.

'So many times I'd seen him in goal and he was absolutely fearless,' Leivers says. 'He'd go down head first and he'd get up and go "Woooo…", but his pride wouldn't let him do any more than that.

'At Wembley he did his usual thing and went down for the ball head first. When he came round I was saying to myself, "He's really badly hurt", because he kept feeling his neck, which he wouldn't normally have done.'

Trautmann kept playing until the end of the match and it was not until four days later that he was found to have dislocated five vertebrae – the second of which was broken. His recovery took seven months.

During this time, Leivers became his chauffeur. 'Bert had a plaster on right down to his waist with four pins into his skull.'

And then, in the 1960 final, came Dave Whelan's horrific mishap.

What Whelan remembers with searing clarity about that day was not the abnormal heat for May or how poorly he was rewarded for his efforts, but the pain he went through after his leg was shattered. The delay in treating Whelan evokes an image of suffering on a scale endured by soldiers in nineteenth-century battlefield hospitals.

Wolverhampton Wanderers, who had just finished runners-up in the Football League, having been champions in 1958 and '59, were clear favourites to beat Whelan's team, Blackburn, who had not had a good season. Two events in the closing minutes of the first half put the result beyond doubt.

Whelan, who was playing out of position at left-back, describes them: 'First, four minutes before the interval we went behind because their outside-left played the ball right across the face of the goal and

Mick McGrath, our midfield player, tried to put it out for a corner but knocked it straight in the back of the net. One-nil to Wolves.

'Not long after this a ball came between me and a winger called Norman Deeley. He'd appeared for England and was a good player, quick. I'd already clogged him once, really hurt him, but I never used to go for the player, only for the ball, and I went for the ball then.

'He didn't. He went for me. I got the ball and he got me. Studs. Stud marks are still on my shin. He came a foot over the ball. Bang. Both bones gone.'

In an instant Blackburn were reduced to ten men for the rest of the match. Whelan's distress, though, was much, much worse.

'My leg swung back and I managed to grab the lower part of it before I hit the ground,' he says. 'If I hadn't the bone would have been protruding, coming out, because it just snapped straight in two. It was so painful and it was constant.

'They had no injections then. Nowadays the doctor will come on and if you've got a break he'll give you an injection immediately – just to kill the pain before they get you off. None of that.

'They put me on a stretcher, which was two poles with a canvas in the middle, carried me off and in the Wembley dressing rooms they had about six baths in a row and they put me across one of the baths. Well, the canvas went up and it moved the bone. I screamed – and that happened just as our players were coming in at half-time.

'They put me on the floor then, but I still hadn't had anything to kill the pain, and even in the ambulance they didn't have anything either.'

Whelan was taken to Wembley hospital where a doctor was waiting for him. He had been watching the match on TV, seen the incident and knew where Whelan would be heading. 'When I arrived there,'

Whelan says, 'he came into the ambulance, took one look and injected me straight in the leg.

'It killed the pain within thirty seconds, there and then – while I was still in the ambulance. I said thank you to him afterwards because he was a very good doctor. He was from Poland.'

Whelan recalls being taken into surgery to be operated on and coming round as he was being wheeled along a hospital corridor. 'The doctor was right beside me,' he says. 'I opened my eyes and the first thing I said to him was, "How did we get on, doctor?" He said, "I'm sorry, you've lost 3–0."

'And I started to cry [he indicates tears shooting from his eyes – complete with a 'Whoosh' sound effect]. I couldn't stop it. I just started crying, "Oh dear, we've lost 3–0."'

Whelan's suffering did not end there. He was moved to a hospital in central London where a specialist encased Whelan's leg in plaster up to the hip as part of an experiment aimed at having him walking again straightaway.

Whelan recalls what happened when the doctor came in the next day.

Doctor: 'Right, I want you to walk now.'

Whelan, disbelievingly: 'You want me to walk?!'

Doctor: 'Oh yes, you can walk.'

Whelan: 'I can't walk.'

Doctor: 'Yes, you can. Will you get on your feet?'

Whelan: 'I can get on my feet, yes, but I want crutches.'

Doctor, having given Whelan crutches: 'Right, now I want you to practise with the crutches. Left foot down, take your weight and swing your right leg forward like you're walking.'

Whelan swung his right leg forward.

Doctor: 'Right, now pull that one forward… do it again…'

Whelan took three strides and fell over.

Doctor: 'Right, you've taken three strides and you've proved everything I'm saying. Your hip can carry your weight.'

'I don't think so,' Whelan thinks.

Soon after Whelan returned home, he went to Blackburn Infirmary in a lot of pain. Two doctors there argued whether they should remove the plaster without consulting the London specialist. The argument ended when one of them suggested that if the plaster was not removed gangrene could set in and Whelan might lose his leg. At this point Whelan told them to cut the plaster off regardless of what the specialist thought.

The weight of the plaster had caused it to dig into Whelan's instep, which had gone septic.

'Sure enough,' Whelan says, 'when the doctor took the plaster off, gangrene had just started. Absolutely spot on that doctor. Otherwise I'd have lost my leg.'

Whelan discovered later that he might well have missed the 1960 final that so changed his life. 'I was nearly signed by Man United in 1959 when I'd just come out of the army,' he says. 'I found out two or three years later that Matt Busby, the United boss, had enquired whether he could sign me. Blackburn never told me. They wouldn't negotiate.'

Bill Slater's retreat from Wembley after his appearance in the 1951 FA Cup final tells a very different story of quite how ordinary the professional footballer's life used to be.

While Whelan had to suffer like any other punter injured that

Saturday afternoon, falling off a ladder or whatever, Slater found that travelling on a Saturday night could be a public-transport nightmare even for someone who had played in the day's big sporting event.

Slater, brought up in the village of Waddington – then in Yorkshire, now in Lancashire – started playing for Blackpool as a seventeen-year-old during the war when the Football League was suspended.

By the 1951 FA Cup final he had just turned twenty-four. He had done national service in the army and was studying physical education at college in Leeds. He was playing on an irregular basis for Blackpool and his selection to play against Newcastle would make him the last amateur to appear in the final.

'There were some injuries,' Slater says, 'which is why I played and why the manager, Joe Smith, picked me at inside-left when my best position was left-half.'

Newcastle won 2–0, a comfortable victory, according to Slater, although not one-sided. But the thing he remembers most vividly about the day was the journey back to his student digs in Leeds.

'The rules about being out of college were rather more strict than they are now,' he says, 'and I had to be back by midnight on the Saturday night. The principal insisted on it.

'I had to miss the Cup final dinner and the awful thing was my train to Leeds was going on to Newcastle. It was absolutely packed with Newcastle supporters celebrating. I sat in the corner of a carriage and no one recognised me – why should they? – but I had to suffer two or three hours of Newcastle celebrations.'

When the Cup was king, it was not just the final that reigned. Matches right from the start of each competition stirred great excitement, far greater than today.

One good reason, on top of the Cup's gilded reputation, was the higher probability of upsets. With what little money there was to buy success being thinly spread, Football League and top non-League teams were far more evenly matched. This much narrower difference in quality and a knockout draw without seedings gave endless scope for giant-killing.

Terry Allcock enjoyed one of the great Cup runs with Norwich City in 1958–59, when Norwich were in the Third Division. It featured yet another episode that underscored the dangers of being a goalkeeper in the febrile action of the FA Cup.

What Allcock says he did not realise when he signed for Norwich in March 1958 was that, a year earlier, a public appeal had helped to save the club, which was virtually bankrupt. 'I'm told the local press contributed too, by paying the wages on a couple of occasions, but it was the Cup run that re-established the club financially.

'All our home games were a complete sell-out with the capacity limited to 38,000 by the police.'

Norwich started their run in November by beating the non-League club Ilford 3–1, having been behind at half-time; in the second round they defeated Swindon, also of the Third Division, 1–0 in a replay, having drawn 1–1 at Swindon. So far, pretty ordinary.

'Then all hell broke loose,' Allcock says, 'because we drew Manchester United in the third round.'

Allcock adds the aside that he never lost a match against United, although at this point it was only as a Bolton player that he had played against them. Nearly a decade later, in 1966–67, he would maintain this unbeaten record when he led Norwich to a 2–1 win in an FA Cup fourth-round tie at Old Trafford.

But this was 1959, and United's visit to Carrow Road was possibly the most exciting thing that had happened to Norwich since the railway arrived there in the middle of the previous century. Tickets were at a premium, Allcock says, and there was quite a bit of black-market activity.

The match took place in January on a snow-covered pitch. 'They'd swept the lines clear and put a blue dye down,' Allcock says. 'We managed to hold our footings a lot better than they did, probably because, unknown to anyone other than ourselves, we removed the top two tiers of leather from our studs and left the nails protruding so that we got a grip.'

This was quite a common practice, in fact. Bolton's Tommy Banks certainly knew about it, not only from playing football. After leaving school at fourteen, his first job was delivering coal from a cart pulled by a horse, Drummer, who was liable to do the splits on frozen surfaces. To prevent this, some of the nails holding Drummer's shoes in place were not driven right home.

Allcock gives credit to Archie Macaulay, one of seven managers he played under at Norwich, for other decisive contributions:

'He was a great confidence-booster. He never talked about the op-position, he always told you how good you were. And another thing he did for the Man U game was change the system, making us almost certainly one of the first teams in the country to play four-four-two, which England used to win the World Cup in 1966.'

Norwich tried it the week before the Cup tie, Allcock says, when they beat Southend 4–0. This convinced them that it was a good idea. It turned into a brilliant one as they used it to beat United 3–0 and progress deeper and deeper into the competition.

They had a close win over Cardiff in the fourth round before putting out Tottenham in a replay that Norwich nicked 1–0 at home.

In the quarter-final at Sheffield United, Norwich trailed 1–0 when their goalkeeper, Ken Nethercott, dislocated his shoulder. The obvious solution would have been to stick Nethercott on the wing to make a nuisance of himself, just as Ray Wood had done in the final against Aston Villa two years earlier.

'But Ken insisted he stayed in goal and played with one hand for most of the second half,' Allcock says, 'and we forced a one-one draw.'

Allcock describes the replay as probably the most emotional night of all. 'The crowd had really got behind us by then and they were singing the national anthem before we started. It made your hair stand on end really. It was a lovely atmosphere.' Norwich won 3–2 after going two up in the first half.

Drawn against Luton in the semi-final at White Hart Lane, Allcock recalls feeling disappointed even though the match ended 1–1: 'We drew but we didn't think we performed as well as we could have done. Maybe it was nerves, I don't know. The second game in Birmingham we were well on top but unfortunately we did everything bar score and we finished up losing 1–0.'

The atmosphere of Norwich's Cup run is beautifully conveyed by the Pathé newsreels that so captured the essence of Britain in the 1940s, '50s and '60s.

The brutally edited black-and-white action sequences and the cut-away shots of the packed terraces emphasise an audience that would have wrestled with the concept of a prawn sandwich, let alone have eaten one. The disconnect between the commentators' posh, man-nered accents and the grittiness of the images merely accentuates this, the toff separated from reality by being stuck in the commentary box.

He signs off with clipped insincerity: 'So Luton go into the final. What a pity it's at the expense of gallant Norwich City.'

Like Allcock, Gordon Milne didn't quite make it to the final, even if the team did. The year was 1965 and Milne was in peak form for Liverpool, the League champions. They were seeking to put behind them unexpected defeats in recent seasons that had thwarted their efforts to win the Cup for the first time.

They came desperately close to being upset again in the fourth round against Stockport County, who would end the season bottom of the Football League in ninety-second place. Bill Shankly was so confident his team would beat Stockport that he went to Germany to spy on Cologne, Liverpool's next European Cup opponents.

'It was a frosty January day,' Milne says, 'and it ended one each. But in the last minute, at the Kop end, Stockport had a corner and their centre-forward, a Scottish lad, hit the bar with a header. It came down on the line and we scooped it away. We could have been out.'

Liverpool won the replay four days later and kept going strongly all the way through to the final without conceding another goal.

Milne, who played in all the games, was feeling good. 'I was always quite keen on my fitness,' he says, 'I was brought up that way. I looked after myself. And I got myself into the England team. So I was playing for England and I was playing for Liverpool and not missing any games.'

Milne needed to be fit. Liverpool's 2–0 win over Chelsea in the Cup semi-final took place on Saturday 27 March – and between then and the Cup final on Saturday 1 May, the Liverpool players submitted, uncomplainingly, to a breathless fixture list.

Confirming something that nineteenth-century mill owners knew only too well – that people work harder the more skint they are – the players slogged their way through ten League games in the first twenty-six days of April.

Under the weight of this backlog of fixtures, a result of FA and European Cup commitments, the players squeezed out just two victories. In other words, no one made more than a tenner, over and above their skimpy wages, in win bonuses. Nor did anyone think of asking for overtime.

Some things inevitably had to give – and one of these was Milne's knee, fifteen days before the Cup final.

It was Good Friday and Liverpool, again playing Chelsea, this time in the League, were up to game six of their April ordeal. The sun shone brightly on a bone-hard pitch at Stamford Bridge. 'I've gone to take a ball,' Milne says. 'At the same time Eddie McCreadie, their left-back, came and just clattered it and I've done my knee ligament.

'When we came back on the train to Lime Street, I had a big ice pack on my knee and I knew that I wasn't going to make the final. Having never missed games, that was a major blow. I remember people telling me not to worry because we'd be there again next season, but it didn't happen.'

On the day of the final against Leeds, Milne says he felt lost. 'All the build-up to the Cup is fantastic and, although I was with the team wearing my tracksuit, I had my suit on underneath it, which was daft really. I felt on the outside looking in, which wasn't how it was for the other lads.'

Yet again the Cup final worked its malign injury magic when Liverpool's left-back Gerry Byrne broke his collarbone in the opening minutes. 'It was strapped up,' Milne says, 'and Gerry played like that

LEFT Jimmy Hill in 1949 when, at the age of twenty, he began his Football League career at Brentford. Twelve years later – by now a Fulham player – he led the Professional Footballers' Association's fight, which included the threat of strike action, against the maximum wage. Hill died in 2015 aged eighty-seven.

BELOW Jimmy Hill in action for Fulham in February 1961, a few weeks after his key role in persuading the Football League to end the restriction on players' wages. Here, in a match at Stamford Bridge, he tussles for the ball with Chelsea goalkeeper Peter Bonetti. Johnny Key is in close attendance.

Colin Collindridge, born in November 1920, is presented with the tie of the Coventry City Former Players' Association by Mike Young in 2011. COURTESY OF MIKE YOUNG/CCFPA

Colin Collindridge during his playing days with his third and final Football League club, Coventry City (1954–56). Previously he had played for Sheffield United (1938–50) and Nottingham Forest (1950–54).

Johnny Paton's time as a Celtic player was interrupted by the Second World War, when he was posted to Canada. Here he is seen in RAF uniform on a visit to New York, where he played in a bad-tempered match for a local team. COURTESY OF THE PATON FAMILY

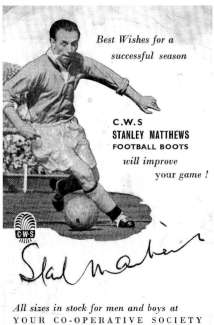

Best Wishes for a
successful season

C.W.S
STANLEY MATTHEWS
FOOTBALL BOOTS
will improve
your game !

All sizes in stock for men and boys at
YOUR CO-OPERATIVE SOCIETY
CWS—46655 R

Johnny Paton (right) with his father, also Johnny, in Trafalgar Square in 1946 after Johnny Jr, a Celtic player, had signed a one-season contract with Chelsea. COURTESY OF THE PATON FAMILY

Stanley Matthews was one of the first players to use his celebrity to boost his earnings – including a deal with the Co-operative Society to endorse boots. AUTHOR'S COLLECTION

G·O·A·L!
...yells Greaves, of Chelsea.
But Leeds goalkeeper Wood
was there to stop it.

Roy Wood, ever-present in the Leeds United goal for two successive Football League seasons in the 1950s, disappoints Chelsea's Jimmy Greaves (left) with a save. Leeds defenders Jack Charlton (second right) and Billy Cush look on. COURTESY OF ROY WOOD

LEFT Tony McNamara, who played for Everton and Liverpool in the 1950s, takes his turn at heading on a low-tech piece of apparatus during his Everton days.
COURTESY OF THE McNAMARA FAMILY

BELOW A heading tennis match was the only Merseyside derby in which Tony McNamara (front second left) played, despite a decade first at Everton and then at Liverpool. He was on the winning Everton side in the 'tennis' contest. The Liverpool team included one of their greatest players, Billy Liddell (back left), and Bob Paisley (front left), who went on to manage the club. Also in the photograph are (back row from right) Cyril Done (Liverpool, referee), Bill Jones (Liverpool), John Willie Parker (Everton), Tommy E. Jones (Everton); and (front row from right) Phil Taylor (Liverpool) and Dave Hickson (Everton).
COURTESY OF THE McNAMARA FAMILY

LEFT Farm boy… Tommy Banks, who signed for Bolton in 1947, supplemented his meagre football wages by working on a farm near his home in Farnworth, Lancashire.
COURTESY OF TOMMY BANKS

BELOW LEFT Cover boy… Banks looks more choirboy than notoriously hard-tackling Bolton Wanderers defender on the front of *Charles Buchan's Football Monthly*.
COURTESY OF TOMMY BANKS

BELOW RIGHT Stan Anderson leads out Sunderland for a fifth-round FA Cup tie at Norwich in 1961. Sunderland won 1–0. Anderson would become the first player to captain all three big clubs in the north-east, moving first to Newcastle and then to Middlesbrough.
PA IMAGES

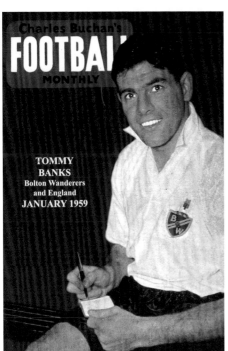

Alec Jackson was discovered playing for a church team near his home in Tipton. Soon afterwards, in November 1954, he scored on his First Division debut for West Bromwich Albion against Charlton Athletic. COURTESY OF ALEC JACKSON

Peter McParland was an outstanding finisher for Aston Villa and Northern Ireland. He scored five of the six goals Northern Ireland registered at the 1958 World Cup in reaching the quarter-finals. COURTESY OF PETER McPARLAND

The collision between Peter McParland of Aston Villa (striped shirt) and the Manchester United goalkeeper Ray Wood after six minutes of the 1957 FA Cup final. Wood, who left the field with a fractured cheekbone, was back in goal by the end of the match. McParland scored both goals in his side's 2–1 win. PA IMAGES

Dave Whelan of Blackburn Rovers is carried off with a badly broken leg in the 1960 FA Cup final against Wolverhampton Wanderers, who won 3–0. While recovering, Whelan worked on a market stall developing the business skills that served him so well in later life. PA IMAGES

Cliff Lloyd (left), secretary of the Professional Footballers' Association, and George Eastham of Arsenal outside the High Court in 1963. Their action ended the 'slavery' rule that had tied players to clubs even when they were out of contract. PA IMAGES

Terry Allcock (left), once a free-scoring forward, had switched to being an influential member of Norwich City's defence by the time of this 1966–67 FA Cup tie at Old Trafford. Here the Manchester United forward Denis Law lines up a header but Norwich held on for a giant-killing 2–1 win in front of a crowd of 63,405. Kevin Keelan is the Norwich goalkeeper. COURTESY OF TERRY ALLCOCK

Hotshots Jimmy Greaves (left) and Cliff Jones when they were members of Tottenham Hotspur's formidable forward line in the 1960s. PA IMAGES

Liverpool players Gerry Byrne (front left), Ian Callaghan (centre) and Gordon Milne (right) with England at Lilleshall before the final squad was named for the 1966 World Cup finals. Milne, the only one of the trio not to make the squad, said it was one of the biggest disappointments of his life. Roger Hunt (left background), also of Liverpool, played in all six England games in the finals. COURTESY OF GORDON MILNE for the rest of the match, which included added time. He was hard as nails, Gerry, and he even got involved in the build-up for our first goal at the start of extra time.'

Roger Hunt scored that goal and, after Billy Bremner equalised for Leeds, Ian St John's header sealed Liverpool's 2–1 victory. (The Pathé News commentator showed his true class by calling St John 'Sinjun'.)

Milne's compensation for having to sit out the Wembley match included not only receiving a win bonus – at least he thinks he received the few extra pounds – despite being out of the side, but, far more memorably, what happened three days later.

On the Tuesday after the final, Liverpool were at home to Inter Milan in the first leg of their European Cup semi-final. 'In all my time I never experienced an atmosphere like the one at Anfield that night,' Milne says. 'And Shanks built it up. He got Gerry and me to walk around the pitch with the FA Cup before the game.

'You could nearly touch the atmosphere, it was that electric, the noise. Liverpool had never won the Cup before, Gerry had played on with a broken collarbone and there he was carrying the Cup. I hadn't been able to play … It seemed to take us for ever to carry it around. And for the final bit we came down in front of the Kop … so what Inter Milan must have felt in the dressing room listening to that noise. They couldn't have missed it. It was a clever move by Shanks.'

(Liverpool won 3–1 but went out after losing the second leg, controversially, 3–0.)

Milne recovered over the summer and regained his place in the first team, although, he says, he never really regained the sharpness he had before. He was still playing for England, but the big prize, selection for the 1966 World Cup finals, would elude him.

Alf Ramsey, the England manager, had already told Milne about his decision when he heard it announced publicly.

'We were driving back from the Lilleshall training centre. Peter Thompson was in the car, Gerry Byrne, Roger Hunt, myself and Ian Callaghan. And the radio came on announcing the World Cup squad: "…and the five unlucky players are: Gordon Milne, Peter Thompson, Johnny Byrne, Keith Newton and Bobby Tambling."

'It was one of the biggest disappointments in my life – a double whammy in a short space of time, missing the Cup final and then this.'

Not everyone signed up to the FA Cup's regal status. Maybe if there had been a significant trickle-down from the spoils clubs received for Cup success to the small brown envelopes players picked up each week, loyalty would have been universal.

Dave Whelan was one who thought unconditional devotion to the Cup was overdone and is even scathing about Blackburn's allegiance to it in the year they reached Wembley.

He refers to Blackburn's fifth-round victory at White Hart Lane in February 1960, the start of the Spurs' glory years. 'It was the most brilliant game,' he says. 'We were the underdogs – Tottenham were favourites to win the League and Cup that season – but we battered them 3–1.'

What still riles Whelan is how some of his teammates reacted. 'The following Saturday we played Spurs again,' he says. 'This time in the League at Ewood, and they beat us 4–1, because, although we were then high up in the League, we wanted the FA Cup and the lads stopped playing.'

Whelan is one of those people who somehow communicates the depth of his disgust by not showing any emotion. He reflects evenly on the fact that Blackburn won only two out of thirteen League matches between the fifth-round win over Spurs and the Cup final: 'We fell into the bottom half of the table in getting to Wembley because the team wouldn't play. They all wanted to go and win the Cup. Amazing.'

Johnny Carey had left by then to go to manage Everton. 'We had Dally Duncan in his place and he didn't know what to do,' Whelan says. 'He should have dropped half the team and put the reserves in to send the message, "You're not playing for the first team again until you start to play."

'They all stopped playing. Midfield, up front – no fight in League matches – and we dropped into the bottom half of the League very quickly.'

'It's difficult to explain this now,' Stan Anderson says, 'but the League was of very little importance in those days. Everybody wanted to play at Wembley so the FA Cup was the prime target. And there was only the League and the FA Cup. That was it.'

As a younger player, he says, you would sit back at players' meetings and listen to what everybody else said, 'but as you got a little bit older you started to have a word yourself'.

He tells how in 1954–55, when Sunderland were in the quarter-finals of the Cup and pushing for the League title, he and Len Shackleton argued at a players' meeting over what the team's priority should be.

'We need to concentrate on Wembley and reaching the Cup final,' Shackleton said.

'Why can't we win them both?' Anderson chipped in.

'Impossible. Never been done.'

'So what? We have the players. We're the most consistent team in the League.'

'No, we're going to concentrate on the Cup.'

'And that seemed to be the decision,' Anderson says.

Sunderland won their quarter-final against Wolves but then won only one of their next eight matches – suffering defeat by Manchester City in the Cup semi-final and losing four out of seven League matches – as their season disintegrated.

'All of a sudden attitudes changed: "Oh, now we're going to try to win the League." Too bloody late,' Anderson says. 'It was ridiculous, but that was the attitude in those days. The FA Cup, that was it. League matches, they were, "Ah well, yeah, if we win those, fine – but, if we don't, it doesn't matter."'

When the Cup was king, the serfs may have been skint, but not all were awestruck.

CHAPTER NINE

A MATCH TO REMEMBER

In which fans pack Goodison AND Anfield to watch live as Gordon Milne commits a howler – the Wales winger forgets his effing boots before scoring his greatest goal against England – the Arsenal new boy who cried himself to sleep feels much better after his volley into the top corner – a keeper plays so well the papers get his name wrong.

Warwick Rimmer has said he will pick me up from outside Hamilton Square underground station. Travelling from Liverpool Lime Street, Hamilton Square is the first stop on the Wirral Line on the Birkenhead side of the Mersey. From in front of the station there is a commanding view across the great expanse of river in the direction of Albert Dock. It is a waterway that has shaped British history. It makes a riveting spectacle.

Right on time, Rimmer pulls up. He has a full head of white hair and hobbles a bit, the legacy of twenty years of professional football, but is trim enough to be playing still. Although he played for Football League clubs Bolton and Crewe – he signed for Bolton as a fifteen-year-old in 1956 – he is a Birkenhead man born and bred and when we meet is working for Tranmere Rovers.

When his playing career ended he became commercial manager at Tranmere before spending twenty-six years as their youth development manager. Latterly he has worked part-time as their child protection officer and recruitment officer.

As we drive through Birkenhead he slows down to point out where his father and uncle, Syd and Ellis Rimmer, once had what would have been grandly known as a turf accountant's office (betting shops were not legalised until 1961). We are heading for Tranmere's ground, Prenton Park, which is more than 100 years old and, despite several rebuilds, still has plenty of room for improvement.

We make our way along a warren of narrow passages under the stands before finding a room we can talk in without being disturbed. It is about ten feet square and probably has not changed much over several years, apart from the fridge filled with beers in the corner. It is where the opposing managers, assuming they are still talking to each other, have their post-match chat.

If this sounds a sombre setting to introduce a chapter about matches to remember, there is a reason. Rimmer has continued a surprising trend: the regularity with which my veterans have identified as their memorable matches those that they might be expected to want to forget.

In fact, it has been striking how many of them have only fleeting recall of the great games in which they featured, such as World Cup matches and FA Cup finals. They choose to hark back to some of the less obvious ones because of their salutary lessons.

When players shared with so many the daily grind of making a modest living, maybe it is hardly surprising that these matches had a deeper, more durable meaning.

A game that has clearly stayed with Rimmer in a more meaningful way than perhaps any other took place right at the start of his professional career.

Rimmer had appeared at youth level for England, including a big win over Spain in the Bernabéu when he played alongside Bobby Moore. He was impatient to make his first-team debut for Bolton, which he did eventually at the start of 1960–61, 'but not before I'd got a bit of a lesson'.

He says it is a lesson he now passes on to the apprentice players at Tranmere so they don't repeat his mistakes.

'I'd been in the reserves for quite a while and then somehow, I don't know what had happened, I found I'd slipped back into the A team playing a match at Stockport on a Saturday morning. And my first reaction was to think, "Oh bugger this, nobody'll be watching." I contemplated acting top dog and not bothering.

'But in the end I decided, "Well, it's a game like any other and I'm going to try my hardest." I put my mind to it properly and we won and I did well. And it was because of this, and the fact that two senior players were injured, that a week and a half later I found myself playing my first game for the first team against Hull City in the League Cup.

'So I tell the young boys these days not to cut off their noses to spite their faces. You never know who's watching you in training, friendly matches or whatever.'

This experience of being demoted to the A team has left a far greater impression on Rimmer than how he fared in his long-awaited first-team debut. 'All I remember about the match against Hull was that it was a very, very tight game, a goalless draw, and I did OK,' he says. He also recalls the disappointment of being dropped for the replay because the player he replaced, Derek Hennin, was fit again.

Gordon Milne comes right out with it: 'I always seem to remember the things that went wrong in my Liverpool days.'

He could not have chosen a worse fixture in which to make a memorable blunder than a fifth-round FA Cup tie against Everton at Goodison. 'It was that finely balanced, as derby games always were, and I decided in my wisdom to play the ball back to Tommy Lawrence,' he says. 'I played it short, Alan Ball got it, went past Big Ron and scored. And we lose one-nothing.

'So I'm responsible for defeat and I can remember that dressing room afterwards. I don't think Shanks said a word.'

To make matters even more painful for Milne, Liverpool showed live coverage on massive screens at Anfield, which meant that capacity crowds at both the great Merseyside grounds witnessed his howler.

Today players can retire to their electric-gated mansions in leafy suburbs and live out their shame in comfort. Milne was imprisoned in his two-up, two-down. 'I remember for weeks I couldn't go into town,' he says. 'If I had all the Evertonians would have said, "Oh well played, Gordon, great pass back." Liverpool fans wouldn't have wanted to talk to me.

'I remember having to come through that but I did play in the next game, which made me think about Shanks's philosophy.'

While Milne suffered, the Liverpool club banked the best part of £12,000 from their live-coverage experiment.

The match that made an indelible impression on Johnny Paton was a Second Division fixture for Brentford against Southampton over the 1951 Christmas holiday when Brentford were 'going great guns' near the top of the table.

'It was a heavy day. Raining,' Paton says. 'It was a terrible pitch, muddy, hardly any grass on it. We were drawing and it was just before half-time.

'Southampton had an inside-right, Frank Dudley, who was a big fellow. Not a great player but dangerous, unpredictable. He got the ball in his own half and started running with it and I thought, "He's too far away for me, I can't chase him. He's thirty yards away." It was heavy mud and in any case it wasn't my job.'

The problem was that it was no one else's job either, the consequence of a system devised by Ron Greenwood, later to become the England manager but at this point still playing as a defender for Brentford.

'Ron, a great tactician, had evolved a system at Brentford known as the retreating defence,' Paton says. 'So no one went out and tackled big Dudley and he kept running with it, running with it, running with it. Then I think he must have shut his eyes and taken a big a swing at it. The ball flew into the net.'

In Paton's estimation, the effect of Dudley's blind swing at the ball has reverberated down the decades for Brentford FC. 'We came in at half-time and I think that what happened next ruined Brentford Football Club right to the present day,' he says.

Jackie Gibbons, the Brentford manager, turned on Greenwood, holding him responsible, as captain and author of the retreating de-fence, for Dudley's goal. 'Why the hell didn't someone go and tackle Dudley?!' Gibbons said. 'Ron Greenwood, you're the captain.'

Greenwood pointed out that it was thanks to the retreating defence that Brentford had one of the best defensive records in the League.

Paton kept his mouth shut, 'but, unfortunately, poor old Jimmy Hill, who couldn't resist giving his opinion, joined in and took Ron Green-wood's side'.

'You don't know what's going on. You don't even come in for the team meetings on a Friday,' Hill said, referring to the fact that it was Greenwood who took charge of these meetings.

'Shut up,' Gibbons snapped at Hill.

And that was the end of Hill and Greenwood as Brentford players. Hill moved to Fulham and Greenwood headed to Chelsea.

Not only that, Paton says, his memories still deeply etched, 'we sank from near the top to down in the middle of the table and the atmosphere at the club was never the same.

'The next home match after Dudley's goal – and I have a picture in my mind of this – I came running out of the tunnel before kick-off and passed Ron and Jimmy in their civvies. I'm not sure about Jimmy, but Ron never kicked another ball for Brentford.

'It's almost unbelievable but the club never recovered from that defeat. You look at the history books and that was the highest up the Football League Brentford have ever got since their First Division peak in the late '30s.'

Bill Leivers's debut for Manchester City did not disappoint in being memorable – but this was mostly for reasons, personal and one other, he would prefer to forget.

What spoiled it on a personal level for Leivers was that not only did City lose 5–0 at Preston North End on Saturday 21 August 1954, but he also suffered an injury that would have a lasting physical effect.

'I went up for a high ball,' Leivers says, 'and this other player made a back for me. I went straight over the top and landed on the bottom of my spine. I have now got three collapsed discs at the bottom of my spine and I'm full of arthritis.' He moves uneasily in his armchair.

'I didn't go off – but you didn't in those days, you just walked about – but it put me out for quite a while, at least five months.'

What also still rankles is that the match has a place in English football history as the fixture that launched the so-called Revie Plan, which Leivers considers a bad case of giving credit where it was not due.

He accepts the match's significance but is annoyed that it stands as a monument to Don Revie, a Manchester City regular in the early '50s who as a manager succeeded Alf Ramsey in the England job.

The 'Revie Plan' was the City players' response to the way Hungary had played a year earlier when they beat England 6–3 in London.

The victory made Hungary the first Continental team to win at Wembley and disturbed not only the English game's deeply entrenched complacency, but also its understanding of where players should be deployed on the pitch. This understanding dated back to football's emergence in the nineteenth century as a passing game.

Most significantly, Hungary deployed a deep-lying, freewheeling centre-forward, Nándor Hidegkuti. This completely flummoxed England's defence, who were drilled to mark a No. 9 who occupied a fixed point and who led the attack from a central, forward-lying position.

'I think most of the players who played for City in that match against Preston weren't very pleased that it is now known as the Revie Plan because it most certainly wasn't called that at the time,' Leivers says.

The two players who came up with the idea, Leivers says, were Ken Barnes, a skilful right-half who never tackled, and Johnny Williamson, a slow but clever forward. There was 'absolutely no question' that they were the ones who introduced the new system, with a great deal of success, when they played together in the reserves.

'It became known as the Revie Plan because Don was the one who played as the deep-lying forward when the first team took it over. Don was down as centre-forward but played in the middle of the park and no one came with him to mark him. It's astonishing when you think about it.'

Despite the inauspicious start against Preston, City prospered as the players grew used to the system. They finished the 1954–55 season seventh in the First Division, seven places ahead of Preston, and reached the 1955 and '56 FA Cup finals.

For all the salutary lessons, though, many more matches are best remembered for being celebrations of a player's skill, most commonly when it combined with the scoring of a priceless goal.

Years later memories of these moments – and the matches that contained them – are as precise as if they were taken from scripts of commentaries delivered at the time.

Terry Neill, the Arsenal new boy, was in need of bucking up after being uprooted from his happy childhood in Northern Ireland. He was mournful and finding it hard to adjust to living in digs in London.

'I was terribly homesick living in the digs the club found me up near Muswell Hill,' he says. 'It wasn't my landlady's fault that they were horrible. She was a widow and had a hard life. There was no central heating, it was cold in the bedroom and I used to cry myself to sleep. I wrote to my parents every day.'

Things improved when, through a contact, Neill's father found him accommodation with a north London solicitor's family. 'They were lovely,' he says. 'I think I would have absconded back home if the Martins had not taken me in and treated me like one of the family.'

But what really settled Neill was when he made it into the Arsenal first team. 'I loved the Arsenal club and loved the training,' he says. 'The youth team coaches – George Male, Ernie Collett, Alf Fields – were great people, really looked after us. Under their guidance I progressed to making my first-team debut in 1960, when I was eighteen.'

He had played in the reserves regularly and had started to train with the first team under Ron Greenwood, who by now was Arsenal's assistant manager. On 23 December he travelled with the first team to play Sheffield Wednesday.

'We were about to play a Wednesday team that included players like Springett, Kay, Swan and Bronco Layne,' Neill says, 'and, after the pre-match meal, George Swindin sought me out in the hotel lobby, sat me down and asked if I thought I was ready to play in the first team.'

Neill says his immediate reaction was to say he needed a little longer. But he declared his readiness without being convinced, which is when Swindin passed on the really shocking news: Neill was going to take Tommy Docherty's place.

'Ah Jesus!' was Neill's reaction, which he still clearly recalls. 'What is going to happen? Tommy is going to punch my lights out.'

It occurred to Neill that this was no way to repay Docherty for all his kindness when he, Neill, had arrived at the club, and Docherty 'put his arm around me, being concerned about my welfare…

'But Tommy sought me out ten minutes later – George Swindin must have told him, "You're out. Young Terry's taking your place" – and, true to form, he sat me down and reassured me: "You'll be fine, just continue what you've been doing, I've been watching you in the reserve games."'

So, Neill played against Sheffield Wednesday. 'We were struggling after John Snedden, a young Scots lad who could have been another

John Charles – could play anywhere, a good athlete, great in the air, skilful and a bit of pace – had to go off with an ankle injury.

'Down to ten men, we had a corner, the ball was headed out, by Swan, I think, and I cushioned the ball on my thigh and volleyed it into the top corner. Don't ask me where I got it from. I don't think I ever did it again.'

After his part in a 1–1 draw, away from home, against a star-studded Sheffield Wednesday team, Neill reckons Swindin was sitting on the bench calculating that for two and a half grand he had landed the club a steal. 'If I remember it took me another four months to score my second goal,' Neill says, 'but for the moment, anyway, George thought he'd got a bargain.'

For Cliff Jones, a match for Wales against England, in which he scored a 'great goal' – his assessment, corroborated by film footage – stands out among all the others, and there were a lot of those in his fifty-nine appearances for his country and more than 500 in the Football League for Swansea, Spurs and Fulham.

'For me, being a Welshman, putting on the Wales shirt was my biggest honour,' he says. 'It still stays with me. My first game was against Austria in Vienna in 1954. I was nineteen. I struggled in that game a bit. We got beaten 2–0. So I didn't get picked again for more than a year.'

He was brought back for the British Home Championship match against a powerful England side – Stanley Matthews, Tom Finney, Nat Lofthouse and Billy Wright – in Cardiff. 'It was 1955 and I was twenty years of age,' he says, 'and the funny thing was I'd forgotten my boots.'

In a panic he rang his wife, Joan – they were still newlyweds – to ask her to deliver the boots to him at Ninian Park as quickly as possible.

'It's just before the game,' Jones says, 'and I'm sort of darting about waiting for my wife and the manager's looking at me.'

'What's up, Cliff? Don't worry about tickets,' the manager told Jones. It was now about an hour before kick-off. 'Just give the tickets to the bloke on the door and he'll let your wife and family have the tickets.'

'It's not the tickets,' Jones said.

'Well, what is it?'

'I've forgotten my boots.'

'What?! You forgot your fuckin' boots? We're playing against England, Stanley Matthews, Tom Finney, and you forgot your fuckin' boots!'

'He went off on one, didn't he,' Jones says.

The upshot was that the boots arrived in time and Wales won 2–1, their first victory over England in seventeen years, with Jones scoring the winning goal.

He details how he did it as exactly as if telling me what he had just had for breakfast.

'I cut in from the left and Roy Paul, a brilliant wing-half, slanted a ball over. I could see it coming and I came across Billy Wright, the England centre-half, got up and went bang with my head.

'It went straight in at the far post. Great goal! Billy Wright had no chance. I was carried off shoulder-high at the end. Amazing! One of my great moments in football.'

Like many of the former players I meet, Tony McNamara says that somewhere in his home in Huyton there is a scrapbook of cuttings containing reports and photographs of his playing days. Also like most of the others, he says the book was the work of other family members; he wasn't that bothered about chronicling his career.

His wife, the kindly Doreen, goes to find Tony's scrapbook. The importance of these tattered collections is not that they fill in details mislaid by fading memories, rather that they tell me things the player never would.

In McNamara's case, it is things such as the assessment of a newspaper columnist who described McNamara as 'an outstanding young prospect to challenge Stan Matthews for England honours'.

Sadly it was not to be. Although he served Everton on the wing with distinction over seven seasons, before crossing the trenches between Goodison and Anfield, he suffered a series of leg injuries at key moments of his career.

As we sit talking, he taps the two new knees that have kept him walking into old age. He shows no resentment that his injuries prevented him from realising his full potential. Instead there is a dignified acceptance of his misfortune: that he played in an era when injured players were encouraged to bite the bullet rather than react as if they had been hit by one – and full-backs considered it their duty to shorten the careers of opposing wingers.

One match for Everton still brings a slow smile to McNamara's face: a 5–2 win over League champions Manchester United at Old Trafford in October 1956. His goal was the pick of the five, sealing United's first home defeat in two years.

Everton were back in the First Division and McNamara was having his best season for the club, playing more than thirty games and scoring ten goals.

'I can still picture my goal at Old Trafford,' he says. 'The Man United goalkeeper cleared the ball and it came to about the halfway line. I moved in from the wing, picked it up and was looking for someone to play it to when I noticed the goalkeeper had come past the penalty spot and was just sort of watching the game.

'So I thought I'd have a go. I lobbed the ball high in the air and the goalie went as though he was going to catch it when he realised he wasn't going to get to it. He turned round to race after it and he and the centre-half finished up in the back of the net with the ball. And as well as scoring that goal I made a couple of others.

'They even mentioned that win over Manchester United at my teammate Dave Hickson's funeral nearly sixty years later.'

Goalkeepers have been known to score memorable goals – to experience the giddy rush usually reserved for some fancy-pants forward – but not many. Opportunities are limited to being a designated penalty-taker, getting lucky with a speculative hack downfield or being summoned to the front line in a desperate ploy to secure a late winner.

Otherwise goalies tend to be mildly deranged misfits, condemned to wander the world playing *foot*ball with their hands and thus excluded from the joy of bulging the onion bag.

There is, of course, a goalkeeping equivalent to scoring, an epic moment that makes a keeper's match 'memorable': the great save – or, in the case of Sunderland goalkeeper Jim Montgomery, the great saves he made in the 1973 Cup final.

Montgomery's double stop, the second part of which was miraculous, was memorable enough on its own without factoring in that it underpinned Sunderland's improbable 1–0 win over the unforgivingly successful Leeds team of the early '70s.

By the time Montgomery parried Peter Lorimer's close-range thunderbolt onto the crossbar, having moments earlier palmed away Trevor Cherry's header, footballers had started to earn a half-decent wage. This was very different from when Roy Wood was manning the last line of Leeds United's defence and earning little more than he had done crushing brick and loading lime.

Wood is partial to playing down his achievements in goal for Leeds. But even he cannot disguise pride in his own double stop in a FA Cup tie against Aston Villa, after which the headline writer confused him with *Ray* Wood, Manchester United's better-known goalie.

The sub-editor's error may have had something to do with the fact that by the time of the Cup tie at Villa, Roy Wood's star had begun to decline, the match being one of only seven first-team appearances he made in 1959–60. He was no longer the regular keeper, having been brought back into the side only because Ted Burgin was injured.

Of his many saves against Villa, the show-stealer was one of Montgomeryesque proportions.

'The Villa winger Peter McParland was cutting in from the left and hit this shot, wham!' Wood says, ramping up the drama. 'I went down and parried it and then someone else came in and hit the rebound. How the heck I got up and flew across the goal I'll never know. I don't remember seeing the ball but I went one-handed and sent it flying into the stand.'

As an exercise in being recognised as a brilliant stopper, the penalty save represents the acme of goalkeeping achievement. Wood made many, including one in a rare away win over the great Wolverhampton Wanderers side of the 1950s, a decade in which Wolves won three First Division titles and were twice runners-up.

'I saved a penalty from Bill Slater,' Wood says, recalling a match played in September 1956. 'I pushed the ball onto the bar and it went over. Wolves were a great side then and hadn't lost at home for several months. On some impulse I decided to dive to the right when Slater placed the ball on the spot, which proved correct.'

He remembers this goal for something else. At the end, the Wolves captain Billy Wright immediately took his leave and disappeared down the tunnel. Wood does not criticise Wright but his tone tells me exactly what he thought. 'It was unlike him,' he says, 'because he was usually such a gentleman – and a great centre-half.'

Not all of Wood's penalty saves had a happy ending.

'I saved a penalty from Tom Finney, but I gave it him back with the rebound. I went the right way but obviously I couldn't hold it. The unlucky part about it was that it could have gone anywhere but it went straight back to his foot and he scored. We still won 2–1, though, and that was at Deepdale [in 1958] where Preston very rarely lost in those days. I had a good game that day.

'I saw Tom at a football dinner soon afterwards and he signed the programme for me.'

Wood says he once had quite a collection of programmes but has given most of them away to charity.

CHAPTER TEN

STARS WHO EARNED THE
SAME AS THE CHORUS LINE

In which Stanley Matthews's reward for giving his autograph is the promise of another clogging – Howard Riley makes the case against his teammate being labelled 'One Save Banks' – Danny Blanchflower feels compelled to tell a teammate the ball is round – John Charles gets away with terrifying a Leeds director.

A telephone rings just after lunch at Blackpool cricket club. The caller, knowing it has been raining in the area, asks whether that afternoon's game has been cancelled. Told that it has, he replies, 'Right, well send Slater over here quickly. We're about to kick off and have only got ten men.'

So it was that seventeen-year-old Bill Slater, who had hoped to spend the day enhancing his reputation as a budding cricketer, made one of his earliest first-team appearances for Blackpool Football Club. He hurried across town in time to take the field midway through the first half.

'Although it was 1944 and Britain was still at war, there were big crowds because watching football was something for people to do,'

Slater says. 'The match had been going for about twenty minutes and there was a huge cheer when I ran onto the field.'

Moments before running onto the Bloomfield Road pitch, Slater had been taken aside by Joe Smith, the Blackpool manager, to be told he was playing at inside right to Stanley Matthews.

It was a bit like a young actor being summoned to play Horatio to Olivier's Hamlet, although Slater, already a promising member of Blackpool's youth team, says it made him even more determined to show off a few moves. This proved a mistake.

'At school I'd been taught it was a useful tactic for an inside-forward, when the wing man came back to collect the ball, to occasionally run up the wing ahead of him,' Slater says. 'So I did this a couple of times.'

Matthews, though, was distinctly unimpressed. 'He came across – he didn't know my name,' Slater says, 'and told me, "Sonny, I would prefer it if you didn't run up the wing like that because you're just getting in my way."'

'He was so polite about it but it was still quite a shock. Can you imagine the star player telling you this?'

Consolation for the slightly crestfallen Slater came late on when, with Blackpool holding a comfortable lead, they were awarded a penalty. At Stan Mortensen's suggestion, Matthews and the other Blackpool stars stood aside while Slater took it – and scored.

By some distance Stanley Matthews, who made his first Football League appearance aged seventeen in 1932 and his final one aged fifty in 1965, was the name that cropped up the most when I asked former players the question, 'Who were the great ones you played with or against?'

Sixty years ago, when the stars earned the same as those in the chorus line, their fellow players' estimation of them was untainted by wage-packet envy. It was based, pure and simple, on how good they were at playing football and, to a lesser but important extent, how they were perceived as people.

What stands out in Matthews's case is not just that nearly everyone I interviewed recognises him as a player of conspicuous brilliance for his two clubs, Stoke City and Blackpool. Also, almost without exception, they treasure a clearly recalled Matthews anecdote – and not necessarily one that ends with them on the seat of their pants as 'The Wizard of Dribble' disappears over the horizon.

Although there are, of course, plenty of these.

Bill Leivers remembers when Manchester City played Blackpool in the 1950s:

'Roy Paul, who was our captain, a Welsh international, played left half. Before the game against Blackpool, Roy said to the manager, "Let me play against Matthews, let me play left full-back," which the manager let him do and I don't think Roy hardly touched the ball. Matthews ran the legs off him.

'He always did the same thing, Matthews. He'd move over to the left and you knew he was going that way. He got everyone who played against him feeling, "There's no way he can come back from over there and go that way." But he did – time after time after time.'

Goalkeeper Roy Wood sympathises with Roy Paul. 'I played against some great forwards for Leeds,' he says, 'but that forward line of Blackpool's that included Stanley Matthews and Stan Mortensen was marvellous.

'On one occasion Matthews was coming along the by-line at me with the ball and I dived at his feet, but when I opened my eyes there was no ball and no Matthews. He'd gone. I remember thinking to myself, "What the hell's going on here?"'

Johnny Paton tells me about when he tried to tease out of Matthews how he did it. Paton played on the opposite wing to Matthews – Matthews on the right, Paton on the left – when they were members of an RAF team that toured Europe after the Second World War. 'They were football-mad in Europe,' Paton says, 'and the Football Association thought sending the RAF team, which had a lot of top international players, would give their morale a lift after it had been lowered by Hitler and his evil Nazi crowd.'

Paton says that when he first met Matthews 'it was like meeting God, because Stanley was God. But, also, he was so ordinary that we used to be ashamed of him sometimes. You could hardly believe he was a footballer he was such a nice fellow and full of humility. Everywhere we went on that tour the only person the people wanted to see was Stanley Matthews, the great Stanley Matthews.'

Only on the pitch would Matthews get irritable, Paton says. He never let this irritation boil over into a show of temper but Paton recalls Matthews's reaction when he marked the great man in five-a-side practice games.

'Being a student of the game who went on to be a coach, I'd studied Stanley and reckoned there was only one way to mark him.

'You had to lean on his shoulder, almost jump on his back, breathe down his neck, never leave him or give him any space. And Stanley used to say, "For Chrissake, Johnny, go away will you. Get lost."'

Mostly, though, Paton says, Matthews was so endlessly obliging that he reckoned with a little persistence he should be able to discover the secret of Matthews's hypnotic skill; how, as Leivers put it, he made others do what he wanted.

Matthews was known for practising on his own. It was during these solitary sessions, Paton reasoned, that he perfected the magic by which he induced full-backs to fall over without making contact with them. So he worked on Matthews – 'I won't bother you, Stan. I'll keep quiet' – until he received permission to practise with him.

This was it, Paton thought: 'Now I'm going to learn the secrets of the greatest man of all time in football.'

He asked Matthews, 'Can you show me your secrets, Stan? How is it you can beat your man all the time, ten out of ten? No one else can.'

'If I had to pay for this lesson,' Paton says, 'even £100 would be cheap.'

Matthews said, 'Right, you're there, you're the full-back, you're the defender. Now, I take the ball up to you, I drag it with the inside of my right foot and I lean over. Your instinct is to do the same, at which point I whip it with the outside of my right into the open space and I'm away. By doing this it gives me that split second to look up and see the position of my forwards.'

'And I'm thinking,' Paton says, 'how fantastic it is that I am learning the secrets of how to become the world's greatest winger.'

But then Matthews said, 'And that's it, Johnny. I just do that all the time. The full-back mistakenly goes that way and sometimes he even falls on the ground because he loses his balance.'

At the time, Paton said, 'Come on, there must be more to it than that, Stan.'

'But, no,' he says now, 'that was it – that was the secret of the great Stanley Matthews. Although, mark you, he would, occasionally, do it five or six times and then go the other way.

'And I noticed something else, which I don't think many others did. For the first maybe ten minutes of a match he would do different things. First ball he got he'd pass it back to Harry Johnston at half-back, second ball he'd find Stan Mortensen in the middle, third ball he'd cross it right away.

'The full-back would be thinking, "Matthews isn't that great"and start to relax and then, oh, oh, and for the rest of the match he'd have his marker in a state of complete confusion.'

Paton, whose twinkling affability has survived unimpaired into old age, may have been one of the few professionals who managed to draw Matthews out of himself.

Bill Slater expresses a more familiar view of Matthews when he says he never got to know him well: 'He was very distant. I don't mean he was unpopular, just that he was rather distant. He sort of lived his own life.'

He recalls an incident when Blackpool were playing Aston Villa in Birmingham, where they stayed the night before the game. 'In the morning people were asking, "Where's Stanley?" He'd had some breakfast but then just disappeared. Even Joe Smith didn't know where he was and I got the impression this wasn't at all a rare event.

'Anyway, one or two of us went to stretch our legs and there was Stanley in a bookshop signing books.'

Despite this remoteness, plenty of stories exist of Matthews's special brand of thoughtfulness.

One of these is told by Don Ratcliffe who was in the Stoke City side to which Matthews returned in 1961. 'I kept asking Stan if I could have some of his handmade boots,' Ratcliffe says. 'He wouldn't give me them. "No, you'll hurt yourself," he said. They were very soft, you see, just like skin. Very light.

'Anyhow, when I signed for Middlesbrough and was leaving Stoke he gave me two pairs – two, brand-new pairs. I was really chuffed with them but when I took them to Boro somebody pinched them, one of the players.'

Even if Matthews could be tetchy at times, Ratcliffe says the mood soon passed. 'I remember playing the ball to Stan and he came running up to me, "Don't you ever pass a ball like that to me again," he said. "Just remember I've got three gorillas trying to kill me. If you're going to give me the ball just smack it straight to me, very hard."

'Anyhow, soon afterwards I got this ball and I was ten yards away from him and I thought, "Yeah, I'll show you for telling me off." So I smacked it really hard, but mis-hit it and it was going about four-foot high into the crowd. And he just put his foot up and killed it dead.

'I couldn't believe it. He got it on the end of his toe. "That's better," he said and put his arm up to say thanks.'

Howard Riley of Leicester has a curiously touching Matthews anecdote. 'It was only towards the end of his career that I played against him,' Riley says, 'and when he turned up to play in a testimonial at Filbert Street he said to me, "All right, Howard?"

'He played against so many other players more than he did against me that I hadn't really expected him to remember who I was. I considered it a compliment.'

Colin Collindridge testifies to Matthews's 'gentleman's way of doing things'. The occasion was an FA Cup tie in 1945–46 – the only season when ties were played over two legs. Collindridge scored three times in the second leg but Sheffield United still lost 4–3 on aggregate to a Matthews-inspired Stoke City.

'As I was running off the pitch this fella came up to me,' Collindridge says. 'I looked round and it was Stanley Matthews, who was the best right-winger for years. He shook my hand and said, "I know you've lost, Colin, but thanks for a great match." And that was it; off he went.

'Now I thank Matthews for this. I wasn't in his class as a footballer but he still had the time to congratulate me.'

Matthews's capacity for being courteous brought a rather different reaction from Dave 'Crunch' Whelan after a match between Blackpool, Matthews's club from 1947–61, and visitors Blackburn in the 1950s.

Whelan, Blackburn's young right-back, says he clogged Matthews in the match itself – 'I cleaned him out, got the ball and took a bit of him with it' – then sought him out afterwards for his autograph. 'I mean he was a legend, still playing in his forties.'

But had Matthews been able to read Whelan's mind he might not have been quite so charitable in obliging his impudent assailant.

Whelan recounts his conversation with Matthews in the doorway of the Blackpool dressing room:

Matthews: 'You're Dave Whelan, aren't you?'

Whelan: 'Yes, I'm Dave Whelan. Can I have your autograph, please?'

Matthews: 'You kicked me out there and you kicked me quite deliberately, didn't you?'

Whelan: 'Yes, sir.'

Matthews: 'But that's against the rules.'

Whelan: 'I know but it's the only way I could stop you.'

Matthews: 'You won't do it again, will you?'

Whelan: 'Oh, no.'

Matthews: 'Give me your book.'

'And he signed it, "Best wishes, Stan Matthews",' Whelan says. 'And next time, I thought, you're going to get clogged. He was a great player.'

Though Matthews achieved international cult status – songwriters and poets lauded him, a novel *They Kidnapped Stanley Matthews* sold well and Ghana's Prime Minister crowned him 'Soccerthone' the King of Soccer – he did have a contender, selected by those I interviewed, for the starriest of the stars.

Tom Finney was born in 1922, seven years after Matthews, and had a much shorter Football League career with his only club, Preston North End. It began in 1946, after a delayed start because of the war, and ended in 1960. But his ability and personality were such that comparing him to Matthews became something of a national pastime.

Certainly, Finney gave a more potent portrayal of the star who slummed it with the rest of the cast. He quietly pursued his second profession as a plumber throughout his playing career, while Matthews was far less accepting of his lot as a brother in downtrodden arms with those who watched him play.

The principals themselves could not always avoid being drawn into the Matthews/Finney debate. Finney would relate how he was often quizzed on it by clients while out on a plumbing job. 'On one occasion,' he said, 'I remember defending Stanley Matthews's corner while I changed the ballcock on a WC.'

The media and even academics found it an irresistible talking point. In 1946, the widely read *Picture Post* scrutinised the two, deciding that Finney was 'less spectacular [than Matthews], less of an individual, less of a one-man circus. Perhaps his greatest asset is that highly developed feeling for collective play that some critics miss in Matthews.'

Much more recently the cultural historian Joyce Woolridge referred to Matthews's quirkiness and extreme self-discipline, which, she reckoned, gave him an ascetic gloss, while Finney's image was more that of an 'ordinary bloke' with an exceptional talent.

Leivers, who played against both men, comes down firmly on Finney's side. 'He was something out of the ordinary,' he says. 'Everyone looked at Stan Matthews and said what a wonderful player he was, which is true, but from the players' point of view the better player was Tom.

'Tom was so much more versatile – equally effective playing in any of the forward positions. And he was a lovely bloke, too.'

Frank O'Farrell enjoyed the privilege, as he puts it, of appearing with Finney for Preston. 'He never made headlines in any detrimental way to the game,' O'Farrell says. 'He trained and after training he'd go off with his workbag to do his plumbing. The odd cistern might be leaking or something.'

On the field, O'Farrell adds, 'there wasn't anything you could find fault with. He had the perfect temperament. He got kicked by full-backs at a time when wingers didn't always get the protection they get now, but he never used bad language or swore. He just showed what a good player he was.

'He played on both wings and could score goals as well as make goals for other people. When I joined Preston he was playing at centre-forward – and he was devastating.'

If he did do harm to opponents, it was of the psychological variety. O'Farrell recalls a match when Preston won handsomely at Tottenham with Finney scoring a hat-trick: 'Harry Clarke was the Spurs centre-half that day and I met Harry some years later. "You remember the game when you beat us down here," he said. "That finished my career." Finney played against him and destroyed him. Playing at centre-forward, Tom could go both ways and Harry just couldn't cope.'

Finney was aware of the psychological damage he could cause as he demonstrated when he played against Dave Whelan, a meeting that might have been billed as the merciful against the merciless.

The occasion was a pre-season practice match when Whelan was coming back from an injury.

'I'd played a couple of practice matches and I was getting by,' Whelan says, 'and then who should I be up against when Blackburn played Preston but the great Tom Finney. He never took me on, though; he never brought the ball to me. He'd pass it, which wasn't his normal game.

'So, when I was going off at half-time, I said, "Tom, you've not taken me on at all." And he said, "No, I'm not going to either. This is one of your first matches back. I want you to feel confident."

'A great gentleman. He did it the whole game. He stayed away from me, used the ball. Never went round me at all. Very professional. A great man.'

Of course, given Whelan's reputation for clogging, Finney may have been staying out of harm's way rather than being kind. Whelan may have reached this conclusion, too. But this was Finney, and even an opponent perfectly capable of harsh thoughts was inclined to think Preston's star man was treading the path of righteousness.

While Matthews went on playing until he was fifty, and said he could have gone on longer, Finney retired in 1960, aged thirty-eight, after falling out with his manager. If he had possessed Matthews's cussed streak – Matthews made a habit of falling out with managers – Finney would almost certainly have kept going for two or three more seasons.

Gordon Milne says it was pretty obvious at the time that Finney stopped when he did because of the manager, Cliff Britton. 'Britton was a pretty dour sort of bloke,' Milne says. 'I think he knocked two years off Tom Finney's career.'

Later Finney confirmed this, discarding his normal reticence in a ghosted autobiography. He described Britton as power-mad and ridiculously strict and unsympathetic. He said it wasn't long before he regretted his decision to retire and could have been talked into playing again. But his wife, the strong-minded Elsie, decreed otherwise.

It is hard to imagine she would have delivered such a ruling fifty years later.

Picture a 21st-century Elsie. She would have been on the phone to Tom's agent demanding he get her man a lucrative transfer because his manager was being nasty to him. He could return to plumbing later on, if he really wanted to.

Not everyone has taken the Matthews/Finney debate as seriously as they should. Recently this appeared on a football website: 'Personally I always rated Albert Finney and Bernard Matthews.'

Basing the selection on the answers given by my interviewees, a Stellar Paupers XI made up of players who appeared in the First Division between the end of the war in 1945 and the abolition of the maximum wage in 1961 would have looked something like this (traditional line-up: goalkeeper, two full-backs, three half-backs and five forwards):

Goalkeeper
Gordon Banks (Chesterfield, Leicester City, Stoke City)

Full-backs
Bill Leivers (Chesterfield, Manchester City, Doncaster Rovers); Walley Barnes (Arsenal)

Half-backs

Danny Blanchflower (Barnsley, Aston Villa, Tottenham Hotspur); John Charles (Leeds United, Juventus, Roma, Cardiff City); Duncan Edwards (Manchester United)

Forwards

Stanley Matthews (Stoke City, Blackpool); Jimmy Greaves (Chelsea, AC Milan, Tottenham Hotspur, West Ham United); Brian Clough (Middlesbrough, Sunderland); Jimmy Hagan (Derby County, Sheffield United); Tom Finney (Preston North End).

GOALKEEPER: GORDON BANKS

As a fellow Leicester player for a number of years, Howard Riley knew Banks well. 'He didn't have much of a reputation when he arrived at Filbert Street from Chesterfield in 1959,' Riley says, 'but once he started playing we all knew he was something special.

'The best game I ever saw him play was when we beat Liverpool 1–0 in the semi-finals of the FA Cup in 1963. After we took the lead in the first half, Liverpool put us under a lot of pressure, which we survived mainly thanks to Gordon.

'He was consistently excellent but I was talking to him the other week and he said, "They still call me One Save Banks because of that save against Pelé in the 1970 World Cup. It's the only one they remember." They should have seen him against Liverpool that day. He was absolutely tremendous.'

Sheffield-born Banks played his first Football League match for Chesterfield of the Third Division in 1958 after an early life that offered few clues to his eventual destination as one of the world's most renowned keepers. He left school aged fifteen and his first job was bagging coal for a local coal merchant. His first match in goal for Rawmarsh Welfare in the Yorkshire League ended in a 12–2 defeat and he was dropped soon afterwards.

Without any formal coaching, Banks persevered to the point where, eighteen months after leaving school, Chesterfield offered him a £3-a-week part-time contract. Once he broke into the Derbyshire club's first team his progress accelerated.

He played only twenty-three games for Chesterfield before Matt Gillies, manager of First Division Leicester City, spotted potential in him that not even Banks himself was sure he possessed. Banks was possibly more impressed by his increased wages, upped to £15 a week, than he was by his move.

Gillies was right, though. By the time Banks celebrated his twenty-second birthday on 30 December 1959, he was Leicester's first-choice number one. In 1963, he quickly established himself as 'Banks of England' and in 1966 he was the keeper of the nation's dreams when England won the World Cup.

At the 1970 World Cup in Mexico, Banks crucially missed England's defeat by West Germany in the quarter-finals, but still placed an indelible stamp on the tournament with the Pelé save. Pelé's close-range, downward header, delivered with a force that would have served him well in a pub brawl, seemed to have been perfectly executed with precision as well as power.

The ball bounced just short of the goal line and wide to Banks's right. It was pretty remarkable that Banks managed to reach the ball, how he then directed it straight upwards and over the bar is hard to comprehend, even when watched in slow motion.

'He was the best goalkeeper I played with or against,' Riley says. 'His positioning was uncanny. A lot of goalkeepers dive around and make spectacular saves but he'd anticipate and didn't have to do that. He would make his brilliant saves, flick the ball over the crossbar or whatever, but he just seemed to know in advance where the ball was coming.'

In common with many of England's 1966 World Cup team, Banks sold his winner's medal in 2001. It fetched £125,000. He did it, he says, to help his three children buy their first houses.

FULL-BACKS: BILL LEIVERS, WALLEY BARNES

'There was a lad who played for Manchester City called Bill Leivers,' Peter McParland says. 'He was a big, strong, no-nonsense sort of player. I liked the way he applied himself.'

McParland nominations for the full-back positions both make the Stellar Paupers XI. He is particularly well qualified to do so having been a winger admired for his swift, direct running. He gives the left-back spot to Walley Barnes.

Generally McParland subscribes to the view that full-backs were brick outhouses who doubled as footballers but in Leivers and Barnes he recognised defenders who were a cut above.

Leivers himself says that he was a reluctant right-back. 'When I was at Chesterfield, playing at centre-half, I told them if they moved me to full-back I'd walk out of the club and not come back.

'Then I went to Manchester City and ended up playing at right-back for ten years. I hated it.'

At City he started playing at centre-half in the reserves and says, 'I honestly believed I was as good as any other centre-half in the country, which is why I wanted to stay there. But then Jimmy Meadows was badly injured in the 1955 Cup final against Newcastle and they put me in the first team at right-back.'

Despite Leivers's preference for playing centre-half, his competence as a right-back does not have only McParland's word for it. After the 1956 Cup final, in which Manchester City beat Birmingham 3–1, the City veterans who attended the game voted Leivers the best player on the pitch. This was despite his needing pain-killing injections in his right ankle, which he badly twisted two weeks earlier.

The press also approved of Leivers's performance with notices that attested to the fact that he was more than just a forceful defender.

Roy Peskett of the *Daily Mail* was not an easy man to please. He made a name for himself as Matthews's sternest critic, regularly accusing him of hindering teams with his selfish play. Peskett singled out Leivers for his Cup final performance, which he said was notable for 'accurate and intelligent passing'.

Frank Coles in the *Daily Telegraph* said Leivers was the sheet anchor of the Manchester City defence. Not only was he strong in the air but also he used the ball to advantage when clearing it.

'I still didn't like playing at right-back,' Leivers says. 'They used to grumble at you if you went over the halfway line.'

Like Leivers, Walley Barnes was a player who arrived in professional football down one of those unbeaten paths that now makes the game of that era seem unbelievably quaint. A Portsmouth scout, on a cycling trip before the war, spotted some lads playing in a field. As he watched he became increasingly impressed by one player in particular.

This led to Barnes's recruitment as a wartime player for Portsmouth – he was nineteen when war broke out in 1939 – and later for

Southampton, before he joined Arsenal in 1943. As an Arsenal fixture for more than ten years, he played in nearly every position for the club, including goalkeeper in a wartime game. Finally installed as left-back he developed into a player for club and country, Wales, who defied the popular notion that no intelligent player ever ended up as a full-back.

'Walley was coming up to veteran age when I first played against him,' McParland says, 'and I was told by someone who'd watched him the previous Saturday that it would be my birthday playing against him. But I went out and didn't get a kick.

'He was a great reader of the game and had done his homework on me. He must have said to himself, "If this fella gets the ball, he's going to take me." So he put himself in positions to cut out the service to me. I had a great admiration for this.'

As a member of Arsenal's 'Iron Curtain' defence, Barnes received much of the credit for keeping out the dangerous Liverpool attack in the 1950 FA Cup final. Arsenal, beaten in their two League matches by Liverpool, won 2–0.

HALF-BACKS: DANNY BLANCHFLOWER, JOHN CHARLES, DUNCAN EDWARDS

'There we are, typical Blanchflower.' This, says Cliff Jones, is how Bill Nicholson, the Tottenham Hotspur manager, reacted to Danny Blanchflower's refusal to appear on the massively popular TV show *This Is Your Life* in 1961. The episode became an instant *cause célèbre* – and it is not hard to imagine the sound of splintering furniture in the Spurs PR office if such a thing happened today.

The Northern Irishman, with no concept of positive image promotion, snubbed the show's presenter, Eamonn Andrews, live on air.

'We were all up there at Shepherd's Bush studios,' Jones says. 'People had come from everywhere – Canada, Ireland, of course … Then on came the announcer and said, "Well, I'm sorry, for the first time in the history of *This Is Your Life* our subject has refused to appear." Bill was not impressed.

'But that was it. Danny was a special character, great intelligence and a brilliant player, too. We all sparked off him.'

The *This Is Your Life* incident came towards the end of Blanchflower's defining season as captain of a great Spurs side – and, as Jones suggests, their greatness was as much a tribute to Blanchflower as anyone. Not only was he an original thinker but he regarded professional football as good an arena as any in which to apply innovative ideas.

Spurs launched their glory years with a record run of eleven First Division victories at the start of the 1960–61 season, laying the foundation for winning the title by eight points. They then went on to win the FA Cup, completing a Double not achieved since 1897.

What most impressed Jones about Blanchflower was the way 'he would make changes out on the field during a game. These days the captain wears the armband and that's it. He'll make no changes.

'But Danny, he would do it. He might switch a player – move somebody forward or bring somebody back.'

Jones says also that Blanchflower had his own oblique way of telling you things. He remembers him asking during a match, 'Cliff, do you know the ball is round?' When Jones looked puzzled, Blanchflower said, 'The ball is round – try passing the bloody thing now and again, son.'

After retiring as a player, Blanchflower became a perceptive commentator on football and life in general. Sadly he died as a result of Alzheimer's disease in 1993 aged sixty-seven. His illness and early death deprived us of what would surely have been many a sardonic reflection on the amount he earned playing football and the inflated sums on offer today.

For his intelligence, playing ability and complete lack of pretension, Blanchflower not only makes the Stellar Paupers XI as right-half, but also as captain.

Alongside Blanchflower at centre-half is John Charles, a rather different character but a character none the less. Had he chosen to be an actor, the Welshman had the looks, physique and personality to take the sort of parts Charlton Heston made famous. As a footballer he had world-class ability as a defender and attacker. He also gained a reputation for maintaining the highest levels of sportsmanship.

'He was extraordinary,' Giampiero Boniperti, a Juventus teammate, said of him, 'I would say from another world because of his human qualities.'

Roy Wood, who saw Charles at close quarters when the two played together for Leeds, is a huge admirer, but his iconoclastic tendencies permit him a few contrary insights into the sainted one.

'He was phenomenal really,' Wood says, 'but he wasn't a big fan of training. He'd jog; he didn't do sprints or anything like that. The only reason he liked playing in practice matches was so he could kick everybody, even though on the park he was a gentleman.

'But as a player, well, the height he could jump and his general athleticism were unbelievable. He was so aware, too. When he was playing at centre-half he just seemed to know where I was. He would regularly head the ball back to me from just outside the six-yard box.'

His status, Wood says, meant Charles was able to take liberties at Leeds that no other player would have got away with unpunished – a fact he illustrates with a story: 'We were playing at Tottenham and stayed at a hotel by King's Cross Station. We had to go for a morning walk and these three directors were walking side by side ahead of us along this wide footpath.

'Anyway, a chap with an Alsatian was coming up and as this Alsatian passed you could see one of the directors move in, nervously. John noticed this, too, and said, "Watch this, watch this." He crept up on the director and went, "Grr-GRRRRRR." Poor bugger jumped up in the bloody air.

'If anyone else had done it they wouldn't have played, but being John Charles he'd get away with anything.'

As an anecdote this says as much about the hierarchical state of professional football in the 1940s and '50s – much nearer the nineteenth century than the twenty-first – as any other in this book.

Duncan Edwards completes the half-back trio, a player whose character was mostly expressed in the way he played the game, rather than in standing up TV programmes or scaring the wits out of club directors.

Cliff Jones remembers Edwards from the British Army team. 'They were a terrific side,' he says. 'I was in the team with Duncan Edwards, the great Duncan Edwards. What a player he was going to be. The best there's ever been.'

In his tributes to Edwards, Bobby Charlton, Edwards's Manchester United teammate, has said, 'If you asked such players as Stanley Matthews and Tom Finney about Duncan their answers were always the same: they had seen nothing like him.'

Walter Winterbottom, the manager who made Edwards England's youngest international for more than seventy years when he picked him in 1955 aged 18 years 183 days, was banking on Edwards: 'It was in the character and spirit of Duncan Edwards that I saw the true revival of British football.'

Winterbottom's revival hopes ended with the Munich air crash in February 1958, fifteen days after which Edwards died from kidney damage. Seven of Edwards's Manchester United teammates had died in the crash itself.

Edwards bestrode the football field, a 6 ft 3 in. athlete with strength and stamina, who dribbled with the deftness of a much smaller man, hit long, precise passes and shot with meaning with either foot.

Interestingly, though most of my interviewees mentioned Edwards among their favourite players, there were few anecdotes, just expressions of quite how formidable he was.

Jackie Sewell is the only one of my interviewees who recalls an episode involving Edwards. It took place during the 1957 Charity Shield match at Old Trafford between Manchester United and Aston Villa – won 4–0 by United – and disposes of the idea that Edwards was without a single rough edge.

Not only did United handsomely avenge their 2–1 Cup final defeat at Wembley earlier in the year, in which Ray Wood was injured, Edwards exacted a little retribution of his own. Having felled Sewell with a clonking tackle, he told his stricken opponent, 'That one's for Wembley.'

FORWARDS: STANLEY MATTHEWS, JIMMY GREAVES, BRIAN CLOUGH, JIMMY HAGAN, TOM FINNEY

Matthews and Finney are chosen on the wings having been nominated, as already stated, by nearly every member of the selection committee.

Jimmy Greaves is included at inside-right as another popular choice. Brian Clough and Jimmy Hagan each owe their inclusion, at centre-forward and inside-right, to the pressing support of a particular individual.

Jimmy Greaves, I would hazard, is the footballer who most closely resembles our image of how we would want our brilliant player who made measly money to be: a chirpy chappy who revelled in going to matches on public transport with the fans, who ungrudgingly accepted being unable to buy his own house even after his transfer to Tottenham for £99,999 – and who appeared far less impressed than just about everybody else by his dazzlingly intuitive skills as a goalscorer.

He was still only nineteen and playing for his first club, Chelsea, when he dazzled Gordon Milne in a match at Preston in December 1959.

Milne remembers it well. The Preston manager, Cliff Britton, Finney's nemesis, who liked to address his players by their surnames, took him aside before kick-off: 'Milne, your job today is to be within one foot of Jimmy Greaves. Where he goes, you go. Don't worry about anything else. If he drops off, you drop off; if he goes wide, you go wide. He's clever but generally he's in or around the box. Stay close to him.'

'As you get more experienced,' Milne says, 'you realise to do this is not that easy. Especially if you've got a bit of imagination yourself you tend to wander off.'

The result: Preston North End: 4; Chelsea: 5, with all the visitors' goals scored by Greaves. 'I don't think I was ever further from him than I am from you now [a couple of feet]. But remember Jimmy with his side-footers? He'd come across you in the six-yard box, just get a touch and it was in.

'None of his goals were scored from outside the box, none of the goals was a rocket. One was a little glancing header. He was just in front of me and glanced it in.

'I can remember the dressing room afterwards and I'm looking round and I can see Tom Finney there and Tommy Thompson – Tommy scored three that day ... Christ! I can't remember what Cliff Britton said to me, I don't think he needed to say anything.

'I played against Greavsie later in life. I played with him for England. He was just something else. He was great, quite compassionate. He laughed and joked about it afterwards. That was what Jimmy was like, "They were all flukes..."'

Greaves, seventeen years old when he first played for Chelsea, scored 124 First Division goals for the club in just four seasons before being sold to AC Milan in 1961. It was a flow that never really slackened with his record of being top scorer in the First Division in six seasons and his six hat-tricks for England still unsurpassed.

But the match he would have most liked to score a goal in, the 1966 World Cup final, he didn't. He wasn't picked having been injured earlier in the tournament.

Greaves's missing out on the big one at Wembley has tended to overshadow his phenomenal record as a goalscorer, a record that makes him a key selection for the Stellar Paupers XI.

It was only in later life that Greaves's misfortune of playing in the era when even players of his towering ability were skint was most painfully felt. His battle with alcoholism followed by serious illness in old age led to medical bills that he and his family struggled to meet.

The most pathetic consequence of this was that, in 2014, Greaves, like Banks, sold his World Cup winner's medal, only five years after he received it. The sale, which realised £44,000, was seen by some as an ungrateful response to the efforts of campaigners who fought for him to be given it despite his missing the final.

Greaves's action left only three of England's World Cup winners – the Charlton brothers, Bobby and Jack, and Roger Hunt – still in possession of their medals.

Brian Clough wins selection as centre-forward in the Stellar Paupers XI as a result of the enthusiastic backing of Stan Anderson, who overlapped with Clough at Sunderland for three years. Denis Law and Nat Lofthouse are unlucky to miss out.

Clough is sometimes underestimated as a player because so much emphasis is placed on his many managerial successes. But as a goalscorer he was up there with the best, even bearing in mind that only one of his League goals was scored in the First Division.

He scored 197 League goals in 213 appearances for Middlesbrough and fifty-four in sixty-one for Sunderland. This is a better strike rate than Greaves's but maintained over a shorter period when Clough was in his prime.

'People either liked or disliked Brian Clough and I admit that when he first came along I thought what a pain in the arse he was,' Anderson says. 'And when he said things like, "If you get it and knock it in the box, I'll stick it in the net for you," you'd think, "Is he bloody kidding or what?"

'But then you got to know the bloke and that's what he did. A number of times playing alongside Brian I used to think, "What the hell's he going there for?"'

Anderson cites an occasion during a Sunderland match when he pushed a pass down the line for Harry Hooper to run after. 'Harry then hit this ball that struck the full-back, came out, hit somebody else, and there was Brian standing three yards out and side-footed it into the net. I was thinking, "How the hell did you manage to be in the right place for that one?"

'It's a knack, I suppose, being in the right place at the right time even though it looks as though it's the wrong place. Somehow the ball seemed to fall to him and he knocked it in.'

Anderson was injured and sitting in the stand, when on Boxing Day 1962, Clough, who at the time 'was scoring goals for fun', received the injury that effectively ended his career. The match was against Bury at Roker Park.

'The match wouldn't have been played if it was today,' Anderson says. 'There was ice all over the pitch.

'Chris Harker, the Bury goalkeeper, came out and went down for the ball. No problem at all. But because Cloughie couldn't stop he went over the top of Harker and tore all his knee ligaments. That was the end of his career and cost us promotion. We'd have walked promotion if Cloughie had played the rest of that season.' They would miss out on goal average to Chelsea.

Surgeons operated on Clough's knee soon afterwards to repair the torn medial and cruciate ligaments – and it is hard to argue with the likely accuracy of thoughts attributed to Clough by David Peace in his novel *The Damned United*:

But no one tells you anything, anything you don't already know –
That this is bloody bad. This is very fucking bad –
The worst day of your life.

Clough did play again but only a handful of games before retiring as a player aged twenty-nine. 'But football is a life of disappointments really,' Anderson says.

Jimmy Hagan, born in 1918, would be better known had his best years not coincided with the Second World War and had he not been quite so obdurate. He played in sixteen wartime internationals – classified as unofficial and so barely recorded – giving performances that stood comparison with teammates Matthews and Finney.

But while he glittered brilliantly on the outside as a two-footed inside-forward, his propensity for awkwardness meant officialdom were leery of him. He played in only one full international for England, a pitiful return for one so talented.

On a weekly wage of seven pounds, Hagan made his debut for Sheffield United in 1938 and for the next twenty years built a cult following at Bramall Lane. 'Jimmy Hagan was the very heart of Sheffield United,' his biographer, Roger Barnard, wrote, 'the conductor, the orchestra leader and virtuoso soloist combined.'

And yet, straight after the war, Hagan almost walked away from a game that paid him so little for the embellishment he gave it. He joined a local architects to train as a surveyor and for a few years gave the club only part-time service. In the end, though, he missed the game too much to be put off by its frugal rewards.

'What made Jimmy Hagan so outstanding was that he had a brain, for a start. And he could be in a room no bigger than this one with three other people,' Colin Collindridge says, seated in his small front room, 'and, with the ball at his feet, he'd dribble round the lot of them.'

Collindridge is the selector who makes the incontrovertible case for picking Hagan, although he admits that there was a drawback to playing alongside him: 'Opponents wouldn't be able to get the ball off him and I'd stand watching him in amazement and then wouldn't be ready when he passed the ball to me.'

But Collindridge and Hagan did perfect one double act: 'After the war Jimmy and I had a routine going that appealed to Jimmy because it meant using his brain.

'A German bomb had landed on the Bramall Lane pitch and where the crater had been filled in the surface was always a bit soft. I'd manoeuvre my full-back so he was standing on this bit of ground and when he was properly bogged down Jimmy would slip the ball past him for me to run on to.'

Had there been a substitutes bench there would have been any number of candidates: Lofthouse and Law, of course, Bobby Moore, Bobby Charlton, Billy Wright and Johnny Haynes... and it has been particularly hard to resist Cliff Jones's nomination of Dave Mackay to play as one of the half-backs.

'I would say that of all the players the most influential to that Tottenham side was Dave Mackay,' Jones says. 'He was a winner, totally committed. When Bill Nicholson signed him from Hearts in 1959 we were a very good side, but you could say that we possibly lacked that little bit of commitment, that spirit that Dave brought with him.

'Everyone's seen that photograph of Dave holding Billy Bremner by the neck, but I say to people about Mackay: there was no one harder, tougher – or more skilful. You must never, ever forget the skilful side of Dave Mackay.'

When I interviewed Mackay for a newspaper in 2004, shortly before his seventieth birthday, his comments on most things were trenchant, but he was quietly accepting of his fate as a stellar pauper.

He was surprised when he arrived at Tottenham that the players used to drink in a pub, the Bell and Hare, just around the corner from White Hart Lane, a practice that would have been out of the question at Hearts. At Spurs what was out of the question was the players going to the West End for a drink. 'Too expensive,' he said.

CHAPTER ELEVEN

KEEP IT ON THE ISLAND

In which Puskás's smile tells Billy Wright his England team are in trouble – Northern Ireland's goalie chases his own teammate during a World Cup match – Stan Anderson's trip to Chile ends in farce – Spurs give a performance that 'no team there's ever been or ever will be' could have lived with.

A small group of young players from Watford Football Club, shepherded by player-coach Johnny Paton, arrive at the Empire Stadium, Wembley, in the early afternoon of Wednesday 25 November 1953.

They are in good time for the 2.15 p.m. kick-off of the match between England and Hungary, a game that Paton is particularly keen his charges should see. 'Hungary are an exciting team,' he tells them, 'and you're going to learn something about the game from them today.'

Others are less convinced. Charles Buchan, a former England player and one of the most respected commentators on the game, has written in the build-up to the match, 'The clever ball-control and close passing of the Hungarians do not alarm me in any way.'

Buchan's smugness reflects the insularity that pervaded English football at this time, a mulish refusal to admire Hungary in spite of the evidence: unbeaten in twenty-four games, unofficially ranked number one in the world and holders of the Olympic title. They are damned by being foreign.

Paton is not so blinkered. Having seen more of the world than most footballers during his service in the RAF, which included playing a great deal of football overseas, he is well aware that antiquated coaching methods and tactical dogma among English clubs are a serious worry for the prospects of the domestic game.

With his professional playing career coming to an end, he has acted on this concern by enrolling on the Football Association's first coaching course at Lilleshall, one of the few initiatives that points towards a more enlightened future.

On this November afternoon Paton takes his unease with him to Wembley. He has no faith in the argument that because England have never lost at home against a team from outside the British Isles that Hungary are heading for defeat.

It is impossible to be sure but almost certainly Paton is at odds with most of the crowd of 100,000. He can tell from the banter that the majority, informed only by views such as Buchan's, are expecting to witness confirmation of English football's superiority.

Only some of them have taken much notice of reports that Hungary will parade a new style of football. Those who have and are unimpressed are in good company. Billy Wright, the England captain, says afterwards, 'We completely underestimated the advances Hungary had made.'

He also confesses he ridiculed Hungary after the two teams first came onto the Wembley pitch. He told teammate Stan Mortensen, 'We should be all right here, Stan,' having observed the visitors wearing what looked more like shoes than boots. 'They haven't even got the proper kit.'

Outside the ground, people are paying the ticket touts good money to see Hungary put in their place: a tenner for the £2 10s top-priced tickets and more than £1 for the cheapest ones, sold originally for 3s. 6d.

Paton and his group have seats at one end, behind a goal. They watch the Hungary team warm up before kick-off, not by dashing about but by juggling the ball. Paton pays special attention to Ferenc Puskás. He notices that Hungary's captain and emblematic star is all one-footed, but reckons that if he wanted to Puskás could keep the ball up all day with his foot, head, knee and shoulder. Around him Paton senses the spectators' awe at what they are watching – and the match hasn't even started.

Puskás continues to demonstrate his trickery until Wright, his fellow captain, joins him in the centre circle to toss the coin. It is the first time the two men have met. Puskás, having been intricately working the ball with his left foot, signs off by nonchalantly transferring it to his thigh and letting it run down his shin onto the centre spot.

Wright says afterwards that when Puskás then gave him a charming, you've-been-warned smile, he realised his earlier ridicule had been misjudged.

It is arguable that English football has never properly recovered from the stagnation that led to the 6–3 drubbing by Hungary in 1953 – and two defeats that followed in 1954: 7–1 to Hungary in a return friendly in Budapest and a 4–2 loss to Uruguay that eliminated England from the World Cup in Switzerland.

The 1966 World Cup triumph, greeted at the time as a new dawn, has become an ironic symbol of our continuing deficiencies. The

English game is still admired for its commitment and endeavour, but neither of these dated virtues has done us much good in international tournaments, where technically superior sides have prospered.

For years the clubs had done little to make the job of a professional footballer significantly more rewarding than clipping tickets on a bus. At the same time they appeared bewitched by the idea that football was – and always would be – as much a game of brawn as refinement, even in the matter of committing fouls: while English footballers openly clogged, the rest did nasty little things on the quiet.

Keep the ball on the island, went the unofficial motto, let the foreigners fiddle, fake and fudge if they wished.

England refused an invitation from Uruguay, the hosts, to take part in the first World Cup in 1930 and remained snootily resistant to doing so in 1934 and '38 when the finals were held much closer to home, in Italy and France.

Their absence from the inaugural championship was particularly damaging. It meant they did not witness the performances of the outstanding Uruguay team, who played a style of football recognisable as the genetic forerunner of the modern game.

Bernard Joy, like Buchan a former England international turned journalist but with a more discerning eye, was one of the first English commentators who did recognise this. After seeing Uruguay play he wrote, 'By marrying short passing to intelligent positional play, the Uruguayans made the ball do all the work, and so kept their opponents on the run.'

It was hardly surprising then that when England did finally agree to play in the first post-war World Cup in 1950, and qualified for the finals in Brazil, their set-up and performances proved woefully inadequate.

As was the Football Association's way, it was not the manager, Walter Winterbottom, but the FA's one representative on the trip, Arthur Drewry, a Grimsby fish merchant, who chose the England teams who played in the three group matches in Brazil. A fortunate win over Chile and 1–0 defeats by the United States (the derided outsiders of the group) and Spain meant England were out of the competition.

England's elimination was bad enough. Worse still, though, was that no one seemed particularly interested in the important lessons that were to be gleaned from that 1950 competition, which saw Uruguay crowned champions for the second time.

The FA flew everybody straight back home after England's third defeat. And with no television and only limited press coverage, the derelict state of English football remained a ridiculously kept secret from domestic coaches and the general public.

Of the very few who did reflect on what had gone wrong and how things might be put right, the defender Alf Ramsey was the most significant. He would be appointed England manager twelve years later and four years after that would win the World Cup.

One or two also noticed other things beyond the South American style of play. The ever-astute Stanley Matthews picked up on the lightweight boots worn by the Brazilians and took a pair to the Co-operative Wholesale Society in Manchester who agreed to copy them.

And Matthews and others could not fail to register that not all overseas sportsmen were as skint as English footballers. On his way to Brazil, via Canada, Matthews had caused amazement among Canada's press corps when he revealed how little he earned compared to ice hockey players of Matthews's equivalent stature.

For the World Cup finals in Brazil, while the FA fought hard to peg the England players' match fees at £20, the host nation's players were on £200 a man in the group stages. More envy-inducing still, each Brazil player was on a promise of £10,000 to win the title.

England did qualify from their groups to reach the quarter-finals at the 1954 and 1962 World Cups, but both times went no further. In 1958, when the four home nations qualified for the finals and were kept apart in the groups, it was Northern Ireland and Wales who reached the quarter-finals, while England and Scotland were eliminated. As in 1954, the Scots finished bottom of their group.

The 1958 World Cup, particularly the finals in Sweden, was the first time the British public became properly engaged in the global game. Not only were the successes of Northern Ireland and Wales widely reported, so was the dazzling brilliance of Brazil, especially that of their seventeen-year-old forward Edson Arantes do Nascimento, aka Pelé.

Playing on European soil, the Brazilians, gaudy in dress and deed, transformed the idea that football need be a monochrome exercise in hoofing the ball about. The South Americans demonstrated technical talent, which included sleight of foot, that was still a novelty in Europe despite the efforts of Hungary. Their exuberance and deft execution were captured on newsreel and disseminated around the world.

Brazil hammered Sweden 5–2 in the final after conceding an early goal. The match's defining images were photos of Pelé, still not filled out into full-blown manhood, weeping uncontrollably on the shoulders of teammates. He was utterly overcome by his own success, which included two outstanding goals, and that of the team.

Of the four home teams who played in those 1958 finals, Northern Ireland, whose record of being the least populous country to reach the finals would survive until Trinidad and Tobago did it in 2006, were the most impressive.

Their success in reaching the last eight, against tough opposition all the way, owed much to their adapting better than the others to the way the game was being played beyond the British Isles. And this was mainly down to their captain, Danny Blanchflower, who, just as he had started doing at Tottenham, took over managing the side once the players were on the field.

McParland says that while the majority of Football League clubs deployed their players in the rigid formations that had been laid down in the 1920s – and which Hungary had deftly picked to pieces at Wembley five years earlier – Northern Ireland were trying new things.

'We had four or five players who could play in midfield,' McParland says, 'and Danny would set it all up, crowding the middle of the park when necessary, but also getting players forward at the right time.'

It is impossible to say whether English football would have prospered if it had followed Blanchflower's creed: that the game was not about battering and/or boring opponents to death but playing, as Hungary and the South Americans did, with style and a flourish and being tactically inventive.

It did not happen because English clubs failed to connect the Irishman's presence with the success of the teams in which he played and dominated with his personality. Or, if they did make the connection, they ignored it out of an inbred distrust of what they saw as too much swank and not enough graft.

After he retired as a player Blanchflower turned to being a manager, but soon despaired of setting English football on a new course. In frustration he switched to making a living as a shrewd media observer.

Blanchflower's role in helping to steer Northern Ireland to the quarter-finals of the World Cup in Sweden was at least the equal of what he achieved as the captain of Spurs.

Northern Ireland's heroics had started in the qualifying competition when they eliminated Italy, which was, quite simply, an extraordinary result.

The Italians had been world champions in 1934 and 1938 and had reached the finals of every World Cup they had entered. A draw against the Irish would have seen them through. The fact that the match was being played in Belfast was not expected to be nearly enough of an advantage for Blanchflower's team to survive.

What undermined Italy's effort was that the tie, instead of being wrapped up in ninety minutes on the afternoon of Wednesday 4 December 1957, mutated into a six-week saga. This was after the Belfast-bound match referee, István Zsolt of Hungary, became stranded in fog in London.

Although the match went ahead in Zsolt's absence, it was downgraded to a friendly when the Italians refused to give official recognition to a substitute ref. It ended 2–2, which would have been enough for Italy to go through.

The long delay would play right into Northern Ireland's hands, partly because it must have rattled Italy that the so-called friendly was such an ugly affair. Having to come back to Belfast could not have been an enticing prospect.

Not only did 'both teams kick lumps out of one another', as McParland puts it, in that first fixture, serious crowd trouble at the end incensed the visitors. One Italian newspaper described the Belfast troublemakers as 'barbarians of a primitive epoch' and the debate about what should happen next reached government level in both countries.

On top of this the extended pause before the rearranged fixture in late January ideally suited the artful Blanchflower.

He had marked the visitors' vulnerabilities in the friendly and insisted the Northern Ireland team gather three days before the rescheduled match. During this unusually long time to prepare, Blanchflower drummed into the players tactics that involved disregarding the formations that English club teams regarded as sacrosanct. They would ambush the Italians with swift breaks from midfield.

In this way Northern Ireland controlled the game, demonstrating that the virtues of the traditional British way could be successfully allied to new ideas. Italy even accepted that their 2–1 defeat was down to the Irish being the better team.

Blanchflower's leadership and McParland's goals – he scored five of the team's tally of six – were the foundations of Northern Ireland's feat of reaching the quarter-finals of the 1958 world finals. That they reached the knockout stage at all surpassed most expectations after they were drawn in a group with holders West Germany and Argentina, the 1957 South American champions, who flopped badly to finish in last place.

The one time Blanchflower lost control of his team was during an incident that was pure pantomime but went virtually unnoticed. If it had happened in a World Cup today, newspapers everywhere would have carried the story. McParland describes the shenanigans in Northern Ireland's ranks in their opening match, a 1–0 win over Czechoslovakia:

'Czechoslovakia bombed us for about ten, fifteen minutes, but it didn't help that our little left-half, Bertie Peacock of Celtic, got on to Harry Gregg, our goalkeeper, for not coming off his line to take a ball that had come across the goalmouth.

'Bertie was the next-door neighbour to Harry where he was born in Ireland, but this did not stop Harry from taking offence and running after Bertie.

'Meanwhile their outside-right's got the ball. I'd come across to stop him from getting a cross in, holding him out on the wing, but behind me Harry's still running after Bertie to give him a punch and Alfie McMichael, our left-back, is shouting, "Get back in the goal, Harry!" Luckily they did not score. If they had they might have destroyed our World Cup.'

For their five matches in those 1958 finals, which were crammed into twelve days in three different cities, the Northern Ireland players each received £250 – 'Subject to tax', McParland points out, with feeling.

The scale of what Alf Ramsey and his team achieved in 1966 should be judged bearing in mind that, even as late as the 1962 World Cup in Chile, England's national team was a relic from its 'keep it on the island' past.

The lessons of the 1953 Hungary defeat still had not been fully learnt. Walter Winterbottom, the England manager, complained that it remained impossible to modernise the team when most club managers were frightened of the risks involved in trying new things.

These risks included the fairly common one of offending fogeyish members of the club board, stern keepers of the rule that nothing good ever came from innovation. They were suspicious of everything from messing with how teams lined up to the very idea that players should earn more than their lowly pegged wage.

It was no better at national level. England selection had stayed in the hands of the butchers, bakers and candlestick makers who made up the membership of the Football Association. In 1962, Winterbottom experienced the same frustration he had twelve years earlier in Brazil when having to defer to a fish merchant over picking the team.

And being chosen to play for England was reward enough. The players should accept what money they were offered for the priceless honour of representing their country.

Stan Anderson, who was a member of England's World Cup squad in 1962, still sounds pained when he talks about this priceless honour, particularly the way the FA treated him throughout his disjointed international career.

His problems started in 1957 when, appearing in an under-23 international against Bulgaria in Sofia, he became the first player in an England shirt to be sent off.

Towards the end of the match, Anderson says, he went over to take a throw-in. As he did so, a Bulgarian player ran across him, spitting at him for good measure. 'So I just went bang and hit him. And, of course, he went down as though I'd killed him and the referee sent me off.'

Bill Nicholson, who was in charge of the team, confronted Anderson later: 'What the hell were you doing, Stan?'

Anderson said that no one had ever spat at him before and he wasn't going to let it pass without a response. 'I told Bill that if I went outside now and he did it again I'd thump him again.'

Nicholson was sympathetic but said the FA would want to know what happened. They would send him, Anderson, a letter.

In fact, the only thing Anderson received from the FA was an indefinite suspension. Nothing else. No letter ever arrived. 'They just made their decision and that was it. I never got the opportunity to go down to London to tell them what happened.

'I did whack him and he went down like a ton of bricks but nobody should spit at people. What aggrieved me at the time was that this fella was apparently well known as a thug who went round spitting at people.'

The suspension lasted until 1962, by which time Sunderland had been in the Second Division since 1958. At the end of March Anderson took a call from a friend who told him he had been picked to play for the full England team.

'Piss off, that's ridiculous,' Anderson said, although he knew he had been playing well. 'They're not going to pick me. I'm in the Second Division.'

'I'm telling you, Stan,' the friend said, 'you've been picked for England to play against Austria at Wembley.'

The friend was right and Anderson achieved his life's ambition to play at Wembley in what was a comfortable 3–1 win.

It would no doubt have dismayed Anderson to be told at this point that he would play only once more for England. This was ten days later against Scotland in Glasgow, a match that Anderson says was an education with more than 130,000 packed into Hampden Park.

Although he does not say as much, by the way he tells the story of the rest of his international career, he feels he was harshly treated. His resentment clearly resides with those inexplicably qualified officers who, in his estimation, ran the English game applying an unfathomable logic. These were the same men who, without a word, had cast him adrift for so long after his 1957 sending-off.

He starts his account of what happened in his second and last full international with the match almost over: 'Scotland were winning one-nil with a few minutes to go when the ball came across and Johnny Haynes, running in, met it with probably his best ever header. It hit the underside of the bar and dropped in – and no one will ever change my mind that it did drop in. But the ball span back out and the linesman didn't give it. Scotland then went down our end, scored a penalty and we got beat 2–0.'

Anderson then went to Chile for the 1962 World Cup but never played. And he remains convinced that if England had drawn at Hampden he would have kept his place in the side. 'I know I would,' he says.

Anderson tells the story of his World Cup experience with an anecdote that encapsulates the sort of logic that so frustrated him.

He sat out the three preliminary games – defeat by Hungary, victory over Argentina and a draw with Bulgaria – but then received a boost to his hopes of being picked for the quarter-final against Brazil.

Harold Shepherdson, the trainer, came to his room to tell him that Walter Winterbottom wanted him to attend the next day's training. 'And when I turned up,' Anderson says, 'there was Gerry Hitchens, Jimmy Greaves, Bryan Douglas and me – only four of us – and I thought I was in the side for the Brazil game.'

Shepherdson was on the halfway line with several balls around him. 'Come with me, Stan,' he said. 'I want you to serve balls to these three players.' And again Anderson thought he must be in the side. 'Good ball, Stan. Now send one to Bryan…'

'But I wasn't picked and I couldn't understand why they'd got me to feed them the balls when it should have been the player who was going to play. What was the point in me doing it?'

England lost 3–1 to Brazil, who went on to retain their world title, and Anderson was not called on again; his final service to his country having been what he clearly felt was an exercise in futility.

No one epitomised English football's 'keep it on the island' mentality quite like Alan Hardaker, the Football League's long-standing secretary.

Hardaker started working for the League in 1951, before taking over as full-time secretary in 1957. Previously he had been an ordinary player who, aged twenty-three, declined professional terms offered by Hull City in order to start his apprenticeship as a bureaucrat working as secretary to the Lord Mayor of Hull.

As Football League secretary, Hardaker displayed his unattractive brand of conservatism with his comment to a national newspaper that having to deal with 'wogs and dagos' was the reason he opposed English clubs entering international competitions.

Largely as a result of this attitude, Chelsea were persuaded not to enter the inaugural European Cup in 1955. The French sports newspaper *L'Équipe* had nominated the English champions, along with fifteen other European sides, to represent the cream of the Continent's clubs.

Polish team Gwardia Warszawa took Chelsea's place – to the satisfaction of Little Englanders and to the detriment of the English game's prospects of keeping up with foreign competition. Nor, on reflection, can the Chelsea club and players have been particularly happy to miss out on the financial benefit.

The resounding success of the first European Cup, won in style by Real Madrid, instantly instated the Spanish champions as the Continent's most glamorous club and ensured the competition's future.

Despite this Hardaker and his ilk still wanted nothing to do with it. But Manchester United, the new English champions, refused to be bullied into following Chelsea's example. They went ahead and entered the 1956–57 competition.

But it was not until ten years later that Celtic, directed by their impressive manager Jock Stein, became the first British club to reach a European Cup final – a feat they celebrated with a spectacular victory.

Like Blanchflower, Stein had the vision to stray beyond the traditional British way of playing. He worked on ideas such as zonal marking, before the name existed, but above all he stressed the importance of players expressing themselves outside the confines of any particular system.

Stein assembled a team of players who came from within 30 miles of the club's Glasgow ground. And after Celtic's exhilarating 2–1 win in Lisbon over the cynically efficient Italian side Inter Milan in the 1967 final, their manager said, 'We did it playing football – pure, beautiful, inventive football.'

A year later, a George Best-inspired Manchester United, directed by another exceptional Scottish manager, Matt Busby, succeeded Celtic as European Cup winners, thrashing the Continent's former masters Benfica 4–1 at Wembley.

If there were a British team who might have conquered Europe before Celtic, it was the Tottenham side operating under Blanchflower's enlightened on-field leadership.

Spurs qualified for the 1961–62 European Cup and their participation alerted an unsuspecting Cliff Jones to what riches, in every sense, international club competition had to offer. His account of Spurs' first two European matches, a preliminary round tie against Polish side Górnik Zabrze, is full of wide-eyed wonder at the world that Hardaker would have rather Jones did not glimpse.

Jones had played with distinction for Wales at the 1958 World Cup finals in Sweden, where visiting teams received limited support. But a home tie against foreign opposition in a club competition was of a completely different order. He describes the second leg against Górnik at White Hart Lane as the 'one match that stood out for me during my time at Spurs'.

The away leg, Tottenham's debut in Europe, was dramatic enough. Spurs came back from 4–0 down soon after the break to narrow the deficit to 4–2 with Jones's goal the first by a Tottenham player in Europe.

'We were in with a shout, but Bill Nicholson wasn't impressed with us, he wasn't pleased,' Jones says. 'The press, they weren't pleased with us either; they gave us quite a bit of stick. It was because of this, I think, that for the second leg we were really buzzing, we just couldn't wait to get out there.

'As we came out onto the White Hart Lane pitch with the Górnik side, the noise from the 62,000 crowd was just incredible. They were amazing; they lifted us.

'We were looking at the Górnik players and straightaway they were on the back foot. In Górnik the atmosphere hadn't been great. There was the ground, then there was the running track, and then there was something else – so the crowd was well away from the playing area. But at White Hart Lane the crowd was on top of them and you could see they were in trouble.

'Right from the off we just got at 'em. Bobby Smith had a shot, the goalkeeper tipped it over the bar and from then on the noise was just one complete roar.

'I was fortunate to get a hat-trick and I would say I have never experienced an atmosphere like it. The final score was 8–1, 10–5 on aggregate.

'It was the start of the glory nights as they were called, and that night we played ... I don't think there's any team who's been or will ever be – and I'm including Barcelona, Real Madrid, Man United – who could have lived with us. That night we would have beaten anybody, I don't care who they were. We just slaughtered them. And Górnik, they were a top side. The majority of them were Polish internationals. But they just never stood a chance. We overran them.'

Tottenham also swept through the next two rounds, against Feyenoord and Dukla Prague, victories that put them into a semi-final against Benfica, the defending champions.

Two towering contests followed. Benfica won the first leg in Lisbon 3–1 in front of 86,000. Jimmy Greaves and Bobby Smith had goals ruled out for offside. Unconfirmed reports have it that Smith's was disallowed despite two defenders being posted on the line.

Benfica went 4–1 up on aggregate in the second leg at White Hart Lane, where 64,448 spectators jammed the stands. Spurs then hit back with two goals, the second a Blanchflower penalty, but in a desperate finish – in which the post twice saved Benfica and Dave Mackay's header landed on the crossbar – the visitors held out.

Blanchflower observed later of the European Cup that it was hard to imagine 'a more potent or popular soccer competition', and described playing in it as 'the greatest emotional experience of my career'.

It did not matter anymore that Alan Hardaker was not listening. His island kingdom was crumbling. Players and fans had experienced something they would not be denied and the English game was on the move.

CHAPTER TWELVE

END OF THE MAX FACTOR

In which Johnny Haynes resists Italians bearing lavish gifts to stay put at Fulham – cricket gives Terry Allcock a summer job and an unlikely batting partner – Cliff Jones has his wage demand turned down flat by Spurs and is told to close the door on his way out – Ron Wylie gives his guide to telling a player's true nature: 'Watch how he plays cards.'

Tommy Trinder is probably the funniest man ever to be chairman of a Football League club, about as different a character from Alan Hardaker as it is possible to imagine. His comical, wide-eyed stare and turned-up clown's mouth contrasted pleasingly with Hardaker's impression of a frosty-faced Dickensian clerk.

Born in 1909 in south London, Trinder deployed his rubber features in a double act with his quick wit. He started working in music hall in the 1920s and went on to become one of the country's best-loved comedians, renowned for his catchphrase, 'You lucky people'. He was also well known for his association with Fulham Football Club, serving as its chairman for nearly twenty years.

In the 1950s, when Trinder was appearing in a show on the south coast, Field Marshal Bernard Law Montgomery, the president of

Portsmouth FC, asked him to watch a match at the Portsmouth ground.

Although Trinder accepted Monty's invitation, he was more interested in the match Fulham were playing elsewhere that day. In fact he was even more interested than usual because it marked an early appearance by Fulham's notable young prospect Johnny Haynes. When the result came through, a Fulham win in which Haynes had scored two goals, Trinder told Montgomery that Haynes would one day captain England.

Montgomery seemed less fascinated by this than by how old Haynes was and Trinder told him off-guardedly that the player was only eighteen.

'Shouldn't he be doing national service?' Montgomery said.

Back on guard, Trinder's razor-sharp repartee came to his rescue: 'That's the other thing about him – he's a cripple.'

As already recounted, legend has it that, some years later, the performer in Trinder and his high regard for Haynes steered him towards another corner. The problem stemmed from his constant eulogising to anyone who would listen about just how good a player the Fulham and, by now, England forward was.

Crucially, he eulogised to Haynes himself. 'If I could pay you more than twenty quid a week, Johnny, you know I would,' Trinder supposedly told Haynes, confident that football's wage cap was set in reinforced concrete. 'With your skills you're worth 100 quid a week. Easy.'

And not only did he tell Haynes, he told the press – and Haynes kept the cuttings to prove it.

But there is much more than this to why Trinder ended up paying Haynes over the odds when maximum earnings disappeared and pay bargaining arrived in 1961. It was far more an act of pragmatism than a consequence of an arm being wrung.

The fact is that at the end of the 1960–61 season, three months after the demise of the regulated wage, the Italian club AC Milan were trying hard to sign Haynes, as well as Jimmy Greaves, then of Chelsea, for a record-shattering transfer fee of £100,000. Milan were prepared to pay Haynes a £15,000 signing-on fee and a weekly wage of more than £200.

Trinder's offer to Haynes was made in response to this. The size of the salary he promised the Fulham captain varied according to which newspaper you read: anywhere from £4,000 a year to £100 a week. And the *London Evening Standard* reported that, by staying in England, Haynes could top up his annual income to £7,000 with a few little earners on the side: ghosted newspaper articles, advertising – Haynes replaced the cricketer Denis Compton as Brylcreem's shiny-haired pin-up – and business interests.

Haynes himself confirmed that reasons beyond football were what were keeping him in London, among them a 22-year-old cabaret dancer called Eileen Farmer.

Inevitably, other clubs moaned about Trinder's largesse. Bill Jones, the Cardiff City manager, for example, wondered sourly how his generosity would be funded. 'Gates are the only income clubs receive,' Jones pointed out, 'and these are dropping.'

On the other hand, the press generally praised the Fulham chairman for being more than just a funny man. At last someone was recognising that if clubs did not start to pay wages that were competitive with other countries, the English game would fall further behind than it had already.

J. L. Manning, the *Daily Mail*'s trenchant and influential columnist, described Trinder's action as a 'bold, brave and sensible application of soccer's New Deal'. Manning warmed to his theme: 'It took the issue of strike notices by the players' union and the whip of parliamentary and public condemnation of our football system to wring from the clubs the concessions that now help to keep England's captain here.'

He might have added that Trinder was not as daft as he looked.

Campaigning to have the cap on weekly earnings removed had been going on since the Football League first imposed a maximum wage, of £4, in 1901. But it was not until after the Second World War that these efforts gained unstoppable momentum.

The first signs of the unrest that brought about this progress were to be found in the club dressing rooms.

Johnny Paton gives an example: 'When I joined Chelsea in 1946, I had a magnificent rise in wages from £8 a week for Celtic to £10. There were 40,000 every week at Stamford Bridge and we were getting paid ten quid, which caused a lot of trouble.

'For the star players, like Tommy Lawton, only getting a tenner a week was a big issue. The money was the reason, and I know this, that Tommy left Chelsea in 1947 and went right down the leagues. I mean he was the world's greatest centre-forward and he joined Notts County of the Third Division. I know he did it for money.

'A lot of deals were being made in those days around transfers and one of Tommy's best friends was the manager of Notts County, a man called Arthur Stollery, who had been the physiotherapist at Chelsea.

'Stollery said, "Come to Notts County", and Tommy Lawton ruined his career by going there for money when he was still in his twenties.'

Paton adds that Lawton 'didn't last too long at the top after that', which is essentially true. Lawton did play for England again, the first player from outside the top two divisions to do so, but only four times, and had a brief spell at Arsenal towards the end of his career.

Paton offers another story about Lawton at this time that illustrates how the top players managed to skim off a little extra: 'Although Tommy was only on £10 a week, he came in one day and threw 400 Players cigarettes on the table: "There you are, lads, help yourselves."

'Tommy was advertising them. He didn't smoke at all – but there was a picture of him with a cigarette in his hand. Other big players were doing the same sort of thing to earn money on the side. I mean how did Stanley Matthews get his hotel at Blackpool? He didn't get that out of his wages.'

Paton may be right about star players being restless for improved pay, but Matthews was not one of them. He was certainly more accepting of the status quo than Lawton, probably because his fame meant he had more avenues for extra-curricular earning than anyone else. Rather than advocate a general hike in wages, Matthews quietly exploited ways to improve his own lot.

Like Lawton, he advertised cigarettes, despite being a dedicated non-smoker, and was the first player to be paid to 'write' a national newspaper column – it was, of course, ghosted – and received payment for producing autobiographies, also ghosted.

He endorsed football boots and asked for money to play in testimonial matches. He took to charging a hefty £100 appearance fee for these matches, a sum easily recouped at the turnstiles by the beneficiary when the public heard Matthews was playing.

On one occasion, when he charged this amount, it did not even matter that he was too injured to play. Instead of taking part in the 1954 testimonial for Ben Collins, the former Northampton Town full-back, Matthews ran the line in an overcoat. The many additional spectators who came especially to watch him easily covered the £100 fee. Matthews did his bit by happily exchanging banter with members of the crowd and adding his autograph to their collections. Everyone left as satisfied as if football's greatest star had been on the pitch.

Matthews and Lawton were not unique in accumulating extra benefits, but because they were so well known, no one really minded their having 'an eye for financial benefit', as one player said of Matthews.

Lesser players bolstering their incomes by more than the norm could cause offence.

When the Scotland international Billy Steel joined Derby County in 1947, he developed a lucrative sideline writing articles for several newspapers. This meant he enjoyed a noticeably superior lifestyle to his teammates', and he only narrowly escaped the retribution of envy. A fellow Derby player threatened to hang Steel from a dressing room peg for his crime of excessive earning.

While the vast majority of players supported the idea of ending the maximum wage, none was entirely sure when or if it would ever happen. The general feeling was, 'We'll believe it when we see it.' And until it did – and for several seasons after it did, when improvement in pay moved ahead only slowly – they found a variety of ways of topping up their incomes, particularly in the summers.

'Most players spent the close season working on the building sites,' Terry Allcock says, 'to keep up their strength and get a suntan.'

Tommy Banks, who had been used to rugged manual work since he was a small boy, was one of these.

But the ever-resourceful Bolton man did not restrict himself to

labouring for local builders to cash in on the close season. He cultivated his own allotment, invested in chickens – 'I had 100 hens who used
to lay for me. I sold eggs all over Farnworth and in the Bolton dressing
room' – milked cows for a local farmer and even landed an unexpected
one-off bonus starring as a model.

The year 1958 had already been a good one for Banks, an FA Cup
winner's medal followed by appearances for England in the World
Cup finals, when his rugged looks saw him chosen to feature in a
razor-blade advertising campaign. Jimmy Hill had picked him out
after being approached by Gillette to recommend a footballer with a
distinctive face.

Gillette liked Hill's choice, put Banks up at the smart Waldorf
Hotel in central London and sent him off to the studios. With ads
appearing on prime-time TV on Sunday nights and billboards, Banks
received close to £400 in payments and expenses.

This represented a windfall payment for the Bolton man, although,
as he says, 'I bet David Beckham and Thierry Henry got a bit more
when they did Gillette ads recently.' The Beckham deal was worth £40
million – 100,000 times more than Banks received.

Banks's main memory of the shoot was the director rejecting the
vest he was wearing. 'It were a white one,' he explains, 'and because TV
weren't as good then it appeared dirty grey on the screen. They sent a
lad out to buy a blue one. It came out white when they filmed it.'

The waggish Roy Wood would no doubt have relished a role in
a TV ad, but had to settle for work as a cobbler in Leeds once the
football season ended. 'The workshop was next to the Templer pub
in Vicar Lane,' he says. 'Each morning we'd receive paper bags full
of old shoes that needed new soles. I worked on the stitching and

channelling machines that sewed the soles to the uppers and made channels for the leather to go into.

'I haven't a clue how much I earned. It wasn't enough to remember.'

A few players, Terry Allcock included, occupied their summers putting their all-round sporting skills to professional use in the other great national sport. Not only did Allcock play cricket professionally, he coached it at a prestigious private school.

The grassy acres of Gresham's School in rural Norfolk became Allcock's place of employment from the summer of 1958. As a working environment, it must have felt like another world to the lad whose earliest sporting experience was playing backstreet football in Leeds and who, for five years in the 1950s, played for Bolton Wanderers.

Today no Football League player would have the time to pursue a parallel career in cricket, even in the unlikely event his club gave him permission.

In the days of the long close season, though, players such as the Compton brothers, Denis and Leslie, could commit themselves to County Championship cricket for Middlesex throughout the summer before reporting back to Arsenal for the football season.

The Comptons are among a select group of professional footballers who played first-class cricket and gained FA Cup winners' medals, for Arsenal in 1950. Since 1964, though, when Jim Standen and Geoff Hurst, he of the 1966 World Cup final hat-trick, played in the Cup final for West Ham, no one else has achieved this distinction.

Standen, a goalkeeper who appeared 178 times for the Hammers, played as a dependable medium-pace bowler for Worcestershire from 1959–70, while the details of Hurst's first-class cricket career are beloved of pub quiz compilers. It consisted of one match for Essex in 1962 in which he batted twice and did not score a run, nor did he bowl a a single ball. He is described as having been an outstanding fielder and an occasional wicketkeeper.

In the 1980s, Ian Botham was one of the last people to play for a Football League club and be a professional cricketer at the same time. But Botham's eleven appearances as a defender for Scunthorpe hardly qualified the cricketing giant to be regarded also as a colossus of football.

While still a Bolton player, Allcock turned out for Blackpool in Lancashire League cricket matches for five years. 'I played against some great Test players,' he says. 'Australia's fast bowler Ray Lindwall and the West Indians Ramadhin, Valentine, Walcott, Weekes and Worrell. I played against them all. I made sixty-seven not out against Lindwall.'

Allcock says the best way to make money playing cricket for Black-pool was to do well in front of a big holiday crowd. 'I wasn't paid very much and we didn't receive bonuses,' he says, 'but if you scored fifty or took five wickets for less than thirty-five runs they took a bucket round the crowd making a collection. You could make quite a bit this way.'

When Allcock joined Norwich, he played cricket for Norfolk in addition to coaching at Gresham's School. Between 1959 and '75 he made forty-five appearances in the minor counties competition as one of the team's most consistent batsmen. He often batted with Bill Edrich when the veteran opening batsman returned to his native East Anglia after an outstanding first-class career with Middlesex and England.

Allcock made one appearance against a first-class county when, in

1965, Norfolk played Hampshire in the Gillette Cup, the first major one-day competition for counties. The match was on the day of the FA Cup final in which Gerry Byrne played almost throughout with a broken collarbone. Allcock had also appeared in that season's competition, but Norwich were eliminated early on at Nottingham Forest.

So instead of turning out in shorts on Saturday 1 May, Allcock found himself clad in white flannels and cast among cricketers. These included Henry Blofeld, the Old Etonian who would become an eminent commentator on the game.

Allcock has fond memories of Blofeld. He recalls the day when they were both dismissed cheaply playing for Norfolk in a match at Lakenham. To while away the time they walked together round the boundary, Blofeld wearing the newly awarded blazer that distinguished him as a Cambridge University cricket Blue.

Telling the story now, Allcock is amused that at the time he was the one, being a Norwich City footballer, who was recognised. 'Every fifteen yards or so we were stopped so I could sign autographs,' he says. 'When we got back to the pavilion, Henry, pretending to be upset at being ignored, took off his blazer and hurled it into a corner.'

Bill Slater also played cricket in the minor counties championship, a handful of games for Warwickshire second XI in the 1950s. But, unlike Allcock, he never earned anything as a cricketer – and for him the end of the maximum wage made only a marginal difference to his standard of living.

During his fifteen years as a Football League player, mostly for Wolverhampton Wanderers, Slater won three First Division titles and an FA Cup, represented Great Britain at the 1952 Olympics and played for England at the 1958 World Cup finals – but he was never a full-time professional. If anything, he regarded his 'proper job' as being a member of staff at Birmingham University's Physical Education department, where in time he became the director.

Slater says it actually cost him money to play in the World Cup finals in Sweden. He had his wages docked by Birmingham University and the expenses the Football Association paid him 'certainly didn't cover what I gave up'.

This did not affect Slater's work rate. He played in all four of England's matches in Sweden and was one of the team's most effective players, although Brazil preferred 'perverse' to 'effective'.

So impeccably mannered off the field, Slater was disliked by the South Americans for being a dangerous nuisance on it. In fact, Brazil were so worried by the way Slater might harry Garrincha that they dropped their star winger from the match. It was the only game the eventual champions did not win, England holding them 0–0 – the first goalless draw in the history of the World Cup finals.

Although there was overwhelming support among the players for an end to the maximum wage, there were a few dissenters. Bill Leivers was one of these.

Leivers recalls clearly the exact amounts he earned when salaries were controlled: 'At Chesterfield I was getting £9 a week and two for a win, one for a draw. When I went to Manchester City I got £11 a week, £13 if I played in the first team.'

At that time the maximum wage was £14; £10 in the close season. This went up to £15 and £12 in 1954, to £17 and £14 in 1957, and then in 1958, until the maximum was scrapped, to £20 and £17.

As the pressure to end the maximum wage mounted in the early '60s, players held meetings in Manchester, Birmingham and London.

Leivers says he thinks he was the only one who voted against abolishing it at the Manchester meeting.

'I did it because I thought a realistic maximum was the way to go about it,' he says. 'I hadn't really thought about what that figure was but I thought it was common sense.'

Leivers reckons the amounts some players now receive justifies the position he took in 1961: 'They're talking about the same sort of thing at football clubs now, aren't they? When you think about players getting 200, 300 thousand a week, it's obscene.'

At the same time Leivers laughs at just how stingy some clubs and their boards were when he was playing. 'I've got to tell you this,' he says. 'I was skipper one day at Newcastle, playing for the reserves. And Newcastle had a good side in those days.

'Fred Jolly, the director who went with us – no one could ever have called him jolly – was sitting in a different compartment from the players on the train. But we obviously got a good result because he came to see us. He congratulated us and handed me what I expected to be some money to buy the lads a drink.

'But when I looked down it was a packet of Polo mints he'd put in my hand. "Share those between you," he said.'

Warwick Rimmer says he was in two minds about ending the maximum wage. Unlike Leivers he was just starting out on his career when the issue came to a head. 'I can fully understand why the players voted to end capping wages,' he says, 'but at that stage I was trying to make a bit of a mark for myself and get established in the first team. The thought of striking just when I was on the verge of making it was a bit worrying.

'But that was a young man's way of thinking, which I never voiced because nearly everyone was unified in what they wanted to do. There was no question of not going with it, but I did have that little bit of feeling, "Crikey, I don't fancy going on strike now."'

Tommy Banks sealed the decision of the Manchester meeting to back strike action with an off-the-cuff intervention that has become part of football's folklore. It swept aside all opposition – bar Leivers's – to such action in the event of the clubs holding out doggedly to retain the wage ceiling.

Stanley Matthews, who was at the meeting, had said originally that on a point of principle he was against players going on strike if the upper limit was not removed. He changed his mind because his Blackpool teammates were overwhelmingly in favour. He said he regarded loyalty to them a superior principle to his objection to striking.

An unassuming type, Matthews attended the Manchester meeting with the sole intention of voting. He was no firebrand and it would have taken something extraordinary for him to stand up to speak. What he could not avoid was another speaker bringing his name into the debate.

A young player put the case for wages continuing to be pegged, his words remembered by Jimmy Armfield, the Blackpool player who was sitting next to Matthews: 'My dad's a miner, earning £10 a week. I play in the lower division and I earn twice as much. I train in the open air and play football on Saturday – he's down the pit for eight hours at a time, five days a week. That can't be right. We earn quite enough as it is.'

This caused Banks, the Bolton and England full-back, to seek permission to speak. 'I didn't go to the meeting with the intention of speaking,' Banks tells me, 'but that young lad's words rang in my ears and so I stood up.'

It was to prove a historic contribution to the debate that has been retold many times. No one recorded Banks's exact words and he happily admits to not remembering precisely what he said. But his biographer, Ian Seddon, himself a former Bolton player, credits him with saying the following (Boltonese first and then a helpful translation):

'Ah think its neaw time ah spokk, Mr Chairmon. Ah'm tellin' thee t'tell thee far'her ah'm on 'ees side, ah noes pits nar fun ah 'avebin theer misell but theer wonn't be 30,000 watchin''im dig owt coal cum Munday morn, theer will be 30,000 peyin gud munny on Setday ut Burnden Park t'si mi tryter stop Brother Matthews 'ere.'

Now Seddon's translation:

'Mr Chairman, I think it's now time that I spoke.

'I'd like to tell your father I know the pits are a tough life having worked below ground myself. However, there will not be 30,000 people watching him extract coal on Monday morning, but there will be 30,000 paying spectators on Saturday at Burnden Park watching my battle with Stanley Matthews.'

No high-earning, massively qualified advocate could have presented a more compelling case or delivered it quite so consummately.

And what made it particularly powerful was that Banks was one of the few full-backs in the Football League who was reckoned to have Matthews's measure.

When it came to the vote on whether to strike, the date for such action being fixed by the Professional Footballers' Association for Saturday 21 January 1961, 'my hand went up', Matthews said.

As the strike date approached, backing for the players widened. Ted Hall, chairman of the Trades Union Congress, was one of those who became involved. He called on the public to boycott any matches that went ahead in defiance of a strike. He warned that any player who broke the strike might encounter difficulty finding work once his playing days were over.

A matter of hours before the strike was due to take place, the clubs caved in to the pressure placed on them by the Football League management committee, who in turn were reacting to the pressure they were under from the PFA and their members.

While Tommy Trinder's decision to dig deep into Fulham's coffers to keep Johnny Haynes at Craven Cottage was a significant point in the progress towards today's off-the-scale wages, the idea that players might immediately start making extravagant demands was never going to become a reality.

A lavish lifestyle was an unknown concept – to professional footballers, anyway. They were so conditioned to low wages in a low-wage society that the next step up was not-quite-so-low wages.

Cliff Jones's manager at Tottenham, Bill Nicholson, gave this reaction at the time to the new deal: 'No one can tell what difference it will make. We have a fair idea of the percentage increase we will offer but it would not be wise for me to disclose it. It is a matter for the club and player and might be some way from the amount we ultimately pay.'

Jones recalls that there was more a sense of wonderment among the players at what was happening than a fierce determination to go out and get what they thought was their due. 'We couldn't believe it,' he says. 'Johnny Haynes getting £100 for playing football! There were lots of jokes flying about, "Haynesy got injured, he tripped over his wallet" and stuff like that.'

As it turned out, Tottenham proved to be one of the more generous clubs, with Spurs' great success at that time undoubtedly a help. But with no agents to do their bidding, Jones, like every other player, had to decide whether to accept what he was offered or go to management to barter for more.

After having a chat with Jimmy Greaves, Jones decided on the latter route. It led to a brief and memorable encounter with Nicholson's hastily devised negotiating technique.

In December 1961, Greaves had joined Spurs after a short, unhappy stay with AC Milan that suggested Haynes had been wise in putting the charms of Eileen Farmer before those of Italian football. Greaves, incidentally, cost Tottenham £99,999, the fee deliberately £1 short of six figures so that the player was not tagged with being the first to achieve this target.

'When the maximum wage was abolished, I went up from £20 a week to £50 a week,' Jones says. 'But it was still exactly the same £10 appearance money, and £4 for a win and £2 for a draw.

'Then when Jimmy came to Tottenham, he was on top money, and I always remember a conversation we had.'

Their exchange, Jones says, went like this:

Greaves: 'What are you getting paid, Cliff?'

Jones: 'Fifty quid a week.'

Greaves: 'You should be getting more than that; you're the best winger in Europe.'

'At the time you could say I wasn't far short of that,' Jones says, 'because I'd had two great seasons.'

Greaves: 'You should go and see Bill [Nicholson] and ask for a rise.'

'I plucked up courage,' Jones says, 'and went in to see Bill. He used to sit at this table and he'd be up there and you'd be down there.'

This time there was a very different conversation from the one Jones had had with Greaves:

Nicholson: 'What's up, Cliff?'

Jones: 'Well, I've come in for a rise.'

Nicholson: 'Oh have you? On what basis do you want to have a rise?'

Jones: 'I think I'm the best winger in Europe.'

Jones says he knew immediately that he had said the wrong thing.

Nicholson: 'Is that right, son? I'll tell you now that's a matter of opinion. On the way out close the door behind you.'

'Yeah, that was it,' Jones says. 'He didn't mess around, Bill. But I had another terrific season, banged in a few goals, Spurs won the European Cup Winners' Cup and Bill said, "Cliff, about that rise. OK, I'll give it to you."

'I went up then to £70 a week. It was a big jump and in a successful week I could be knocking off £100, which was good money compared to the man in the street, the working man.'

These figures, and Jones's reference to the 'top money' Greaves was getting, are interesting. They show that Haynes might not in fact have been that far ahead of some other highly rated players in what he had negotiated. Maybe the Haynes/Fulham arrangement gained the publicity it did, and still does, for being talismanic rather than exceptional.

But a considerable disparity existed between what the good pros now earned, as a story by Peter McParland illustrates. It is also a cautionary tale about the pitfalls players could stumble into before they had agents.

He says most of the Aston Villa players had signed for £25 a week with £5 appearance money. 'But I refused what the club were offering. I was looking to double my wages to £40 a week.

'I was down in Bournemouth at the time on my summer holidays and told Villa that I wasn't prepared to return unless they improved what they'd offered me by a lot. By doing this I got my wages up to £35 a week and £5 per week appearance money.

'But being as I was negotiating on my own, I got caught out. Rather than settling for £5 per week, I should have gone for £5 per appearance, because we were playing two games a week. So I missed out on a fiver, which I'm sure wouldn't have happened if I'd had an agent.'

Unlike McParland, who had been a First Division player for nearly ten years in 1961, Terry Neill was a new boy who thought being on the £20 maximum plus bonuses was 'like having died and gone to heaven'.

'Then, when the maximum wage was lifted, we went up to forty-five quid a week with a huge increase in the win bonus,' Neill says. 'With so much on offer, there were other bonuses; you've never seen the Arsenal players train like they did in that pre-season.'

Neill claims to have been behind a cheeky move that finessed an unlikely perk out of Arsenal at the start of the 1961–62 season.

'I've got to confess it now that I can,' he says, referring to his part in persuading the management that by being third in the table after only two matches the Arsenal players were due a bonus.

'It was only alphabetically that we were in third place after we won 1–0 at Leicester,' Neill says, 'but I said to a couple of the lads, "We're near the top of the league, you know. We're due a bonus for being in the first six. You'd better go in and argue with the manager."

'We'd only played two games. The manager protested but in the end they paid the bonus.'

Neill and Gordon Milne recall that both their clubs preferred to link increases to something tangible, rather than deciding a player's wages by assessing his worth subjectively. Hence Arsenal and Liverpool introduced crowd bonuses.

Milne was not taken in by this and thinks it 'was probably to appease the Liverpool players for their continued low wages despite the success they brought the club'. He says, as far as he recalls, the players received an extra £2 for every 1,000 spectators north of 28,000.

Overall, Milne paints a rather bleaker picture than Jones and Neill of the immediate aftermath of the wage barrier coming down. It is redolent of things being grimmer up north than down south.

'Whenever we played London games,' Milne says, 'we went by train, which meant card schools. We played for nothing in little groups – mine might consist of Roger Hunt, Peter Thompson, Ian St John and me.

'And when we finished with the cards, the conversation was usually about our ambition, which, for most of us, was to have our house paid for. If you could pay off your mortgage then that would be the business.

'There were some you knew wouldn't be able to manage it, they couldn't save a penny, and there were three or four of them whose marriages went sideways.

'Ron Wylie, who became my number two when I managed Coventry, used to say if you watched footballers play cards – they all played cards in those days – you could tell their characters.

'Some would hold their cards up tight, others were more relaxed but cautious, others were casual. It was quite true. I was cautious, I wasn't a risk-taker.'

The end of the maximum wage can be seen as one of the watershed moments in English football in its progress towards the bloated monument to Mammon it would grow into by the close of the century.

But it cannot be represented as an opening of the floodgates; more a highly significant oiling and easing of the hinges. Television money was what would carry away all obstacles to unimagined changes in the game's finances.

Professional footballers were certainly lifted out of the wage-earning bracket of working-class people who still experienced everyday privations, but they continued to live modest lives and went largely unrecognised by all but the most dedicated fans.

Bill Slater gives an interesting picture of what it was like to be a First Division footballer either side of the cap on wages being removed: 'I suppose I felt quite important in the sense that I was playing for a successful club, but players weren't recognised as they are today.

'When playing for Wolves, even living a short distance away in Birmingham meant I wasn't noticed, which I rather welcomed.

'There was one occasion in Birmingham, after some small boys came running after me, I said to my wife it was the first time anyone had recognised me there. When I was in Wolverhampton, young people mostly might come and ask for an autograph. It wasn't something I resented. I was always quite polite. There was always a crowd of them waiting outside the ground after a match.'

CHAPTER THIRTEEN

TOO OLD TO PLAY, TOO POOR TO RETIRE

In which a nasty break sets Dave Whelan on the path to his first million before he gives up football – Alex Dawson, having started in the red shirt of Man Utd, ends up 'a red yeti' – Roy Wood chooses working in a betting office over playing for Liverpool – George Eastham sees the team he put together before being sacked go back to the First Division.

Dave Whelan has agreed to see me at one of his homes. This one, he tells me, after pausing to make a quick mental calculation, cost him £35 million.

It is not his family home, the one where he sleeps, but it is one where he does an awful lot of living, at least it is at the time when we meet.

The DW Stadium is the ground of Wigan Athletic, the football club Whelan owns, and of his beloved Wigan Warriors rugby league team.

Before our chat he orders lunch to be sent upstairs. Having eaten on the train I opt just for tea; he also goes for tea, plus ham sandwiches. 'White or brown bread?' the catering lady asks. 'Either will do,' Whelan replies, 'but no butter.' I end up helping him finish them.

We sit at a large, polished table in the directors' box, a spacious room in the modern style: a glass front looking out over the pitch. The area was once a munitions dump, where, after it was abandoned, Whelan played as a small boy.

Dressed in an open-neck shirt and sleeveless pullover, he is an amiable host. In the reception area I have just watched him greet a family from Australia. He has given them as much time as they want, talking and posing for group photographs.

He is also engaging and unsparing with his time when he talks with me. I remain conscious, though, of the implacable side to his nature. It is a side of him he has demonstrated throughout his adult life as an uncompromising, if ultimately ill-fated, full-back and in his dealings as a pragmatic and conspicuously effective businessman. I am happy ours is a chat and not a negotiation of some kind.

When I call him back two days later to double-check a couple of small points – one or two of his memories about his playing days are at odds with the record books – he does not return my call. I suspect he feels he has given me enough of his valuable time.

I have never completely trusted the old adage about something or someone being the exception that proves the rule, but it is hard to deny that Whelan fits it pretty well.

Before footballers made enough to finish their playing days with a life of leisure stretched out before them – a bit of punditry, possibly, and long hours on the golf course – the prospects were not dissimilar from those facing any other man whose working life had been one of physical labour: a prolonged struggle to make ends meet into old age.

Of those I interview, Whelan stands out as the towering exception. Even by the time he had stopped playing he was already on the way to his first self-made million. The starting point was the moment his leg was shattered playing for Blackburn in the 1960 FA Cup final.

'After I was in hospital and came back home, I asked the doctor how long I would be in plaster,' he says.

'He told me it depended on how quickly the leg took to heal, but that I was bound to be in it for six months, minimum. I was actually in it for nine months.

'In that time I was bored, I couldn't do anything. So I went to the market in the centre of Blackburn. I took a look around, saw these two lads who were working on a market stall selling basic toiletries and, knowing I'd got to do something and learn something, I asked if I could work on their stall.'

The Howarth brothers ran the stall and Bill Howarth, the boss, recognised the benefit of having a Blackburn Rovers player, who had appeared in the Cup final, at his side. He paid Whelan ten shillings a day to serve the customers, who, just as Howarth had reckoned they would be, were attracted by his celebrity assistant.

'All the people in Blackburn knew me,' Whelan says, 'and would stop to buy something so they could ask how I was and whether I was getting better. For my part I learnt so much in six months on that stall.'

The key lesson was the paramountcy of the 16 per cent gross margin, or, as he also puts it, 'tuppence in every shilling'.

'I picked it up so quickly,' he says. 'If something cost you one and eleven [one shilling and eleven pence], you sold it for two and three – four pence profit, 16 per cent.'

Clearly Whelan had happened upon something that deeply interested him. 'I came to look at Wigan, where I found they had no outside market. There were none of the stalls they used to make out of metal and then cover in tarpaulin. They were all inside stalls.'

The market superintendent told Whelan there was nothing to stop him having an outside stall. And so, for a rent of fifteen shillings a day, he set up two of them by the main entrance.

'I was selling toiletries – I bought them off the lads in Blackburn, they supplied me – and the first day I took 200 quid. So I'd made like thirty-two quid in a day.'

Whelan had hoped to resume his playing career with Blackburn, but after a couple of comeback games in the reserves he cracked his leg again. In 1962 he was transferred to Crewe Alexandra, stalwarts of the Fourth Division, although in 1963 they gained promotion for the first time in their history.

'The leg got stronger,' he says, 'but the pace never came back.' He quit playing professional football in 1966, just short of his thirtieth birthday.

By then his life was already set on an entirely different trajectory. 'The last two years while I was at Crewe I had the market stall in Wigan. I trained in the mornings and my sister ran the stall for me until I got back at one o'clock.

'Then, when I retired from Crewe, I knew what I wanted to do and I went to America to learn. I was aware from what I'd read that they were five to six years ahead of us in the retail section.

'I went to New York, I went to Chicago and looked at what they were doing – and they had just started supermarkets, selling food in one area and non-foods in another. They piled goods up and you helped yourself.

'It made you wonder, "How do they help themselves to things? They must steal them." We were used to going into a shop in the UK and saying, "Can I have that?" Someone would then get it for you.

'But in America it was self-service. Goods were piled up on a pallet and people came in, took two tins of beans, put them in a basket and then paid for what they'd got at the end. It was so different from what we were doing here.'

'Whelan came back to Wigan determined to copy the retail model he had observed in the US. 'I was still working in the market then and earning good, good money – £400, £500 a week. But straightaway I went to look at this building in Wigan and I thought, "Supermarket – Whelan's Discount Store".'

The thought became a reality and, Whelan says, 'was a fantastic success. You had to queue to get in. In two years I'd opened a total of ten. We were the first supermarkets in the land to sell food and, on the next floor, non-foods – toys, furniture, electrical stuff… the items you could sell were being relaxed all the time.'

'I should have stayed in supermarkets,' he says, 'because Asda weren't about then. There was Morrisons but Ken Morrison was only in Yorkshire. He had twelve supermarkets in Yorkshire; I had ten in Lancashire. I should have stayed in them.'

Whelan says he would have gone into business even if he had not broken his leg at Wembley, but the injury meant he started sooner than he would have done.

When we meet he is in his late seventies and says the urge to work is as strong as it has ever been. Although he may have been rich enough to retire many leap years ago, he has no plans to do so just yet.

Whelan's story of gathering riches represents the extreme exception for professional players of his era. For nearly all of his contemporaries the outcome was very different. The place they ended up when they stopped playing may not have been exclusively one of hardship, but nor was it overpopulated with those in a position to retire before reaching old age.

Billy Liddell, the outstanding Scotland winger, is the one other player I came across whose later life was of a completely different order from that of the vast majority – and I only came across him second-hand.

Liddell, who died in 2001 aged seventy-nine, joined his first club, Liverpool, in 1938 and stayed with them until his retirement from the game in 1961. Tony McNamara talks about Liddell as admiringly as if he had been a fan rather than a teammate when he joined Liverpool from Everton.

'Unlike Everton, Liverpool did have a really big star then,' McNamara says. 'He was Billy Liddell from Scotland, a winger who scored more than 200 goals for the club.

'He'd started training as an accountant before leaving Scotland and could have made a good career for himself outside football, which was a rare thing among professional footballers in those days.

'He was coming towards the end of his career when I joined Liverpool and by then his presence and his popularity meant he was in such demand to make speeches and attend functions that you never saw him. I shared a room with him once and even then I don't think I saw him for more than a few moments.

'After he retired from football, he became a Justice of the Peace in Liverpool and did good works and later took a post at the University of Liverpool.'

An obituary by Brian Glanville, the journalist who watched Liddell play, said that he was so esteemed at Liverpool that the team was nick-named Liddellpool.

'He was almost too good to be true,' Glanville said, 'the perfect sportsman – fast, hard but impeccably fair – a convinced Christian; a diligent worker with boys' clubs; a wartime Bomber Command pilot officer and pathfinder; and a teetotaller who, when he beat Liverpool's appearance record held by the illustrious goalkeeper Elisha Scott, was presented with a cocktail cabinet.'

Those former professionals who had successful careers as managers were better rewarded than most, but not excessively so.

Managers' jobs were the only employment most old pros were qualified to do – and the veterans who lined up to be given a mana-gerial break had a neediness that meant boards were almost as penny-pinching in rewarding them as they were their players.

No wonder this was the golden age of footballers regarding club directors with utter disdain, summed up by the empty space in Len Shackleton's autobiography beneath the chapter headed 'The Average Director's Knowledge of Football'.

Like many, Bill Leivers went from being a player to being a player-manager when he joined Fourth Division club Doncaster Rovers in the summer of 1964. It was an assignment that did not last long after Leivers had an almighty row with the sort of director Shackleton damned with his blank page.

The row revolved around a new board member who pushed the first-team claims of a particular player. Leivers told the director that the player in question would 'never make a footballer as long as he's got a hole in his arse'. When the chairman failed to back him, Leivers headed for the exit – with only one regret.

'The next day,' Leivers says, 'I've got the *News of the World* and God knows how many other papers outside my door. The *News of the World* bloke offered me £2,250 to do an article. For that I could have more than bought a house at that time. I said, "I don't care how much you offer me. It'll make no difference whatsoever between me and him."

'And I've wished a million times since that I'd taken the money.'

After this, Leivers's managerial career bumped along with his successes unrewarded in a marketplace teeming with ex-players in search of work.

He missed out on being made manager at Scunthorpe after he and an old pal, who was competing for the same post, agreed they would ask for exactly the same terms: forty quid a week plus £5 expenses. When the board twigged their complicity, they gave it to neither of them.

'They took as their manager a bloke from the Eastern Counties League,' Leivers says. 'He lasted three weeks.'

After a brief spell at Workington, a job Leivers enjoyed having initially been hesitant because the club was 'halfway across the Irish Sea', he took over as manager of Cambridge United when they were in the Southern League.

'I promised Cambridge we wouldn't finish below fourth and I expected to win the League after that and be in the Football League in three years – and I did exactly what I said I would do.'

He spent eight years at Cambridge before 'all of a sudden things started to go wrong for me and, what happens, I get the sack. I was then offered a job at Chelmsford but I didn't like the way Chelmsford were running the club.'

Leivers says he mistrusted the owners' plans for the club, that they were intent on building on the site eventually. 'I'd seen so many

Southern League clubs where they'd done exactly that. So I told them what I thought about them and walked out.'

Eventually he returned to Cambridge, this time to manage Cambridge City, where he served out the rest of his professional life, finally as the club's general manager.

It was hardly the glorious finale that someone who had given so much of himself so wholeheartedly to football deserved, but then this could be said of so many others.

George Eastham's experience of managing Stoke City, after he had represented them with distinction in his later years as a player, drove him into self-imposed exile thousands of miles away from the UK.

And as with Leivers at Doncaster, Eastham's departure was caused by a board who thought they knew better about players than a former top-class player.

'My time as manager of the club wasn't quite so enjoyable as when I played for them,' Eastham says.

'The team was a bit old and needed new blood. So I got everything together, except I felt that we needed a centre-forward and told the directors I wanted to buy this lad called Brendan O'Callaghan.

'But they said they couldn't afford him, gave me the elbow and brought in Alan Durban to replace me. They then bought a centre-forward and who do you think it was? Brendan O'Callaghan. The team that I put together, with O'Callaghan added, went back into the First Division.'

Eastham had had enough. He pushed off to South Africa where he started a sportswear business and showed his contempt for apartheid by going out of his way to coach black kids. 'It's been marvellous,' he says. 'It's forty-odd years now. I think I'm used to it.'

Gordon Milne, who spent nearly thirty years managing, including a stint in charge of the England under-18s during which they won the 1972 European title, acknowledges he was fortunate to be shielded from meddlesome board members.

'In my early days as a manager,' he says, 'when I went to Coventry City with Joe Mercer – Joe was like general manager, director of football, and I was the young coach – he helped me and encouraged me. He was a buffer between me and the board. A lot of managers didn't – and still don't – get that protection.'

Stan Anderson fulfilled his desire to be a manager, although not quite in the manner he can have expected. While others failed to secure their financial futures within the game, Anderson succeeded in doing so by default.

With his playing days at Newcastle coming to an end in 1965, when he was thirty-two, Anderson, who had his coaching badge by then, joined Middlesbrough. Boro wanted to squeeze a few last games out of him while he settled in as first-team coach.

Anderson understood that landing a manager's job, if he managed to at all, would take time. What attracted him to joining Middlesbrough was that Raich Carter, a wonderful player for Sunderland before the war, was the Boro manager.

'Raich had been a multi-talented player,' Anderson says. 'Everybody talked about him, "Ooh, did you ever see Raich Carter play?" All this sort of thing. I thought I must be able to learn something off Raich.'

Anderson has a vivid memory of watching Carter towards the end of his playing career, when he was Hull's player-manager. 'Hull got this free kick just outside the box,' he says, 'and Raich spent ages arranging his players: 'You go there, you go there, you go there.' And then after doing all this he took the kick himself and pinged it straight in the top corner. He knew all the time exactly what he was going to do.

'He was a super player and the whole point of going to Boro, I thought, was I'd be working with a manager I was going to get on well with and who'd appreciate me. It was a disaster.'

He describes going to see Carter in his office when he first arrived at Boro: 'He was reading a paper. He said, "Morning, Stan. I'm nearly finished." He told me to have a look at the photographs while I was waiting.'

The walls were covered with pictures of Carter playing for England, holding up a trophy, shaking hands and so on. All Anderson could think was, 'Very nice, yeah, very nice, but you'd have a job to find any photographs of me in my house.'

When Carter put the paper down, he said, 'Right, Stan, what would you like to know?' Anderson remembers the rest of the conversation going like this:

Anderson: 'I'd just like to know what you're thinking about the match on Saturday. What tactics do you want me to work on with the players?'

Carter: 'Do what you want.'

Anderson: 'No, I've got to work on what *you* want, boss.'

Carter: 'Oh no, just a bit of five-a-side.'

Anderson: 'But tactically what do you do, play four-four-two or four-three-three or…?'

Carter: 'No, you sort it out.'

Anderson: 'This can't be right. You've got to have a system that you're playing.'

Carter: 'No, do what you can.'

'The training ground was a bloody shambles,' Anderson says. 'Raich didn't seem interested in the job.'

Soon afterwards Middlesbrough no longer seemed interested in Carter, sacked him and offered the manager's job to Anderson.

Not surprisingly, Anderson was disconcerted to find the long road to managing a major Football League club reduced so dramatically by an unsignposted shortcut. He was not convinced he was ready for it. 'I said I'd think about it,' he says, 'and went to see Harold Shepherdson. I told him he should take over.'

Shepherdson, a former physical education instructor in the army, was basically a magic-sponge man. He had been an assistant to England managers since 1957, and still would be in 1966 when England won the World Cup, and was Carter's assistant at Boro. He knew his limitations and told Anderson: 'No, I'm not going to be manager.'

It was at this point that Anderson decided he would have a go. 'Somebody had to do it,' he says.

Anderson managed Boro for seven years, guiding them straight back up to Division Two in 1967 after they had been relegated in 1966. He took charge of four more clubs before ending his managerial career in 1981. He joined a distinguished list of players who never quite achieved in a suit what they had in their playing days, but at least managing gave him the gainful employment that eluded so many of his contemporaries.

In retirement Anderson honed his exceptional skill as a golfer. He may well have concluded that, had he known about golf as a small boy, that was the sporting career he should have pursued.

He had never heard of golf before Don Revie introduced him to it in 1956. 'I went and caddied for Don soon after he joined Sunderland,'

Anderson says, 'and watched him and a few others playing. They were hitting the ball all over the place. I thought I could do better than that.'

He was absolutely right. He bought a set of second-hand, left-hander's clubs for £4 and found the game came naturally to him. Briefly, he says, he had a handicap of one. When I meet him, in his eighties, he is still regularly shooting scores lower than his age. He has a best eighteen-hole score of sixty-five and once shot seventy-two on the St Andrews championship course.

Long though the queue was to fill a managerial vacancy, not everyone jumped at the opportunity. For example, Tommy Banks, the one-time male model who had been paid £200 cash to sign for Altrincham after finishing with Bolton in 1961 and received £15 a week for playing, refused the offer to manage the go-ahead Cheshire County League side.

Rather than accept the opening that may well have led to a coveted manager's job in the Football League, Banks set off down the sort of post-football employment route, unmarked and perilous, that was familiar to any number of former pros.

At first he chanced his luck in a building venture with older brother Ralph. T & R Banks Ltd went bust, despite Tommy's tireless efforts, but not before he had built the house in Elsie Street, Farnworth, which is where I visit him.

'He were too soft,' Rita, his wife, interjects gently, referring to Tommy's business acumen.

'Aye, I was,' Tommy says, cheerfully agreeing to the divergence between Banks the footballer and Banks the businessman.

And so he reverted to full-time manual work, once again labouring as wholeheartedly as when he worked down a mine. He sticks out his jaw and lets out a subdued growl when I cast doubts on what he saw as the fun aspects of hard physical graft. I take it as a sort of rebuke coupled with a sadness that he is no longer capable of such work.

He says he enjoyed hod carrying and was, evidently, the sort of labourer every brickie prayed to have as a helper. He earned more doing it than he did when playing for one of England's most eminent First Division teams, but that was by the by.

When he gave it up after a hip replacement, he applied to become a postman. There were no vacancies and so he took over a newsagent's shop close to his home. It was a five-year nightmare that ended in 1986. He advised anyone who would listen that if they thoroughly disliked a person they should buy him or her a newsagent's.

Bolton Wanderers' great left-back, now approaching his sixties, once more returned to what defined his sporting and working lives: physical toil. His final job for the eight years before he retired at the age of sixty-five was as a member of a builder chum's bricklaying gang.

Even in these later years, with an artificial hip, he remained phenomenally strong. 'We were building a water tower,' he says, 'and I'd carry a full hod of bricks up three forty-rung ladders roped together. That was 160 pounds, not far short of a hundredweight.' His eyes sparkle at the memory.

At least Banks had the opportunity to turn down a manager's job. Very few received such an offer and, like Banks, might well have turned it down. The job brought with it a burden of responsibility that many old pros accepted was too much for them.

Without having asked him, I suspect Alex Dawson is the type who would have dismissed, without giving it a second thought, the very idea of being a manager.

Dawson, the 'baby' who had faced Banks in that 1958 Cup final, turned out to be cut from the same tough fabric as the Bolton full-back. He, too, relished strenuous manual labour once he gave up football.

From the battering-ram school of centre-forwards at Manchester United and Preston North End, Dawson found himself what he considered to be ideal employment at Corby steelworks in Northamptonshire. And a healthy dose of overtime meant his first pay packet, containing more than 100 quid, comfortably eclipsed his best weekly wage in nearly twenty years of professional football.

Dawson had finished his football career playing for Corby Town in the Southern League. He and his wife, Clare, still live nearby in a small bungalow in the market town of Rothwell. 'You'd be surprised how many ex-footballers worked at Corby,' he says, although he adds that none he came across had played for one of the big clubs. He recalls one of the old pros saying to him, 'I didn't expect to see you here from Manchester United.'

'I did all the dirty jobs,' Dawson says – and his eyes are as merry as Banks's had been remembering those skyscraper ladders. 'I really enjoyed it.'

Not only dirty jobs, but dangerous ones, too. 'It's amazing how many deaths you saw there,' Dawson says, and describes how one member of his maintenance gang was killed in a tumble-dryer-type device. 'We were cleaning it and they started it up to see if it was all right and this guy hadn't got out.'

Dawson himself came very close to being killed – not on the occasions he hung 200 feet up in an unstable cradle painting gas holders, but when he fell from the top of a 30-foot hopper. 'It was clogged solid until we started drilling it and it all gave way. I fell right through it and out of the gate at the bottom.' Battered and bruised, he refused medical treatment. 'He was like a red yeti when he got home,' Clare says. She and her husband laugh heartily at the memory.

Alec Jackson was another with no managerial pretensions. He left school at fifteen, found employment as a machinist close to his home in Tipton and, from everything he tells me, had no ambition other than living what might be described as a traditional working man's life.

The fact that for more than a decade Jackson's outstanding natural ability as an athlete and footballer took him way beyond the limits of what he felt he might achieve did not fundamentally change him. It did not alter his sense of who he was or where he felt he belonged.

Not much better off when he retired from playing professional football than he was when he started, Jackson wished only to return to his roots.

'When I retired,' he says, 'I went into a mill and since then I've done just about everything, working eighteen hours a day. It needed to be done.'

Jackson was growing up when the population's sense of self-sufficiency was reflected in the numbers who produced their own food on allotments, plots of land made available for non-commercial gardening. There were more than a million of these in Britain after the Second World War.

This number has dwindled to fewer than 300,000, one of them in the possession of Alec Jackson. 'I've had my allotment for thirty-seven years and I've still got it,' he says. 'I still work it but I've had to cut back. Me and a friend share it, one half each. I produce just about everything you can eat.

'And I do other bits and pieces, making things, fishing. I'm lucky because I'm hanging on. There's quite a few of those I used to play with who have gone. Good people have gone.'

As I board a train at Blackpool Station to return to London after meeting Rex Adams, I try to convince myself it has not been a wasted journey.

Three hours earlier on a late September afternoon I have turned up at Adams's home in Bloomfield Road, a few yards from the ground where he once played for Blackpool in the First Division. He has just returned with his wife, Muriel, from a short campervan holiday in Woodstock, the Oxfordshire market town that is the site of Blenheim Palace.

Autumn sunshine warms us as we talk in a small back extension to Adams's house. He is a genial host, but his football story is thin – particularly for someone who was once seen as a successor to Stanley Matthews at a club strong enough to appear in three FA Cup finals around the time he served them.

In three years with Blackpool, 1948–51, Adams would play only sixteen matches before being transferred to Worcester City of the Southern League – quite a tumble for a First Division player. He eventually retired from football at the age of twenty-nine.

When I hear a few weeks later that Adams has died suddenly, just short of his eighty-sixth birthday, I am not only shocked, because despite his age he had seemed in good health, I find myself going back over his story. I am once again struck by the cottage-industry nature of the game not so long ago.

Of course players will always come and go. But it seems unimaginable today with top-flight clubs, such as Blackpool once were, vetting recruits so meticulously or nurturing them from a young age that a player could have come and gone leaving quite so little trace as Adams.

Someone at Blackpool must have thought Adams was a good player when the club signed him from Oxford City in 1948 to understudy the great Matthews, although Adams himself seems nonplussed by this. Throughout our chat he is almost apologetic about his ability.

The most memorable moment of Adams's career was when he scored his only goal for Blackpool against high-flying Portsmouth at Bloomfield Road in front of 20,000 spectators in September 1949. But even this highlight came unadorned with stardust.

Portsmouth, who would be Football League champions that season, had won 5–0 at Newcastle three days before visiting Blackpool. Adams's goal against them was the only one of the match. According to a local newspaper, there was a hint of offside. The Portsmouth defence stood still, but the flag stayed down and Adams ran on alone to score.

Apart from that goal, Adams has few memories of playing for Blackpool. The one anecdote I prise from him is amusingly earthy but with nothing directly to do with football. 'At the time Muriel was expecting our first child,' he says, 'there were about four other players – Tommy Garrett was one – whose wives were expecting and I remember the manager, Joe Smith, saying if it was a competition for effing [his euphemism] we'd be top of the First Division.'

Until pensionable age, Adams was in no position to consider pursuing a leisurely life in retirement. After football he worked as a fitter at the Hawker aircraft factory in Blackpool, ran a newsagent's shop for seven years and for twenty years worked in the Blackpool office of the *Manchester Evening News,* doing a range of jobs from distributing the paper to 'bushing' on the stencil machine.

Roy Wood was lucky when Leeds put him up for sale. He had two choices of what to do next: join Liverpool, where Bill Shankly wanted to have him as a goalkeeper, or work in a betting office.

He plumped for the betting office job as the one to give him a better life.

'No one at Leeds gave me a reason for being put on the transfer list,' Wood says. 'I was just put on it. Although I couldn't prove it, there was one possible reason why Sam Bolton, the Leeds chairman, wanted to get rid of me. I was on the PFA committee by now as the Leeds players' representative and this was at the time the Football League players were pushing for the abolition of the maximum wage.

'During negotiations I remember sitting across the table from Bolton, who was on the FA committee. He was always against me for doing this because, of course, he and the other chairmen were in favour of keeping wages capped.

'When the man who was putting money into the club didn't like you, didn't like your face, that counted for a lot in football.'

Wood says he had the chance to join quite a few clubs, including Liverpool: 'Bill Shankly said I could go there. He told one of his trainers that he needed another goalkeeper and the trainer mentioned my name. Shankly said I'd do because if a man could play every game and get promotion to the First Division [with Leeds] he couldn't be bad.'

Liverpool were prepared to pay a fee for Wood and his accrued benefit. He admits he was attracted to moving back to his home town, but he was only recently married and he and his wife decided to stay in Leeds, where he had just bought a bungalow off Kirkstall Lane.

'Luton, Crewe and Mansfield, where Raich Carter was now manager, were among the other clubs who showed an interest in me,' he says, 'but I wasn't prepared to go anywhere that meant travelling long distances.'

Opposite the Leeds ground there was a greyhound track, which is where Wood became friends with Jack Ash, who was 'one of the bookies who stood up shouting the odds'. One night, when the two men were having a drink, Wood told Ash that Leeds were selling him and that he had a mind to pack in football altogether. But he did not know what to do.

'Roy, if you want a job with me,' Ash said, 'you've got one so long as I'm in business.'

The year was 1960 and betting shops were not set to become legal until the following spring. Up until May 1961 there were betting offices but not shops. These offices were strictly regulated with blacked-out windows; lettering to advertise what the premises were used for could not be more than four inches high. Also, they were subject to the whims of the authorities.

'It was a funny thing,' Wood says, 'in the old days they used to raid the betting offices, take what cash there was, close you down and let you open again on the Monday. It was to fund the Lord Mayor's Ball, I think.'

He started work for Ash on the top floor of his office in Leeds. 'I worked on the credit side, taking bets on the phone,' Wood says. 'I did this to start with just to pick up how things worked, before I went into the offices. By the time Jack died in 1967 I was looking after five offices.

'They then sold the business to a fella called Jim Windsor, who also had betting offices with a head office in the same road as Jack's. Later Jim sold it to William Hill – and that's how it is today.

'I went on my own on the credit side, taking bets on the phone, which was what I knew. I didn't really have an office. It was just a room with a tape machine in it. I did that for a while, into the '80s, and then

I went to work for a fella called Ray Kettlewell doing the same sort of thing.'

Howard Riley provides a variation on the employment quandary that footballers once faced. This was long before soaring wages changed the dilemma to one of how best to invest/fritter away their wealth.

Now in his mid-seventies, Riley is bronzed and chipper. He still looks fit enough to be scampering down the wing for Leicester City, the club for whom he appeared in two FA Cup finals, as he bounds out to greet me while I fumble for my taxi fare. His home on a neat estate in Leicester is a short distance from Wigston where he was born.

Riley's dilemma in the '60s was of an altogether subtler nature than deciding what he would do with himself to keep his family going once he gave up playing.

'If I have a regret about my football career,' he says, 'it's that I finished too early. It had a lot to do with having been to a grammar school.

'I remember reading about Graham Taylor who'd been to one, too, and he seemed to feel the same way – that football as a profession wasn't really looked upon as something desirable for someone with the academic background of a grammar school. I wouldn't say sport was frowned upon, in fact they did encourage it – but more as a recreation than a career path.

'At Kibworth Grammar School there was this attitude: you're going to play professional football...? Why not think of something else? What are you going to do afterwards? All professional footballers do is open pubs and things like that. You should be looking for something higher.'

As a young, impressionable pupil, Riley was influenced by this out-look. 'To some extent it rubbed off on me,' he says, 'although I never gave less than 100 per cent to my football and it was always my ambition to get in the first team. But it was why I started thinking I ought to prepare for a career beyond football while I was still young.'

Riley says the presence of two part-time players in the Leicester team gave him the idea that a similar arrangement could work for him while he qualified to be a PE teacher. So after the 1963 Cup final, he 'took a chance' and enrolled for a three-year teacher-training course at St Peter's College, Saltley, in Birmingham, not far from where Bill Slater was on the university's PE staff.

It was this that led to the premature unravelling of Riley's days as a Leicester player. 'Being part-time meant I was going to lose my first-team place at the club, which is why I went to Walsall for six months at the end of 1965.'

He also had a brief spell playing for Atlanta Chiefs in the newly formed North American Soccer League. 'I took the family over to Atlanta,' Riley says. 'It was very interesting and very different – travelling by jet to away matches for a start and getting home at three in the morning – but you didn't save a lot of money. I earned about the same as I did in England, so I decided to come back after one season.'

Having qualified from Saltley, Riley found a job teaching PE and history at secondary schools in the Wigston area, 'which was very enjoyable – but I still wish I'd gone on playing a bit longer'.

For many players who were born in the 1920s and '30s, retiring from their jobs beyond football never happened. They died young – much younger on average than they do today.

One reason was the acceptance of drinking and smoking as a way of life that should not be denied to sportsmen. This was partly down to the fact that the detrimental side effects were not fully recognised.

Jack Jones, captain of the Spurs side that won the FA Cup in 1901, wrote in his book *Association Football* that beer was 'so much a recognised article of diet that it would be impossible or at least unwise to forbid it'. At half-time in the 1950 Cup final Denis Compton quaffed a fortifying brandy.

Jones was markedly less sparing on the matter of smoking. He wrote that he could not 'find words strong enough to express my disapproval' of a practice that 'once started may lead to grave disasters'. But it was many years before anyone took much notice. Half a century later, in 1957, a ban was mooted – after 11 a.m. on match days.

Another reason for premature deaths, specific to football, we are now finding out, is the risk attached to heading a ball. And it is a risk that has not gone away.

The death in 2002 of Jeff Astle, who started his professional career at Notts County in 1952 and died aged fifty-nine, highlighted the perils of heading the leather ball of old. Astle scored many of his 137 goals in 292 appearances for West Bromwich Albion with headers.

After he died, having been diagnosed with early-onset Alzheimer's, his brain was found to have chronic traumatic encephalopathy. This is a condition normally associated with boxers, who have always taken up their sport well aware of the health risks.

The debate about the extent to which the risks have diminished is ongoing, with plenty of evidence that they remain very real and that action may need to be taken.

In September 2017, the Republic of Ireland international Kevin Doyle retired on medical advice after suffering persistent headaches. Doyle had been a renowned header of the ball.

There is one health risk that has surfaced in recent years that would never have affected the old-timers. A direct result of the immense wealth of the top players, it is the stress brought on by unsound business investments.

When footballers were skint very few of them had enough money to make either a sound or unsound investment. Maybe the flower stall or laundrette idea or, in Tommy Banks's case, the newsagent's didn't quite work out, but that was about it.

Now, the massive amounts of money players have at their disposal when they retire represent the potential for disaster on an equally massive scale.

The pitfalls for the 21st-century footballer are evident from figures broadcast recently by a charity for ex-pros. These show that two out of every five of them are made bankrupt within five years of retiring from the game.

For them a more suitable epitaph might be: too old to play, too rich to retire.

CHAPTER FOURTEEN

ANCIENT AND MODERN

In which Frank O'Farrell loses half his blood and receives the last rites – a player changes clubs over the issue of a few cigarettes – George Graham wakes up unmarried and by kick-off the same day is a husband playing against his best man – the ancients give their frank views on the money earned by players in the twenty-first century.

You went home. No tomorrow. Football again. No tomorrow. Football again. And that was it and we lived for it. I mean the life with those players – money can't pay for it. To become a professional footballer, it's difficult to imagine what it's like. I've told you about the supporters. They bloody treasured you. You couldn't believe them, coming up wanting to help you. The supporters in those days weren't supporters, they were a family. There were fifty, sixty, sometimes eighty thousand come to watch you play football …

And they must have been enjoying what they saw. And, by God, we on the pitch enjoyed what we were doing. So, putting it all together, all of it, them days will never come again. Because, for me, the type of football you're watching

now – thirty passes and they've still created nothing. But
the fans in those days really made my life. There are a lot
of people who still remember and I'm thankful whenever I
do meet them. They say, 'Can't you remember me?' I mean,
sixty or seventy thousand people, it's hard to remember.
But I still say, 'Oh yeah, bloody hell, how are you keeping?'
It's nice. I'm lucky...

ALEC JACKSON, WEST BROMWICH ALBION WINGER 1954–64

T his was one man's answer to my question: how would he compare
today's era with the one in which he played?

Based on all the players' answers to a range of questions, I have com-
piled six areas of comparison: health, medical care and lifestyle; playing
conditions, kit and equipment; standard and style of play; atmosphere,
attitude and approach, which is the one that brought forth Jackson's
stream of consciousness; how would you fare playing today; and, finally,
present-day wages, the subject that generated the most robust answers.

HEALTH, MEDICAL CARE AND LIFESTYLE

Advances in medical care have been significant, although, as mentioned in the previous chapter, the realisation of the harmful effects of
heading a ball has exposed an area where more needs to be done.

More straightforward has been improving the treatment of easily
recognisable injuries such as fractured bones, pulled muscles, cuts
and bruises.

The attention Dave Whelan received after so badly breaking his
leg in the 1960 FA Cup final is just one example of a response that by
today's standards seems almost criminally crude.

Frank O'Farrell tells an equally harrowing tale of a medical emergency that, had it happened today, it is hard to imagine would have come so close to tragedy. It was while he was a Preston player in the late '50s. He had a heavy cold and, during a training session, his nose started to bleed.

'Jimmy Milne took me into the treatment room,' O'Farrell says, 'but he couldn't stop the bleeding. It just kept bleeding, bleeding, bleeding. So they took me to the hospital, Preston Royal Infirmary, and they couldn't stop it either.

'They started injecting me with something that would clot the blood, vitamin K I think it was. I lost half my blood supply, four pints of blood. I had the last rites. The Jesuit priest from the local Catholic Church came in and gave me the last rites. They thought I was going to die. It was that serious. I was in there for a couple of weeks.

'They never found out what it was except that there was a weakness in the blood vessel. They thought this could have been the result of when I had a clash of heads with my own centre-half at West Ham. We were going for the same ball and I needed six stitches in my eyelid, my eyelid was hanging off. I spent a couple of days in London Hospital where they sewed the eyelid back on.'

Grim stuff, but with O'Farrell any story, however dark, usually comes with a humorous twist. 'After I'd recovered,' he says, 'I was talking to some of the men in the ward and they said that when I came in they asked, "Who's that?", and were told, "Oh, some Irishman called O'Farrell."

'So they all thought I was some Irish drunk who'd been in a fight.'

Of the succession of injuries that eventually blighted Tony McNamara's career, a leg wound, incorrectly treated, had particularly disastrous consequences.

McNamara says the trainer strapped up his leg with the wrong side of the tape against his skin. 'It meant my leg couldn't expand and I was in a lot of pain.

'In the end they sent a doctor from the club to the house and when they peeled off the tape the sticky side was against my leg. It pulled off all the skin. The shock of that caused psoriasis to set in.'

McNamara says he doesn't think he ever fully recovered from this, but he compliments Everton on standing by him more than half a century later. 'I have two false knees now,' he says, 'and to give the present Everton set-up their due it was they who paid for me to have them done.

'When the club found out that I was struggling, rather than let me go on an NHS waiting list they looked after things for me. That's one thing about Everton now, they look after their former players.'

Perhaps an even greater factor affecting players' well-being than improved medical care is that it is now irrefutably the case that Jack Jones was right at the start of the century to worry about players' lifestyles.

Jones's concerns about smoking were particularly prescient given that at the time, and for several years to come, some doctors promoted the health benefits of drawing in lungfuls of burnt tobacco fumes.

Although players still smoke and drink, at least they can be in no doubt about the risks. And also on the upside for their welfare, they now enjoy the benefits of improved dietary advice and fitness regimes. Other things, too, have become available as wages have rocketed: luxury accommodation and the chance to chill out during the close season at exotic locations.

But taking advantage of these things was not an option for Jackson's generation, either for the want of facts as yet unproven or of funds to pay for those that come at a price.

We have already seen that sixty years ago it was almost certainly the case that most footballers liked a ciggy or two. While newspapers nowadays love to publish lists of 'Ten Footballers Who Smoke', after the war a more revealing list would have been of ten who didn't.

Heavy drinking was also something that was expected and accepted. Being caught imbibing was not the scandal that makes today's inebriated footballer tottering away from a bar headline news.

Cigarettes were the perfect Christmas present for footballers. Leivers remembers that it was being short-rationed in a Yuletide handout that contributed to his leaving his first club.

Each December a director at Chesterfield gave cigarettes to the players, fifty to each of the first team and twenty to each of the others.

'Well, I'd been in the first team until just before Christmas 1952 when I got injured,' Leivers says, 'and when the manager, Teddy Davison, came to hand out the cigarettes he gave me twenty. I had never smoked a fag in my life and had no intention of doing so, but my dad did and in the past I'd given them to him.'

When Leivers failed in his protest that he deserved fifty because being injured was the only reason he was not in the first team, he said something that he has regretted ever since.

'Teddy Davison was a lovely little chap,' he says, 'but I told him, "You can stick those cigarettes right up your arse – and you can put me on the transfer list at the same time."

'And that's how I came to leave Chesterfield – over a few cigarettes.'

The demon drink prompts Tony McNamara to tell a story about his Everton predecessor Dixie Dean, whose sixty goals in the 1927–28 season remains a monumental Football League record. The story had evidently been passed down as much as a tribute to Dean as anything.

'There were so many of these stories about Dixie's misdemeanours,' McNamara says, 'as many as there were about all the goals he scored.'

This particular story was about a phone call from the police that the Everton trainer, Harry Cook, received one Friday evening. An officer told Cook, 'We've got Dixie Dean here. If you want him to be fit for tomorrow you'd better come and get him.'

Cook duly rescued the royally sozzled Dean and took him back to his house – Cook's house that is – for the night. 'Apparently Harry was going to have a party and there was this big cake on the table,' McNamara says. 'During the night Dixie woke up, saw the cake and ate half of it. The next day Dixie played, scored a hat-trick and played a blinder.'

Dean, incidentally, lived to the comparatively ripe old age for a pre-war footballer of seventy-three.

It is highly unlikely that Dean understood the modern concept of a diet. He would have regarded talk of the sort of meticulous eating that has become integral to a player's fitness as complete claptrap.

Not everyone had this attitude, though. Stanley Matthews was in a very small minority of fastidious eaters. Some days, usually Mondays, he would not eat at all having been convinced by the gains bestowed by fasting.

The majority, however, felt living an energetic outdoor life required regular fry-ups and/or meat pies, chips and peas. It did not even occur to all players that being particular about what they ate in the hours before kick-off might help their performance.

Peter McParland was one of the more forward-looking: 'When we won the Cup in 1957, we had a terrific trainer, but I would have liked to have had all the stuff that they get now.

'I was never comfortable before a game with what I would eat. One of our players, Stan Lynn, would eat a bar of chocolate and a Mars bar. Some had boiled chicken, boiled fish, a bit of rice, but I couldn't eat that stuff because I felt there was a big lump in my belly when I was going to play a game. So I was never comfortable with the food.

'But today they've worked out what you should eat, which is good, and the facilities are great for fitness. I would have liked to have had that to add to what I already had as a player. Then perhaps I'd have been top, top, top.'

As the '60s progressed Terry Neill experienced the stirrings of a concerted new approach to player welfare. He attributes Arsenal's key role in this to the foresight of Bertie Mee, who joined the London club as a physio in 1960 before becoming manager; also, the club's doctor, Alan Bass, who would leave the UK because of disillusionment with the NHS and rise to be FIFA's top medical man.

Neill cites as an example of a more sophisticated outlook Mee's dim view of the widespread use of cortisone injections. 'The squads used to be much smaller,' Neill says, 'and unfortunately a lot of clubs kept their star players playing with injections and this only masked the real problem.

'We were very fortunate at the Arsenal that we always had the best of medical attention and dietary advice.'

For some, though, there was nothing wrong with the old ways. Terry Allcock is one of these. He says, 'The medical attention amounted to an ex-player who was acting as trainer and who used to come on, hit you with a sponge and tell you to get on with it, run it off. I have no regrets.

'I feel sorry for them when I watch them play now. Defenders daren't tackle because they would get a yellow card or get a red card, or someone would fall down in the penalty area.'

PLAYING CONDITIONS, KIT AND EQUIPMENT

Putting aside the pay modern footballers receive, the thing the ancients covet most about the game at the highest level today is never having to squelch through mud.

'It is a different game from when I played,' Roy Wood says. 'For a start, the playing surface is virtually the same every week. I look at the television and they're playing on a blinking billiard table.

'I remember the Chelsea ground. If I stood in one spot for two minutes my feet would start sinking in.'

'Stamford Bridge was always a bog,' Terry Neill says. 'Upton Park was like a beach by the end of September but at least after Ron Greenwood went there as manager it was like a well-rolled beach.'

'You look at White Hart Lane today and the pitch is immaculate. It is unbelievable and it will be like that at the end of the season,' Cliff Jones says. 'When we played, at the start of the season the pitch was OK, come autumn it wasn't too bad, come the winter and it was fuckin' awful.'

But mud was not the only problem. Pitches had quirks. Bolton's was the most notorious. It used to be the widest in the Football League and was cambered so that from one touchline you could not see the other one. The pitch was surrounded by a gravel running track and a three-foot drop, known as the moat.

The bottom of the moat is where many a winger's mazy run came to an end, notably when ushered into it by Tommy Banks and Roy Hartle, Bolton's uncompromising full-back pairing.

Neill recalls another way in which Bolton's pitch created problems for opponents: 'When Brian Pilkington, a five-foot-nothing, tricky little winger, was taking a corner, he'd disappear down this slope and then all of a sudden he'd come up in instalments and the ball would come over … it was one of the greatest tactics ever.'

The ancients are almost as abusive about the ball they used as the pitches. 'As for the ball,' Bill Leivers says, 'when I was at Chesterfield – and this is the gospel truth – they would take the old leather T-ball, fasten a brick to it and put it in the plunge bath with enough water to cover it. This was on Friday, ready for the game on Saturday. So it weighed half a ton to start with.

'They used to do that and people just won't believe it. I don't know why they did it. I never queried why they did it but they did it. If you headed it, it knocked your damned head off.'

The logic behind giving the ball a bath would be interesting to know. The fact is that it was only when it was soaked that the old leather ball became heavier than the non-absorbent synthetic leather ball used now. The dry weight has remained at 14–16 ounces (410–450 grams) since 1937. Which may surprise some, particularly old footballers, but hardly explains why anyone would want to dip a match ball in a plunge bath.

Invariably, given the nature of English winters, the leather ball did absorb some moisture even without a pre-match dousing, which may mean heading has become safer. Time will tell.

As Dave Whelan points out, the weight of a leather ball when wet was not its only unwelcome characteristic.

'In my day,' he says, 'not only did the leather balls become much heavier by taking water in, they had big, protruding laces in them. If you caught that lace on your head it would hurt, cut you even. Bang! But you had no option. The ball now is a constant weight. It doesn't matter if it's raining or whatever – the ball doesn't get any heavier.'

The synthetic ball with its smooth surface also behaves differently. Wood, a goalkeeper who knew where he stood with the old leather ball, says, 'I think a lot of goals today are scored by accident because with the ball they use anything can happen.

'The old ball was a different kettle of fish altogether. If some of them had to play with the old ball on a muddy ground we'd see how good they are. They wouldn't be able to do all the tricks they do today, back-heeling and God knows what.'

Boots have undergone the greatest change in the kit players wear. The heavy, natural materials once used to make shirts, shorts and socks were abandoned long ago, but this was mere window dressing compared to the effect that modifications to footwear would have.

The boots England played in at the 1950 World Cup in Brazil would not have looked out of place on a building site. And three years later, when England played Hungary at Wembley, Billy Wright was deriding the Hungarians before kick-off for wearing boots that looked as though they came from a fashionable shoe shop.

Bolton's policy was to allow each player one pair of what would now be regarded as ludicrously heavy boots. These had to be purchased from Albert Ward's sports shop in the centre of town – and any player paying more than £2 for a pair risked the wrath of the club secretary, who scrutinised receipts.

'At Chesterfield they gave you a pair of boots twelve months in advance,' Leivers says. 'So you had two pairs of boots, one that you were wearing and another pair that you had to wear now and again and they were for the following season. Some of them had metal toecaps inside. Totally different from the carpet slippers they wear nowadays.'

'What we played was football,' Wood says. 'What they play today ought to be given a different name.'

STANDARD AND STYLE OF PLAY

The distinct whiff of damning with faint praise hangs over the players' comparisons between the game as they knew it at the start of Queen Elizabeth II's reign and as it is played in the monarch's twilight years.

The fitness of Premier League players and the speed at which they perform receive admiration, but… there is nearly always a but.

'The game itself is faster now,' George Eastham says, setting the tone. 'Fitness levels have increased, eating habits are a bit different and players now are bigger.

'I've just been to one of my old clubs, Stoke, and found I was looking up at the players I met rather than at them. I was looking up at the Eiffel Tower.

'Some of today's defenders, you think, "My God, if they'd tackled me in the old days, what would have happened?" It's changed in that respect.'

It is worth allowing Terry Allcock to interject here, making it clear that Eastham's observation on size is just that, and not a comment on hostile intent. 'Physically you expected to be clouted, particularly as a forward,' Allcock says. 'If you weren't you thought you were playing against a gentleman, but there weren't many about in those days.'

Eastham pauses, and here comes the but. 'Skill-wise,' he says, 'I don't think the game's as good as it used to be. There were far better players in my day. You would look at the man face on, go at him, take him on and beat him. I don't see that anymore now. It's pass, pass, pass, pass – sideways, backwards, any ways but don't lose the ball, which to me is becoming boring.

'The excitement in football is going for goals, getting down the other end as quickly as possible, having a shot at goal, missing, scoring, whatever.

'The way they play now is killing the game. I haven't got the appetite for it I used to have and for me to say that has got to be something because the only thing I've ever known is football.'

Tony McNamara puts different words to the same tune. 'In my day teams played with five forwards, three half-backs and two full-backs,' he says. 'No one really questioned this for a few more years. So the emphasis was on attack.

'Now defence is the first consideration. The attitude is: don't give a goal away and at least we've got a point. There can be as many as five people ranged along the back to stop the opposition scoring.

'Certain games are pretty good. They're quicker than we were, pass the ball around smartly and get it forward. But in other games you can sit there for ten minutes and all you'll see is them moving the ball sideways and backwards, never forwards.'

This last point becomes a refrain. 'The football we played was more direct than it is today,' Howard Riley says. 'Now it's more about possession and lateral movement across the field – and then eventually looking to pick out a runner.

'Ours was more simple, long balls behind full-backs for wingers to run on to. We very rarely played it back. It was one against one and you'd take them on before getting a cross or a shot in.'

Even Dave Whelan, who is by far the most admiring of what is now on offer, finishes off with a but. 'It's a much quicker game now, the ball is fizzed about much more than we could do it given the conditions,' he says. 'So I think the game today is so much better than when we played.

'But the skill of the players when I played was as great as it is now and those players playing then would still be stars today. I don't think there's any doubt about that.'

Although Terry Neill broadly agrees with the consensus, he does recall being exposed to the influences that would put an end to English football's introversion.

'It's a much more technical game now with the emphasis on passing and movement and that sort of thing,' he says. 'But we weren't total strangers to this because in the early, mid-'60s we had a friendly game for one of the Duke of Edinburgh's charities against the Real Madrid team of Di Stéfano, Puskás, Gento, Santamaría. They stuffed us by the way, but playing them was a bit of a lesson.

'Also I played against Trapattoni, when I made my debut for Northern Ireland in Bologna in 1961, and the Italian players then played a more tactical game. We were a lot more direct in our day despite that fact that we had very skilful players in the Arsenal team such as George Eastham.'

But not everyone was blessed with skills, nor were they expected to be. 'Defenders were basically defenders,' Neill says. 'When I first came into the Northern Ireland team Danny Blanchflower was captain. He nicknamed me Tiger and would say, "Tiger, you go and get the ball and give it to those of us who can play."

'He said it in such way, though, that I would have run through brick walls for him.'

ATMOSPHERE, ATTITUDE AND APPROACH

'They were lovely days to play,' Terry Allcock says, echoing Alec Jackson's elegiac start to this chapter.

'Great atmosphere. There was still a feeling of relief after the Second World War and everybody went to football. All flat caps, everybody walked to the game. All the stadiums were in built-up areas, not on the motorways out of town. Very enjoyable…

'They were great days. I don't think the atmosphere now is the same. There isn't the banter among supporters. They're segregated. Everything's done on the corporate side. It's a completely different attitude.'

Stan Anderson comes at things from a different angle. 'It's an entirely changed atmosphere now,' he says. 'It's not as watchable as it used to be and I think that's probably because of the high price of getting into the ground and so on.'

The steep admission charges have made a fundamental difference, he says. 'When you go and watch matches nowadays there's a lot of anger against the prices people are charged. You know, "I've just spent forty quid on this bloody lot…", and that's bound to make it less enjoyable to watch.

'I look at the attendances now and there are teams who've lost in front of a crowd of 42,000 and the next time there are only 27,000 watching. Where have they all gone? They've just decided, "Bugger it, I'm not going to pay that amount."

'In the days when the Shacks and Milburns were playing, they were on fourteen, fifteen quid a week and the ordinary working people – the miners and so on – were on eight, nine quid a week and they could associate themselves with each other. Now it's just outrageous.'

And there is general agreement that the attitude on the pitch has changed just as much as it has on the terraces, particularly with regard to being clouted, as Allcock puts it.

'We played in tough conditions compared to today and we entertained and we had hard but fair tackling,' Peter McParland says. 'The odd one here and there would go over the top but the majority of my career it was hard but fair and you took that. You knew what was going on.'

McParland recalls a gathering of Aston Villa players in 2007 to mark the fiftieth anniversary of the 1957 FA Cup final in which he scored the winning goals against Manchester United.

'There were a few of us there from the Cup final team,' he says, 'including our great supporter, Merv the Swerve [Mervyn King] from the Bank of England, and [BBC commentator] John Motson. John came over and said he had recently watched a film of the final. "You weren't half getting into one another," he said, "but you all got up after you were tackled." He noticed that. Nobody was rolling about on the ground.

'You had to get up and get on with it. And most times when a fella gave you a belt you didn't let on he'd hurt you. The crowd liked to see fellas going hell for leather into tackles.'

If the attitude on the pitch was to play hard, the attitude towards training was generally less intense, certainly less intense than it is now – and, viewed from today, some of what went on seems positively bizarre. 'We trained hard enough but it was all left to ourselves,' Johnny Paton says. 'Alex Dowdalls, the trainer at Celtic, used to come out with a white coat on, have a look for five minutes, say, "You all right, boys?", then go back in.

'Once when we wanted to play five-a-side behind the goal – you weren't allowed on the pitch – I was detailed to go in and ask Dowdalls for a ball. When I asked him, he said, "Why do you want a ball? You'll see enough of that on a Saturday."'

Running was the staple exercise that kept players fit. Howard Riley's account of how Leicester City trained is fairly typical: 'Clubs have all got academies now and tremendous facilities but our training was basically centred on the Filbert Street ground.

'Early season training might include going up to Bradgate Park for some long-distance running, but mostly we'd report to Filbert Street where we'd train on the track round the pitch – lapping, sprinting and some hurdling – and have five-a-side games in the car park wearing gym shoes.

'We didn't do a lot of training with the ball apart from the games on the car park and the odd practice match on the main pitch during the week.'

Riley would go back in the afternoons to practise crossing the ball with Gordon Banks and one or two other players. 'But that was voluntary,' he says, 'and the groundsman wasn't too happy. You always had to get past him if you wanted to go on the pitch, which seems incredible now.'

In so many other ways the footballer's life was less fraught, more closely related to the everyday grind of those who watched them or the hacks who wrote about them.

'At Liverpool, we played a European match in Bratislava,' Gordon Milne recalls. 'Afterwards the lads went for a beer – we only drank beer, there was no wine or anything – and the five or six journalists who were covering the game came along too.

'They might be criticising us the next day, but we'd all sit together. That was how it was. There wasn't the edge there is today. Journalists are no longer allowed to fly with the players, they don't talk to them, they fall out with them. Our time was really good.'

Cliff Jones puts a different slant on the lives of his generation being rooted in ordinariness. Having been carried shoulder-high from Ninian Park after scoring Wales' winner against England in 1955, he did what most other young men did on the Monday morning after the game – he clocked on for a day's shift.

'At half past seven I went into the fitting shop at the Prince of Wales Dry Dock,' he says. 'I was met by my foreman, Dai Ward, who was a good bloke. He said, "Cliff, well done on Saturday. Now there's your tools, you got proper work to do, son."

'I thought, "Eh, you're right." And that's what shaped me and made me realise how fortunate I was to play football for a living and not, if you like, work for a living, because, as I say, football ain't work.'

And just like Joe Punter on the terraces, players got married on Saturdays during the football season – rather than in high summer in an Italian monastery.

Freddie Steele, the Stoke City striker, had been granted permission to marry on the last day of the 1937–38 season, when Stoke looked safe from relegation. Come the final Saturday things had changed, and Stoke needed to beat Liverpool at home to stay in the First Division.

The full choral church ceremony went ahead as planned, Steele chatting to the priest and church warden about the game that afternoon as they waited for the bride. The one concession to the match was that Steele missed the reception so he could be in good time for kick-off. He then scored with a diving header in a 2–0 win that kept Stoke in the top division.

'In the '60s,' Terry Neill says, 'Arsenal's rivalry with Tottenham was probably greater than it is now and I remember a 4–0 win against Spurs at the old Highbury, a young Pat Jennings playing in goal for them and I scored a penalty. And that was the day George Graham, who also scored a goal for us, was married.

'As footballers did in those days, he got married at eleven o'clock in the morning [at Marylebone Town Hall]. And Terry Venables, who was playing for Tottenham against George in the afternoon, was his best man. George then brought his wife to Highbury to watch the match.'

Neill, who went on to manage Arsenal from 1976 to '83, also brings a manager's perspective to how things have changed. 'I hate this modern aspect of mind games,' he says.

'After Ipswich beat us in a Cup final Bobby Robson apologised for his team's victory while I was congratulating him; and the following year when we nicked victory over Dave Sexton's Manchester United he turned round and congratulated me, gave me a hug and I apologised to them.

'Then the following year, when John Lyall's West Ham beat us 1–0, John was apologising to me and I was congratulating him.

'There were no mind games, which are juvenile. Unfortunately it is a modern trend. I mean one only has to look at Prime Minister's Questions. My grandsons behave better at school than the so-called coalition and I thought coalition roughly translated meant working together – or something akin to that. And these are supposed to be our leaders.

'What leadership, eh? None. Disgraceful.'

HOW WOULD YOU FARE PLAYING TODAY?

One forum where old pros can savour a little of the adulation the modern player does and air their views publicly on changes in the game is the corporate box, that essential addition to the 21st-century stadium. As the star hosts in these boxes on match days, they mingle with champagne-fuelled clientele eager to ask questions.

Cliff Jones says not only does he enjoy doing this but he gets paid more than he did when he played for Tottenham. And the question he is asked more than any other is how he thinks he would have fared in today's game. His reply is that the more relevant question would be: how would the modern footballer have done in the time he, Jones, played?

He says, 'I think players of my period would adjust far better to the modern game than today's modern footballers would to the game of yesteryear, when it was much more physical.

'The game may be quicker today, but when I played the ball went forward quicker. You watch Barcelona today. Sometimes they pass right across the midfield, twenty or thirty passes, and they're still in the midfield.'

Terry Allcock has a similar story: 'These days,' he says, 'I still host the match sponsors at Carrow Road. I look after twenty, twenty-five people and many of them say to me, "Do you think you could play in today's game?" I say, "I'm sure I could because I had two good feet, I could head the ball and I could score goals for fun, really."

'And then I say that they couldn't have played with us because we were too physical.'

Alex Dawson recognises in the modern game the same possibilities that existed for him when he started out for Manchester United in the 1950s: 'In one respect I wouldn't really fit in today because the game's played at a much faster pace. On the other hand, what I did was score goals and I think if you've got that ability it doesn't matter which era you play in, you'll always be successful.'

Like Dawson, Peter McParland was an attacking forward who sees even greater scope in the modern game for his style of play than existed in his day. 'I'd fancy playing against lots of the defenders in England now,' he says, 'because they give you space. I liked a wee bit of space to get a smack at it, get in and score a goal.

'If you gave me space I was always capable of eating it up and getting something out of it. And that's happening now in the game in the goalmouth and my job was to be in there getting touches and that.'

What McParland says he would not enjoy about playing today is 'all the shady stuff that they do, pull your shirt and all that, which is absolutely outrageous as far as I'm concerned.

'And you have to put up with it otherwise you'd probably be off for hitting people. During my career you could probably count on one hand the number of times my shirt was pulled. Nobody pulled your shirt and it's annoying to watch that sort of stuff.

'When someone came to mark you tight for a corner kick, we didn't pull each other and wrestle with each other and all that because the referee would have given a penalty. Now it's a penalty only once in a blue moon.

'I think they've got to look at that now. The managers don't care now if they're doing it because they're getting away with it. If they didn't the manager would have to say, "Hey, you've got to stop pulling shirts and dragging fellas down in the penalty area."'

Howard Riley speaks for 'most of my generation'. He reckons 'we'd have been OK playing the modern game. We'd have adapted. As long as players have got the skills and the speed and the awareness – that's what it's about.'

PRESENT-DAY WAGES

Immoral, unbelievable, barmy, crazy, fantastic… the ancients are mostly unequivocal in their opinions of what top players are paid today, although many qualify their outrage with 'but good luck to them'.

The one man to disagree, without any sort of qualification, is Dave Whelan – and he, of course, is the only one who has been the payer, as owner of Wigan Athletic, as well as the payee, when he played for Blackburn and Crewe.

'My view is simple,' Whelan says. 'I think when you play professional football you are a very special and lucky person. And if you play in the Premier League it means you are watched by billions of people and you earn every penny they give you. I have no hang-ups about paying players, especially in the Premier League. The matches are broadcast all over the world and if that was a pop star they would get billions.

'Now football players get well paid and we all say, "Aw, they get overpaid," and think they're getting money for old rope but they're very special, talented players. You do get the odd one who's arrogant and unaware of how lucky he is to have been given the gifts to play the great game. I wish I could do it all again.'

Such benevolence is in short supply among the payees. Here, in alphabetical order, is what a selection of them have to say about the wages today's players earn:

Terry Allcock

The money they earn? I think it's immoral. From my own generation's point of view we can't identify with what they earn.

A pound is a pound still – unfortunately, being a Yorkshireman. It's outrageous. You just try to imagine the salary payment at the end of the month at clubs like Manchester City, where you've got thirty-odd pros and possibly the lowest paid is on about 100 grand a week.

I think they're ruining a lot of youngsters. The clubs with all the money now are taking them at fifteen, sixteen, seventeen and paying them thousands and thousands and it doesn't do them any good.

But that's only a personal opinion.

Stan Anderson

I'm not being critical. If the clubs want to pay that and they can afford it that's fine, and I don't disagree with people making as much as they can, that's fine.

But then I think the attitude of players must be to put on a performance and work as hard as they possibly can in the match – and I sometimes don't see it.

People say to me, 'Did you see that match last night, Stan?' 'Yeah, I saw it.' 'Sixty, seventy, eighty grand a week and they play like that!'

And that's not even the supporters – it's just people watching it on the telly. 'They're getting all that money every week and I'm lucky if I get 500 quid.' It just doesn't work with them.

Tommy Banks

Wages and transfer fees today are ridiculous. I mean £86 million for Gareth Bale. It's an unknown quantity. In my day, we were even worse off than players had been in the 1920s. You look at photographs in the '20s and they're all well-geared – good overcoats, top-class tailoring. But later on the benefits and wages didn't go up with the times.

Alex Dawson

It's hard to compare what we earned to the ridiculous amounts players earn today. These days the youngsters set out, as we did, thinking about football, but when they receive all that money, with all the distractions it must bring, it must make it difficult for them to concentrate on actually playing the game.

Alec Jackson

I'm not envious of the money, it's just that I can't see why you need to be paid so much. I mean money is money, money makes life, you can't live without it, but I think it has ruined just about everything that goes along with sport.

I love watching golf, tennis, boxing, cricket – and then all of a sudden I pick up a paper... I mean Rooney the other day, I went bloody mad, didn't I? Good luck to the kid, he's got a family and his job is to get as much as he can so he can give them a decent standard of living when they grow up. But I read he's getting half a million for an hour and a half. Half a million for an hour and a half? Do you realise what half a million is? That's your life. And then it says he's got £52 million – just because he can kick a ball better than somebody else.

I agree about wanting to give your family a good standard of living and bring them up right. But I disagree with getting that sort of money just because you can play football. Don't forget, what is football? It's only a game.

Cliff Jones

We all know about the rewards players get today, the amount of money, it's just mind-boggling. Unbelievable.

As I say, getting £200,000 for playing football, when it's not work, they don't realise how fortunate they are. They wouldn't be too impressed now with the twenty quid a week we used to get.

OK, they've got to keep themselves in shape, but that's no big deal, to keep yourself in shape. People go to health centres and fitness clubs, they pay to keep themselves in shape. So they don't realise how fortunate they are, these young men, to be playing football for a living.

Bill Leivers

Most of the players are overpaid. I know it's a very simple thing to say, but how can you have a surgeon who's earning however much it is, and then you've got a bloke because he's good at kicking a ball about can earn…

That's what annoys me, when they say they earn it. They don't earn it at all. That's what they get paid. I mean Yaya Touré, £200,000 a week? The place has gone barmy.

If I were playing now I would never employ an agent. I cannot see for the life of me why you need an agent to do your work for you. [At this point I interject, 'I know you'd be all right, Bill, because you're strong-minded but a lot of players today are…' Leivers leaps in to complete my sentence] …thick, to put it bluntly. If someone came to me and said he could get me a whole load more money I'd tell him, 'If you get it, mate, I can get it.'

Peter McParland

We didn't think then when Jimmy Hill was going around the country talking to players about lifting the maximum wage that it would turn out like this. It's fantastic really. We would all have taken the money if anyone had come up and said, 'Do you want this much?'

Good luck to them, but the thing I don't like about it is that there are kids now getting loads of money. I believe some of them have even gone up into the million class before they have even made the grade.

Gordon Milne

Looking back, I wouldn't change our time for anything. In my early days players went to the ground on the bus still – not many had cars – and we were all on the same money. Money wasn't the god it is today, which meant we were closer to the fans and they were closer to us because there was no talk about how much we were earning.

We were paid more than a carpenter, so we were well-off, but the most I earned was forty, fifty, sixty quid a week towards the tail-end of my spell at Liverpool and then going on to Blackpool. There was an innocence about those times, which I don't think there is today.

Terry Neill

We travelled on public transport, although when we got onto forty-five quid a week we thought we were rich beyond our wildest dreams and all started to get what we thought were fancy cars.

Good luck to them, but it's not the money, it's the effect that money has on them.

I was with a good friend of mine yesterday who's on the committee at the local golf club, Hassocks, where Crawley Town have a golf day. And all the Crawley players book their own caddies in.

What the hell?! Crawley Town, with all due respects, I mean I wish them nothing but good, but I'm thinking when we were players at Arsenal in the '60s – Bob Wilson, Ian Ure, Frank McLintock, George

Graham, Geordie Armstrong – we had a block membership at South Herts Golf Club.

Now they're booking their own caddies. Who the hell do they think they are? And it's a flat course, Hassocks. I play it most weekends. Then I think, 'Hold on here. These guys are probably on a few grand a week.'

Johnny Paton

I never earned as much as twenty quid a week when I was playing football. I had £8 at Celtic, that was my top wage, £10 at Chelsea and £12 at Brentford.

When I got transferred to Watford my top wage was £14 a week, which went up to £18 when I started coaching there.

But I'm not a bit envious of the money they earn today. Not at all. Although I had ups and downs we always paid the rent, we always paid our bills, we're not in debt – everything you see in this room is cash. We've always run cars and managed to keep our heads above water.

Fortunately – and I mean this, sincerely – money has not been my motivation in life. OK, it's important, but I've never been motivated by it. So I can sit with millionaires and not care what they've got. It doesn't seem to mean anything to me. I say, 'Good luck to them.'

The thing is, though, can they [modern players] look after themselves? I never got involved in betting on the horses or on the greyhounds, but I was pals with guys who did. I like a social drink, we have a glass of wine at weekends and an occasional glass of whisky, but I never got involved with alcohol. I had very close friends, I won't mention their names, who were womanisers. I never got involved with women outside of our marriage. We've celebrated our sixty-sixth wedding anniversary. I've got nineteen grandchildren and great-grandchildren and my family have always been more important to me than my football.

There is a danger with the big money today if these boys get carried away in those areas I've just been talking about. I'll tell you something: some of them will finish up in big trouble.

Howard Riley

I think I could have adapted to the money they earn. It's phenomenal, isn't it? Unbelievable really. You have to think of what we got and then multiply by a thousand – or more than that in some cases. It's just out of this world. But fair enough – you're offered it, you accept it.

It's a shame in a way, though, because it's the supporters who are paying for it. I've been reading about the German sides, Bayern Munich and Borussia Dortmund, who have reached the European Cup final. Season tickets over there are only £150, which works out at about £6 a match for top-level football. If they can do it, why can't we?

Roy Wood

Moneywise, it's gone crazy really. I'm not going to blame the players. I blame the people with money for spoiling the game. It'll all blow up in time. I don't know which way it will go but they can't carry on the way they are.

EPILOGUE

Any project that involves meeting good people with interesting histories has to be an agreeable experience, and writing this book did not disappoint.

I was generously treated wherever I went and listened to endless stories, in many instances told with great eloquence. But I was also taken aback by quite what humble lives most of the forgotten stars of Saturday afternoons now led.

I developed a test for taxi drivers who, as we know, know everything. I asked them when they dropped me on a nondescript street or housing estate to name the occupant of the modest bungalow I was about to enter.

'Haven't a clue, mate.'

'You should: he played for Manchester United in an FA Cup final.'

What stands out looking back is that I encountered very little bitterness from these old players about their lot. Trenchant views, yes, expressed with passion, but hardly any rancour.

And if I gained one thing from four years of working on *When Footballers Were Skint*, it was a better understanding of the connection between the present state of professional football in England and its past.

It became clear to me that the Football League's discordant history – especially the struggle over wages – has played a big part in those changes that have shaped the modern game.

The pay struggle between League officials, clubs and players in the early and middle years of the twentieth century ended in 1961 with the abolition of capped earnings.

Somewhere along the line since then things have gone awry.

And I would suggest that a big reason for this is the wide recognition at the time that the players' cause was a just one.

As one contemporary commentator put it, the players' campaign to free up what they were paid was reinforced by 'the whip of parliamentary and public condemnation'.

The right of players to negotiate wages with no upper limit then became as sacrosanct as any other great prize won by working people – even if Cliff Jones, that fine player from Spurs' glory days, argues that football is not a job.

As a result, the players' original objective has become distorted. The struggle was against the maximum wage. It was not, as it now seems to be interpreted, to win the right to scrabble after every last penny of riches the game generates.

And who is it that has suffered most from this distortion?

The supporters, who, arguably, are as much a part of football's success story as the players.

Alec Jackson, a West Bromwich Albion player in the 1950s, tells us in the closing chapter of *When Footballers Were Skint* that when he played fans 'bloody treasured you. You couldn't believe them, coming up wanting to help you. The supporters in those days weren't support-ers, they were family.'

It is not the fans' fault that this important relationship no longer exists. And the players and their agents, indulged by the clubs, have been as complicit as anyone in building a barrier – sandbags stuffed with money – between themselves and those who pay their wages either at the turnstile and/or through TV subscriptions.

No one wants to see players skint again, but the tales in these pages reflect the values that created something special – and that something had a far broader purpose than making footballers rich beyond their wildest aspirations.

ACKNOWLEDGEMENTS

My thanks to all those players who granted me interviews and made writing this book such a rewarding experience. I owe a great deal, too, to the team at Biteback Publishing, who showed the highest standards of midwifery in easing my latest creation into the world, and as ever I am indebted to my agent, Jonathan Conway, for his support and guidance. Mike Collett, a friend and football writer who is more steeped in the game than anyone I know, read the manuscript and swooped on many errors, both schoolboy and recondite. My wife's skill in taking a vaguely presentable photo of me was the least of her contributions. Many more of you have helped to an extent that is poorly rewarded by a general thank-you. I apologise for doing it this way but omitting one deserving name by an oversight is a sin that cannot be forgiven by mentioning any number of others.

SELECT BIBLIOGRAPHY

Barnard, Roger, *The Jimmy Hagan Story* (Stroud: The History Press, 2010)

Chippindale, Peter, and Franks, Suzanne, *Dished! The Rise and Fall of British Satellite Broadcasting* (London: Simon & Schuster, 1992)

Dewhurst, Keith, *Underdogs: The Unlikely Story of Football's First FA Cup Heroes* (London: Yellow Jersey, 2012)

Dixon, Keith, *Jackie Sewell* (Derby: Derby Books, 2010)

Finney, Tom, *Tom Finney: My Autobiography* (London: Headline, 2003)

Harris, Tim, *Sport: Almost Everything You Ever Wanted to Know* (London: Yellow Jersey, 2007)

Harvey, Charles, (ed.) *Almanack of Sport 1966* (London: Sampson Low, 1966)

Huggins, Mike, and Williams, Jack, *Sport and the English, 1918-1939* (Abingdon: Routledge, 2006)

Matthews, Stanley, *The Way It Was* (London: Headline, 2001)

Rippon, Anton, *Gas Masks for Goal Posts* (Stroud: The History Press, 2007)

Roberts, John, *The Team That Wouldn't Die* (London: Aurum, 2008)

Seddon, Ian, *Ah'm tellin' Thee – A Biography of Tommy Banks, Bolton Wanderers and England* (Trowbridge: Paragon, 2012)

Whelan, Dave, *Dave Whelan: Playing To Win – The Autobiography* (London: Aurum, 2009)

INDEX

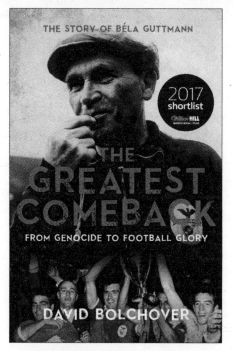

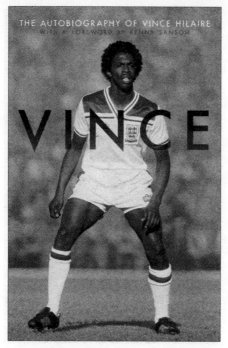